1250
7SP

APPROACHES TO THE THEATER OF CALDERÓN

Edited by

Michael D. McGaha

UNIVERSITY
PRESS OF
AMERICA

LANHAM • NEW YORK • LONDON

Copyright © 1982 by

University Press of America,™ Inc.

4720 Boston Way
Lanham, MD 20706

3 Henrietta Street
London WC2E 8LU England

Library of Congress Cataloging in Publication Data
Main entry under title:

Approaches to the theater of Calderón.

Includes index.
1. Calderón de la Barca, Pedro, 1660–1681–
Criticism and interpretation–Addresses, essays, lectures.
I. McGaha, Michael D., 1941–
PQ6312.A66   862'.3   81–23994
ISBN 0–8191–2277–7   AACR2
ISBN 0–8191–2278–4 (pbk.)

CONTENTS

iii

iv

PREFACE

In April 1979 Professor Susana Hernández-Araico, distressed by the fact that no plans had been announced for a commemoration of the tercentenary of the death of Calderón de la Barca on the West Coast, took the initiative to organize such an observance. She contacted colleagues at a number of Southern California universities, and on May 8 the committee to plan an international symposium on Calderón met for the first time at UCLA. Professor Hernández-Araico and I cochaired the committee. Professor Carroll Johnson of UCLA served as treasurer. The other members of the committee were Professor Juan Corominas, California State University, Dominguez Hills; Professor Julian Palley, University of California, Irvine; Professor James A. Parr, University of Southern California; and Professor Enrique Rodríguez-Cepeda, UCLA.

One of the committee's first actions was to invite seventeen of the world's most distinguished Calderón specialists to participate in the symposium. Only four of the invited speakers--Professors Edwin Honig, R. D. F. Pring-Mill, Jack Sage and N. D. Shergold-- declined our invitation. We also sent a call for papers to Spanish departments all over the United States in the hope of attracting younger and less established scholars to participate. Six of the papers submitted were chosen for presentation.

The symposium took place at UCLA on March 5-7, 1981. Bringing together so many people from such great distances was obviously a very expensive undertaking and would not have been possible without the generous support of the sponsoring institutions and important contributions received from the Ahmanson Foundation, the Spanish Consulate in Los Angeles, the UCLA Center for Medieval and Renaissance Studies and Professor Juan M. Corominas. All printing and mailing expenses were defrayed by California State Polytechnic University, Pomona.

The nineteen papers presented at the symposium and here published for the first time embody a broad spectrum of approaches to Calderón's theater. As Professor Bruce Wardropper commented in his keynote address, "the appraisal of a writer is the best form of commemoration." Together, these papers constitute a valuable and much-needed reappraisal of Calderón's achievement. Though they differ in emphasis and methodology and occasionally arrive at contradictory conclusions, it is remarkable how often they complement and mutually support each other. From this kaleidoscope of varying perspectives, a new panoramic view of Calderón's work gradually emerges, a view which helps us to understand why his work continues to appeal to readers and audiences three hundred years after his death.

It is strange, however, that while Calderón's reputation has continued to rise in England, Germany and the United States, his work has been despised and neglected in his native Spain, particularly in the twentieth century. In his keynote address Professor Bruce Wardropper raises the question of why Calderón has fared so badly in Spain in the last century. He finds that the great liberal writers of modern Spain-- Unamuno, Machado and Ortega--identified Calderón with political absolutism and religious fanaticism. It is hard to understand why Calderón was singled out for this treatment, since most of Spain's Golden Age writers were just as orthodox in their religion and just as ardent in their support of the monarchy. Wardropper finds the answer to this problem in the extraordinary influence and popularity of Marcelino Menéndez y Pelayo's book <u>Calderón y su teatro</u>. Published in 1881, that book purported to be a eulogy of Calderón on his bicentennial. However, Menéndez Pelayo constantly denigrated Calderón by comparing him unfavorably with Lope de Vega. Many modern Spanish writers derived their knowledge of Calderón more from Menéndez Pelayo's book than from personal reading of Calderón's work. Calderón thus became a symbol of all that was hateful and reactionary in Spain's past. Foreign scholars, free from involvement in Spanish politics, were able to view his work more objectively and attain a more unbiased view of its true artistic merits.

Professor Manuel Durán urges that we abandon the traditional Lope-Calderón dichotomy and try instead to judge each writer in terms of his own circumstances, goals and accomplishments. He believes that Calderón's biography offers important clues to a proper understanding of his work. For Durán the central event of Calderón's life was an identity crisis brought on by his parents' insistent desire that he become a priest and his own long resistance to that desire. From his father's death in 1615 until his ordination in 1650, Calderón seems to have alternated between rebellion

and tentative acceptance of his father's will, which
he identified with God's will, and to have suffered
profound feelings of guilt as a consequence. Durán
attributes the ambiguity in the honor plays to
Calderón's own ambivalence about accepting a role
which seemed to violate his natural instinct towards
love and his integrity as an individual. He sees the
constant triumph of duty and honor over passion in
Calderón's plays as the playwright's attempt to con-
vince himself--and God--that he knew what he must do
and would eventually accept it. Far from being the
smug and complacent exponent of orthodoxy whom we
know so well from manuals of literary history,
Calderón was a complex and tortured person who finally
submitted to the sacrifices demanded of him by divine
and paternal authority only after the deaths of his
two brothers and his only son convinced him of the
frailty of human love and the ultimate unreality of
the world of appearances.

Professor Robert ter Horst shares Durán's convic-
tion that Calderón was as much repulsed as attracted
by totalitarianism. Ter Horst perceives a constant
tension between content and form--orthodox ideas and
heterodox art--in Calderón's work. Noting that
Calderón's most vital characters "are all thieves
and usurpers, artists, challengers of divine prerogative," ter Horst finds that the apparent submission
to authority in Calderón's work is in reality a pro-
foundly humane statement of the individual's ability
to resist the tendency toward degradation, which
Calderón saw as the law of nature. For Calderón the
victory over the ungoverned and lustful self was also
the victory of the civilized artist over the brute.

Professor ter Horst observed that in Calderón's
plays honor was presented as a force of nature, of
which the playwright no more approved or disapproved
than he did of death. Professor Cesáreo Bandera finds
that in the three famous and controversial honor plays
--A secreto agravio, secreta venganza, El médico de
su honra and El pintor de su deshonra--Calderón reveals a profounder understanding of the psychology of
love than he is usually credited with. These plays
demonstrate that romantic love and marriage are almost
incompatible. Lurking like a viper within the lover's
desire for happiness is a desire for the opposite.
Violence, the dark side of desire, serves in these
plays as the accomplice to the law of honor. The
honor plays express Calderón's view that nothing is

so fragile as the peaceful happiness of lovers.

Professor Hannah E. Bergman has found ample evidence of the same jaundiced view of matrimony in a number of plays in which the gracioso is a married man. In these plays the boredom and constant bickering of the gracioso couples contrast sharply with the romantic love of the usually not yet married protagonists. Professor Bergman finds it significant that most of the plays she examines were written within ten years after Calderón renounced the possibility of marriage to become a priest.

The three mythological plays--El mayor encanto, amor, El monstruo de los jardines and Fieras afemina amor--studied by Professor Angel Valbuena Briones present a philosophical basis for Calderón's rejection of sexual love. In each of these plays a hero of classical mythology is distracted from his true destiny by sexual passion, which clouds his understanding until he finally overcomes temptation by using his free will. Sexual passion, usually thought of as a virile attribute, is presented in these plays as a form of weakness which can reduce even a Hercules to effeminateness. According to the Neoplatonic philosophy underlying these plays, beauty should raise the intellect toward contemplation of the divine, not serve as an end in itself.

Professor Everett Hesse analyzes the constant presence of illusion in La vida es sueño. The characters in the play are caught in an intricate web of misunderstandings and further complicate matters by deceiving each other and themselves. All ends happily, however. For Hesse, the play's social message is that "it makes no difference whether we deceive ourselves or others, provided that our intentions are good."

La vida es sueño is the play which has most often been considered Calderón's masterpiece, but Professor Susana Hernández-Araico would reserve that title for La hija del aire. The two plays have much in common. Like La vida es sueño, La hija del aire deals with a prisoner--this time female--who rebels against an imprisonment which might have prevented the fulfillment of her gloomy horoscope. Concentrating upon Menón, the only truly tragic character in the play, Professor Hernández-Araico demonstrates how Calderón uses the complex and ambivalent image of the sun-- which at once symbolizes the King, feminine beauty

and reason--to presage Menón's downfall, brought about
by moral blindness and ending in physical blindness.
Menón brings his tragedy upon himself, but his punishment seems disproportionate to his crime.

Professor Francisco Ruiz-Ramón devotes most of his
paper to a study of La cisma de Inglaterra but begins
by defining the Calderonian "tragedy of error," of
which both that play and La hija del aire are among the
most important examples. In these tragedies each character, aiming towards a goal, makes a choice which leads
him away from that goal. The moment of anagnorisis
comes when the character, having arrived at exactly
the situation he had hoped to avoid, recognizes his
irreversible error. The presence of Fate--given dramatic expression in horoscopes, prophecies and dreams--
unifies the action, but the plays' message is conveyed
through dramatic irony, which reveals how each link in
a chain of events contributes to a total pattern of
meaning. These masterfully structured plays express
Calderón's tragic view of human nature as free to
choose but limited in choice by weakness, ignorance,
pride and sensuality.

Just as La hija del aire and La cisma de Inglaterra employ dramatic irony to reveal each episode of
the plot as at once resulting from erroneous human
choice and from the inexorable operation of Fate, La
devoción de la cruz constantly literalizes figurative
language to imbue what on the surface appears to be an
honor play with symbolic religious content. Professor
Edward Friedman examines Calderón's complex and subtle
use of ironic language in this play which contrasts
human and divine laws.

Two of the papers in this volume are devoted to El
príncipe constante, one of Calderón's plays which has
been attracting increasing critical attention in recent
years. Professor William Whitby notes that the final
scenes of this play, in which King Alfonso exchanges
the captive Moorish princess Fénix for the corpse of
Prince Fernando, have sometimes been considered superfluous or unimportant. Most critics have acknowledged
that the play functions on a literal level and on an
abstract, metaphorical one. Bruce Wardropper has
stated that it falls somewhere between comedia and
allegory. It has been suggested that the meaning of
the exchange of Fénix for Fernando's body is that
Beauty (represented by Fénix) is worth no more than a
corpse. Professor Whitby finds a more profound meaning

in the exchange. Fénix's words as the exchange takes place show that she sees the trade as the fulfillment of the mysterious prophecy according to which she would be the price of a dead man. When she says "cumplió el cielo su homenaje," the homenaje she refers to (albeit unawares) is the pact between Fernando and God. Homenaje was a term used to designate a pact which mutually obligated a vassal and a lord. Fernando (the vassal) has defended Ceuta for his lord (God). Now God keeps His part of the bargain by redeeming Fernando from captivity. The exchange is necessary to the fulfillment of poetic justice in the play.

Professor Alberto Porqueras-Mayo focuses his attention on the "bridge character" Muley, who connects the principal and secondary themes of the play. The gallant Moor Muley is adapted from the tradition of the romances fronterizos. He is friendly to Fernando but politically loyal to Fernando's captor, the King of Fez. In the play he performs some of the functions normally carried out by messengers and the chorus in Greek tragedy. By the end of the play, he has become an emblem of Friendship, just as Fernando is emblematic of Constancy and Fénix of Beauty.

Professor Donald Dietz examines how Calderón introduced a greater degree of conflict into his later autos sacramentales and thereby makes them more dramatically interesting. He distinguishes between horizontal conflict--a struggle between allegorical characters from two opposing camps--and vertical conflict, in which allegorical characters in the same camp fight against each other. In his early autos Calderón, like his predecessors, used only the horizontal conflict between the forces of good and evil. Calderón's boldest use of vertical conflict occurs in the auto version of La vida es sueño, in which he introduces dramatic tension among the three persons of the Trinity over the desirability of creating man and, after the fall, of redeeming him.

Professor J. Richards LeVan demonstrates how in the auto historial--an auto based on subjects from the Bible, legend, history or classical mythology-- Calderón adapted familiar stories to express new themes. In these plays a metaphorical pattern of religious ideas (conceptos imaginados) is superimposed upon the known plot. The auto Los encantos de la culpa, like the mythological play El mayor encanto, amor, is based on the myth of Ulysses and Circe.

However, in the auto Circe represents not just sexual passion but sin in general, which seduces the will (Ulysses) through its lust for life. Man's memory reminds him of the fact of death and shatters his hopes for temporal happiness. The Eucharist, a magical counter-charm to sin's encantos, enables man to cope with the fear of death and transform it into a positive spiritual force.

Professor Hans Flasche's paper, a study of Calderón's use of adjectives in the auto La vida es sueño, is the only paper in the volume with a linguistic orientation. According to Flasche, Calderón uses adjectives in extraordinary abundance and has a marked preference for placing the adjective before the noun it modifies. He sometimes places as many as four adjectives before a single substantive and uses adjectives prepositively twice as often as he places them after the noun. Sometimes the prepositive adjective expresses a subjective feeling, but one cannot generalize about this.

With the appearance in the seventeenth century of buildings specially designed and constructed for theatrical performances, a new style of performance, known as the stile rappresentativo, was born. Professor Alicia Amadei Pulice explains how the use of the three-dimensional perspective stage required changes in the very structure of drama. These changes consisted principally of a new emphasis on verisimilitude and an enhancement of the visual and auditory aspects of drama. Calderón was the first great playwright in Spain to write this new type of theater. He was extraordinarily sensitive to sight and sound, and he had scenery, music, histrionics, movement, gestures and facial expressions very much in mind when writing his plays. For this reason his works suffer much more than those of Lope de Vega, which were conceived as dramatic poetry, from an exclusively literary treatment.

Professor John Varey singles out a particular aspect of the staging of Calderón's work, the use of the "discovery space," for detailed study. In the corrales the discovery space was an enclosed area in the center and at the back of the stage, partitioned off by curtains which could be opened to "discover" a scene. Though often employed with shock effect to reveal the results of violence, it was most commonly used to represent a prison or cave. Since it was set back under the balcony and therefore relatively dark,

it served effectively for this purpose. In plays
written for performance at Court, the space repre-
senting the cave or grotto was placed at the rear of
the sets of perspective flats. Calderón was extremely
proficient in exploiting the symbolic possibilities
of the discovery space, using it to represent the
limits of human knowledge, the enslavement of man's
free will, Plato's cave, the womb and the tomb.

Professor Vern Williamsen studies Calderón's
importance as a transition figure between the comedia
nueva of Lope and Neoclassic drama. He begins by
analyzing Calderón's imitations of earlier works,
noting that when Calderón adapted plays by other
authors he improved their structure, achieving a
greater unity of theme, poetic imagery and characterization, and clarified and intensified their didacticism.
These qualities were in turn imitated by Calderón's
successors and were a very important factor in the
development of the Neoclassic esthetic in Spain.

Professor Bruce Wardropper stated in his keynote
address that since Lope's death in 1635, Calderón and
his imitators have reigned supreme in the Spanish
theater. In the concluding paper in this volume,
Professor Eduardo Urbina offers evidence of the per-
sistence of Calderón's influence in the twentieth
century. Most critics of Federico García Lorca's
work have indicated his debt to Lope de Vega but have
ignored, underestimated or even denied any influence
of Calderón on Lorca's work. Urbina, noting that the
auto La vida es sueño was the single work most often
performed by Lorca's theater company La Barraca, goes
on to demonstrate that the auto exerted a decisive
influence on Lorca's play La casa de Bernarda Alba
and that Lorca owed much of his concept of a popular
poetic theater to Calderón.

I believe that the major lesson that emerges from
this collection of critical studies is that even today,
three centuries after his death, Calderón remains a
largely unknown playwright. These trailblazing essays,
full of fresh insights and surprises, give us a glimpse
of the rich rewards awaiting future investigators of
the almost unexplored territory which is Calderón's
theater.

Michael D. McGaha
Pomona College

The Standing of Calderón in the Twentieth Century

Bruce W. Wardropper

Like most people who are not politicians, I am not accustomed to giving keynote addresses. Since I was not sure exactly what was expected of me, instead of asking the organizers of the Symposium about it, I consulted a dictionary. My Webster's tells me that a keynote address is one "that presents the essential issues of interest to the assembly." I have decided that for us there are two essential issues. The first is what has happened to Calderón's standing since his death was last commemorated on the grand scale in 1881. The second is what is going to happen to it at this Symposium of 1981. My address has thus two parts.

In the prologue to their admirable Calderón y la crítica: historia y antología, Manuel Durán and Roberto González Echevarría, addressing their Spanish readers, refer to the ignorance and neglect that had caused Calderón to be almost unknown "to our grandparents and even to our parents."[1] In their historia they seek to explain the neglect. Unlike Góngora, they say, "Calderón is apt to unleash polemics that rise above the purely esthetic plane. . . . Calderón's Catholicism, his undeniable adherence to seventeenth-century Spain, that is to say, to the Spain of the Counter-Reformation convalescence, cannot be sidestepped in the Peninsula" (p. 110). "In a century like ours," they continue, "which looks askance and suspiciously at all religious fanaticism, whether real or apparent . . . , Calderón could not avoid suffering, not now the officially sanctioned attacks of the eighteenth century, but at the very least silence" (p. 112). It is certainly true, as our Yale colleagues point out, that, while a number of Spanish scholars have made contributions to Calderonian studies, only a very few have specialized in them, notably Angel Valbuena Prat and his son Angel Valbuena Briones. Such key figures in Hispanic literary scholarship as Ramón Menéndez Pidal and Américo Castro have treated Calderón's work with a neglect suggesting contempt.

We are come here neither to bury nor to praise Calderón, but rather to appraise him. The appraisal of a writer is the best form of commemoration. For reasons which may or may not be valid, our colleagues in Spain must seem to the presumably committed

1

<u>calderonistas</u> in this hall to have been unjust in their appraisal of the writer whose death--and life--we are today commemorating. Those of us who are not Spaniards are privileged in not having to <u>feel</u> the <u>problema de España</u> as we study Spain's literature; we are privileged to be able to look at it dispassionately, although not all of us do. I think we should at least make the effort. In the case of Calderón, this means that we should begin by trying to understand why this great writer is anathema to so many Spaniards. Is the explanation given by Durán and González Echevarría the right or the only one? Is it really Calderón's commitment to an established and (perhaps) fanatical Church that makes Spanish scholars shy away from him?

The fact is that Calderón is unpopular not only among Spanish scholars but also among Spanish creative writers and intellectuals. One recalls, for example, those grotesquely Calderonian husbands of twentieth-century fiction--Ramón Pérez de Ayala's Tigre Juan and Ramón del Valle-Inclán's Don Friolera--and the non-Christian <u>autos</u> which Rafael Alberti and Miguel Hernández modelled on Calderón's. Calderón is as much the butt as the inspiration of these writers of fiction. Other great writers in this century, authors of essays and other forms of nonfiction, are so mesmerized by what they think he stands for that they cannot refrain from discussing him with high seriousness. Perhaps by considering some of their statements we may come to understand more clearly or more fully the reasons why he has been slighted by literary scholars.

I begin this brief survey with a quotation from José Ortega y Gasset which Durán and González Echevarría cite in their book: ". . . some present-day Spaniards, hearing the word 'Spain,' do not recall Calderón or Lepanto . . . but merely feel, and what they feel is pain. I do not know if there are many or few of these Spaniards; I do know that there are some, and that they would seem to me the best if I did not count myself among them" (p. 111). This is a conceit--and a conceited expression--of which Ortega must have been unusually proud, for he is here repeating, almost verbatim, words from a lecture entitled "Vieja y nueva política" which he delivered in March 1914.[2] The coupling of Lepanto and Calderón, the battle and the writer, as buzz words symbolizing what was rotten in Habsburg Spain, suggests that heroics and propaganda in the cause of religion represent an attitude

2

no longer shared by the "best" Spaniards. Rather than a vigorous active life in the service of faith, Ortega advocates a vigorous meditative life in the search for truth. Calderón is implicitly condemned as the major perpetuator of received--and presumably false--ideas.

In an excursus (originally written in 1947) in his Papeles sobre Velázquez y Goya, published in 1950, Ortega clarifies his earlier intuition about Calderón.[3] "Taken as a whole," he says, "his work and his inspiration (estro) have become exceedingly problematic for us [Spaniards]" (p. 212). Studying this problematic in a chapter on "Formalism," Ortega argues that an extended repetition of natural forms in life and in art results in a pathological "hypertrophy of these forms to the point where their vegetative exuberance covers over their spontaneous vital contents" (p. 201). The cancerous growth of these abnormal forms he calls "formalism." Velázquez, the painter of Calderón's age, was great because he avoided the perils of such formalism. In the royal palace, Velázquez's and Calderón's paths crossed every day, but they never met. Unlike Velázquez, Calderón, the poet of the age, surrendered to formalism.

In those typically Calderonian passages which Dámaso Alonso has studied as examples of correlación y recolección,[4] a catalogue of poetic features which is recapitulated at its end, Ortega sees "a formidable hardware (quincalla) of formalist versifications" (p. 212) which the poet inserts mechanically into the text of his dramas. Another formalism noted by Ortega is found in those passages in which a character makes a syntactically correct statement which is mispunctuated in every line by an emotional aside:

> Entre los brazos
> de mi esposo (¡pena extraña!)
> dormí (¡infelice desdicha!)
> y cuando (¡aliento me falta!),

and so the speech continues. "This reiteration of the asides . . . ," says Ortega, "creates the impression of a pathological tic and converts the second half of the lines into a kind of belching" (p. 216). But formalism of this sick kind is not limited to the verse; it extends to the plot. In plot construction Calderón is such a virtuoso that we grow weary as we watch him not just weaving plots but actually taking pleasure in his "enredismo puro" (p. 216). Now, the

addiction to such formalism of speech and plot was,
Ortega contends, philosophically and politically, a
serious matter; it "was disastrous for our nation . . .
because it turned minds away from their normal pursuit,
which is, quite simply, to understand what things are"
(p. 222). Calderón stands accused of having given
spectators what they had come to expect, of confirming
their prejudices, of distracting their attention from
the reality around them. If one believes that in
Europe the seventeenth century, the century of Galileo
and Descartes, marks the first movement toward the
modern, toward an emancipation from classical and
religious tradition, one must concede that the indict-
ment is not without merit.

A great twentieth-century poet who had no use for
Calderón was Antonio Machado, here considered as a
prose writer. Wearing the mask of his alter ego Juan
de Mairena, he compares one of Jorge Manrique's Coplas
--"¿Qué se hicieron las damas, / sus tocados, sus
vestidos, / sus olores?"--to Calderón's famous sonnet
in El príncipe constante: "Estas que fueron pompa y
alegría."5 The poet who has defined poetry as "la
palabra esencial en el tiempo,"6 now engaged in studying the Ars poetica of his fictional poet, argues that
"time (the vital time of the poet with its own vibration) is what the poet seeks to untemporalize . . . ,
to eternalize" (p. 297). Manrique's ubi sunt? and
Calderón's sonnet to the flowers both try to express
an analogous thought, the transience of time and the
ephemeral nature of human life. The medieval poet
pretends to know nothing; he inquires after ladies,
dresses, perfumes, lovers, thereby placing them in
his vital time. Calderón, evoking the light of dawn
and cold night, has used elements of nature which are
in themselves timeless. "Concepts and conceptual
imagery--thought, not intuited--are," Machado claims,
"outside of the poet's psychic time, outside of the
flow of his own consciousness" (p. 299). The difference between the copla and the sonnet is the difference
between lyric poetry and rhymed logic. In Calderón,
says Machado, poetry "does not sing; it reasons, it
discourses around a few definitions. It is--like all
or almost all of our literary baroque--belated scholasticism" (p. 299). I do not mean to cast doubt on the
sincerity of Machado's poetics; quite the contrary.
But it is, I believe, significant that the censure of
Calderón on esthetic grounds leads to an implied
censure of the mode of his religious thought. For
Machado Calderón's scholasticism was, or should have

been, out-of-date; yet scholasticism was still in Machado's day the official philosophy of the Spanish university. One senses that this great Spanish intellectual is blaming Calderón for perpetuating down to his Spain an outmoded philosophical system and the theological burden which it conveyed. Machado and Ortega agree that Calderón's drama has been instrumental in stifling freedom of thought in their country.

Moving back in time, I turn now to another great Spanish intellectual, Miguel de Unamuno. As all his readers know, Unamuno adored Segismundo almost as much as Don Quijote: they were both dreamers. But he had considerable reservations about the creators of these unsystematic dreamers, and especially about Calderón. The third essay in En torno al casticismo, entitled "El espíritu castellano," begins by asserting that the most castizo segment of castizo writing is the theater, and in it the most castizo drama is Calderón's.[7] This is so because Calderón embodies the local and transitory spirit of castizo Castilian Spain and its reverberations in later centuries. For Unamuno there is a casticismo with a positive value, which contains all humanity, and also one with a negative value, which perpetuates the narrow special interest of an exclusive caste. Calderón is castizo in this second, pejorative, sense: he is a "símbolo de casta" (p. 153) and also a "'símbolo de raza'" (p. 152). To successive generations of Spaniards, Unamuno holds, Calderón transmitted ideals which properly belong only to a privileged group of insiders, the ideals of Church and Court. Once again the playwright is represented as the inhibitor of the freedom of others.

As a writer Calderón does not fare well at Unamuno's hands. In his drama, facts are said to be presented "in a rough state" (en bruto) and "juxtaposed from the outside" (p. 153). The plot line is almost always impoverished and oversimplified; its effectiveness is diminished by too many episodes. Whereas Shakespeare managed to meld the adventitious with the subject of his plays, Calderón pasted it on. Calderón had recourse not to his "nimbus" but to a "realm of concepts," founded on a lifeless dissociative idealism, "not the sea bottom full of life but a cold, stony sky" (pp. 154-55).

I find Unamuno's discussion of Calderón in En torno al casticismo confusing. Unamuno, one must remember, is not a dialectical but an antithetical

5

thinker. He allows his distinction between the two kinds of casticismo to blur. Inadmissibly, he differentiates the Calderón who wrote La vida es sueño from the Calderón who wrote the other works, the angel of light, as it were, from the prince of darkness. Unhelpfully, he compares Calderón to the incomparable Shakespeare. And finally, it is paradoxical that Unamuno's objection to Calderón should be based on his having belonged to a select minority which pretended to speak for the whole nation, when Unamuno, a minority of one, pontificates for all Spaniards. From this narrow, and narrow-minded, perspective, Calderón is adjudged to be an unworthy symbol of what Unamuno takes to be the real Spain.

All three of the twentieth-century intellectuals whose views we have considered maintain that Calderón's influence on his country was pernicious because he endorsed the orthodoxy of his time. But so did Lope de Vega, Francisco de Quevedo, Baltasar Gracián, and all the great writers of the seventeenth century. What is puzzling to the non-Spanish Hispanist is why Calderón was singled out for special attack. One might suppose that it must have been because of the effectiveness of his advocacy of those commonly held ideas. Such is not, however, the case.

What the reader notes, even in the varied approach to Calderón's drama represented by these three thinkers, is a certain repetitiousness of language. For example, Ortega writes that the complexity of Calderón's plots "wearies us" (nos fatiga) (p. 216); for Unamuno, Calderón is the writer "we present-day Spaniards 'read with most weariness'" (leemos con más fatiga) (p. 152). Now, these last words are not Unamuno's own; he quotes them, approvingly, from Marcelino Menéndez Pelayo's Calderón y su teatro.[8] In fact, nearly all of Unamuno's criticism of Calderón is based on this book. Menéndez Pelayo had declared that "Calderón's capital sin" was monotony; Unamuno elaborates on this strange notion (p. 154, and note). There is little evidence that either he or the other intellectual critics had read more than a half-dozen of Calderón's plays. But they most certainly had read Calderón y su teatro. It is not too unfair to say that their criticism of their bugaboo is largely second-hand.

Calderonistas know that Don Marcelino's book is not to be taken seriously. Generations of Spaniards, taught in high school to venerate "the great polygraph,"

6

do not know this. The book has thus had an influence far exceeding its deserts—on intellectuals and lay people alike. The facts about this book are well known, but I will rehearse them briefly to place my argument in context. A hundred years ago, the twenty-five-year-old Menéndez Pelayo gave a series of eight lectures (or lecciones, as at times he arrogantly calls them) to the Unión Católica of Madrid to commemorate the bicentennial of Calderón's death. The lectures alternate praise and blame. Calderón is confidently adjudicated third place among the world's playwrights, after Sophocles and Shakespeare (p. 418). Calderón's glory "is the glory of an entire nation" (p. 408); he is, as Unamuno was to repeat, "símbolo de raza."[9] But he had "great defects (p. 418), such as inverosimilitude and the inability to create characters, which defects the lecturer dwells on at length. These lectures are most revealing when Menéndez Pelayo discloses, as though by accident, his personal prejudices: Calderón is not to him "personally . . . as likeable (simpático) as others among our dramatists"; "no name that we would rather (quisiéramos) prefer, neither Lope's, nor Tirso's, nor Alarcón's, would appear encircled with the halo of national glory" (p. 418), as does Calderón's. The critic obviously viewed his task as having distastefully to laud a patriotic emblem on an occasion of national self-congratulation. He could not, however, resist the temptation repeatedly to emphasize his personal preference for Lope: "To my mind, Lope is a much superior artist to Calderón, not only in his spontaneous and productive talent (vena) and his inexhaustible creation of plots, but even in his characteristic power to create characters, which is Calderón's weak point. . ." (p. 13). As Valbuena Prat has pointed out, the effect of this ambivalent treatment was to "'descalderonizar' a Calderón."[10] Dámaso Alonso has seen the other side of this coin: the lectures, he says, were designed to "overthrow Calderón from the pedestal in order to install Lope in it.[11]

Now, literary historians (and especially Dámaso Alonso) have made much of the alleged fact that Menéndez Pelayo was generous in retracting statements which he later came to regard as mistaken. It is generally supposed that in his foreword to Doña Blanca de los Ríos' book Del Siglo de Oro, published in 1910, he retracted his adverse opinion of Calderón. In fact, he gainsays not his critical judgment of the dramatist but only the "petulancia juvenil" with which

7

he expressed it.[12] Menéndez Pelayo's circumscribed palinode had in any case little effect on Calderón's reputation among Spanish scholars and intellectuals since it was buried in another scholar's rather inaccessible work. In the next year, 1911, Menéndez Pelayo effectively denatured the retraction, such as it was, by authorizing the second edition of Calderón y su teatro, with a few rectifications (as he calls them) in footnotes. These rectifications are designed to strengthen the general esteem for Lope at the expense of Calderón. For example, the original statement of 1881 that Lope's popularity has not been "as deep or lasting" as Calderón's is footnoted in 1911 as follows: "Today this idea does not seem to me correct, far from it. Elsewhere I will rectify it along with several other points touched on in these youthful, improvised lectures" (p. 12, note 1). Las palinodias de don Marcelino were hardly magnanimous: they continue and fortify the campaign against Calderón. And the authority of their author has implanted his prejudices in a century of Spanish intellectual life and literary scholarship. The irony in this sorry episode lies in the fact that the Calderonian values so disparaged by Unamuno, Machado, and Ortega, those of Court and Church, are the very values which Menéndez Pelayo upheld. In these circumstances one sees why it was imperative for non-Spaniards to pursue Calderonian studies at some distance from Spain itself.

The tricentennial will be celebrated not just here in Los Angeles but in many parts of the world, not least in Madrid. For this event it has proved necessary to enlist the services of some eminent Spanish scholars --the main ones being Antonio Domínguez Ortiz, Rafael Lapesa, and Emilio Orozco--who are completely unremarkable for their Calderonian scholarship. Once again, Calderón's drama has become a rallying point for a national piety based on ignorance. The "símbolo de raza" has lost none of its virtue. But, a century after Menéndez Pelayo's exercise in cynicism, the pious event rings hollow. Literary history needs to be realigned to show that since Lope's death in 1635 Calderón and his imitators have reigned supreme in the Spanish theater, not always admired by intellectuals, but nearly always the darlings of the masses. In this sense, it was Calderón, and not Lope, who established the Spanish theater.

It is not at all certain that Calderón would have relished the success of his dramatic formula, but success it was. In the eighteenth century, Cañizares,

8

żamora, and Comella paid him the tribute of their in-
different imitations and refundiciones, while Calderón's
own plays still drew large audiences.[13] Ramón de la
Cruz parodied him, a most sincere form of flattery. In
1785-1786 Vicente García de la Huerta capitalistically
republished his works in his Theatro Hespañol in
response to a known popular demand. The Neoclassic
Ignacio de Luzán, far from damning Calderón, comments
that because of his genius his faults become beauties
(primores), and that he observes the greatest of all
esthetic rules, that of gripping the spectators'
attention. "He served and serves as a model," writes
Luzán, "and his plays are the most renewable capital
(el caudal más redituable) of our theatre."[14] Juan
Pablo Forner has his fictitious Cervantes praise
Calderón's great talent.[15] In La comedia nueva even
the afrancesado Moratín the Younger grudgingly con-
cedes Calderón's mastery. When in 1814 José Joaquín
de Mora and Johann Nikolas von Faber were debating
the issues of Romanticism, Calderón was at the center
of their debate. Juan Eugenio Hartzenbusch edited
(badly, but never mind) Calderón's works at an early
stage in the production of the Biblioteca de Autores
Españoles. In 1870 the now forgotten dramatist
Adelardo López de Ayala gave a once famous eulogy
of Calderón in his reception speech to the Royal
Spanish Academy. And in the bicentennial year of
1881 the enthusiasm for Calderón was unabated.

At the same time that Menéndez Pelayo was demolish-
ing Calderón's stature before the Unión Católica, less
biased minds were testifying to his importance as an
artist. The Universidad Central of Madrid held an
acto público to announce the results of a poetic competition it had organized in celebration of Calderón's
genius. Students had been invited to write poems
honoring Calderón with the enticement of a gold medal
as the prize for the best poem, and silver and bronze
ones for the runners-up. The jury determined that it
could not in good conscience award the gold medal.
Indeed, the Memoria[16] in which the accepted poems were
published is a repository of atrocious verse; but
undergraduate poetry has seldom merited gold medals.
What I find appealing in the Memoria is a "Dialogue
in imitation of the poetic academies of the seventeenth
century," which was performed by students but merci-
fully written by one "Don Juan de Dios de la Rada y
Delgado, Director y Catedrático de la Escuela Superior
de Diplomática." The title of this dialogue is un-
promising--"¡Vítor á don Pedro Calderón!"--but the

dialógue repays a reading. The interlocutors are
Licio, a proponent of Calderón's drama, and Aurelio,
a self-confessed detractor. The style is a delicate
blend of Calderón and Bécquer. Licio declaims:

> Quien mira del ave sólo
> Las leves alas plegadas,
> Mal comprenderá su vuelo
> Cuando al espacio se lanza;
> El que contempla la rosa
> Sin acercarse á besarla,
> Mal percibirá el perfume
> Con que enriquece sus galas;
> Y quien ve la forma sólo
> Y el pensamiento no alcanza
> Sin penetrar el sentido
> Que su valor aquilata,
> Apénas ve lo que mira
> Su inteligencia velada (pp. 78-79).

Aurelio's and Licio's debate over Calderón's weaknesses
and strengths is modelled on Cipriano's debate with El
Demonio in El mágico prodigioso. In the face of Licio's
stubborn arguments in support of Calderón, Aurelio
finally acknowledges defeat, using the Devil's words
to Justina: "Venciste, Licio, venciste / Con no dejarte
vencer" (p. 83). It turns out, happily, that Aurelio
has been convinced all along of Calderón's preeminence
as a dramatist. He has been only testing Licio's
debating skill: "Las razones que me dabas, / Apénas
las formulabas / Eran ya razones mías" (p. 83). It is
a good-humored academic exercise which lets one see
that Rada had a good, even subtle, understanding of
Calderón's art and thought. He must have been quite
taken aback by the publication of Calderón y su teatro.
The disciples of Rada and other forgotten professors
like him were to be denied the evident love and joy for
Calderón that still thrived in 1881. A single mean-
spirited man was to change the course of Spanish
literary history, and leave Calderonian scholarship
stunted in Spain for many decades. Calderón would become the scapegoat of those intellectuals who would
fruitlessly ponder the insoluble problema de España.

Fortunately, those of us who have been banished
from Spanish soil by accident of birth, civil war, or
avarice have not had to cope with this problema de
España, a problem well characterized by José Bergamín's
book title, but not by his beautiful lead essay of the
same title, Calderón y cierra España.[17] Disengaged

from such controversy by our emancipation from an enervating nationalism, we have been freed to view Calderón as a creator of works of art. This Symposium has put aside the distracting and sterile polemic initiated by Menéndez Pelayo, and continued by those who endorsed uncritically his prejudices. It has installed in its place a considerable body of scholarship which seeks--at least seeks--to establish the truth about his art.

I have been privileged to read, in advance of the Symposium, all of the papers that will be delivered. In the remainder of this address, I shall try to whet your appetite for the intellectual feast of which you are about to partake. I hope to give you a general impression of what lies in store for us. I shall mention a few trends and ideas, but no names; and I shall refrain from commending or censuring any of the papers. I have no desire to destroy the pleasure of anticipation.

This Symposium clearly brings Calderonian criticism up to date, but not yet into line with the diverse continental movements known collectively as la nouvelle critique. You will hear mention of semiotics and deconstructionism, but you will not be severely taxed by them. The aggiornamento to which I refer consists rather of some advance beyond the now overworked análisis temático-estructural, Robert Pring-Mill's controversial term for the critical method employed by most British and American Hispanists since the Second World War.[18] There is, however, no need yet to toll a knell for close reading; you will be able to listen to some illuminating exercises in this technique.

The school associated with Edward Wilson and Alexander Parker tended to show us a Calderón whose thought was clear, but unoriginal because it was in accord with Tridentine orthodoxy, a Calderón whose art presented that orthodoxy quite unambiguously. This view of the dramatist is about to be challenged in your hearing. One speaker will tell us that Calderón's art is actually heterodox. Several speakers recognize the "dark side" of his life and his drama. The uneasy, even violent, father-son relationship, first noted by Parker in 1966,[19] is beginning to be seen as a key to understanding the development of his drama. The sense of a lucid, rational Calderón is now yielding to a realization that in the early plays--the

ones we read most--he writes as a tormented, questioning and doubting, questing man.

I have just alluded to that regrettably small number of early plays that have tended to constitute the
Calderonian canon for scholars here and abroad. You
will hear voiced at this Symposium various complaints
about this miniscule canon. One speaker will assure
us that Calderón is "a largely unknown dramatist."
Another will bemoan the neglect suffered by La hija
del aire. In the wake of these complaints, I am happy
to be able to tell you that in many of the papers you
will hear discussions of late mythological and other
court plays, of autos sacramentales, of entremeses.
In this year of commemoration, the old canon has been
dramatically enlarged. One of our colleagues makes
the point that one cannot understand Calderón after
reading only a half-dozen plays; it is necessary to
read every single line he wrote. In opposition to
this view, you will hear it argued that the two
sonnets in El príncipe constante are the microcosm
of Calderón's macrocosmic art, and that they therefore contain the quintessence of his dramatic oeuvre.
El príncipe constante may well be the text most cited
by our speakers; but it is encouraging to be able to
report that La hija del aire does not run far behind.
The expansion of the canon is largely responsible for
the revision of many of the tenets of the Anglo-
American school, if school it was.

In 1981 we are no longer so sure that Calderón
abhorred the cruel code of conjugal honor on the narrow
ground that it was incompatible with Christianity. The
ambiguities in the honor plays are now frankly recognized as such; and so the plays have become one aspect
of Calderón's art which is subject to drastic reinter-
pretation. One speaker sees honor as a duty imposed
on man, which, like so many other social and religious
imperatives, cannot be accepted and performed without
intolerable concomitant suffering. Another sees honor
as a tyrannical social "law" which husbands obey only
because of their jealous desire, a desire which structures all fiction. For still another, honor is one
of Calderón's great subjects, or matières; in his
plays honor functions as a contemporary myth. If
these new perceptions of Calderón's treatment of honor
sound solemn, a more lighthearted contributor to the
Symposium will show you that, even in his serious
mythological plays for the court, he took a dim view
of marriage, one which is strikingly akin to the

12

irreverent attitude to marriage we find expressed in farce.

As I have said, the mythological plays will not be neglected at this Symposium. The whole question of Calderón's treatment of myth receives perceptive attention. Mythology sometimes provides elemental situations to which Calderón returns time and again in his drama. One such case--that of the hero who is temporarily distracted from his heroic mission by dalliance with a lady, nymph, or vixen--will be offered for your inspection. Deep structure of this kind may also be furnished by the myths of Christianity itself; one paper tentatively relates the Christian belief in hell to the discovery-space in corrales, carros, and court theaters.

In the Symposium papers, little attention is paid to actual performances. We will be treated, nevertheless, to a historical survey of how theater construction and changing acting styles helped to produce Calderón's distinctive kind of comedia, leaner and more unified than Lope's, but at the same time more spectacular because it deliberately appeals to the senses of sight and hearing. Several papers adopt such a historical perspective. One of them sees Calderón's work against the background of his so-called minor precursors and contemporaries, pointing toward the regimented official theater of the eighteenth century. Another distinguishes the "horizontal conflict," a frontal assault on Man by adversary forces in the autos sacramentales which preceded Calderón's, from the "vertical conflict" engineered by Calderón, in which the passions and the elements war among themselves as they war against Man.

It is Calderón's language that is underrepresented at this Symposium. You will hear, however, papers on his figurative use of language, and on the significance of his peculiar habit of placing more than one adjective before the noun they modify. Much work remains to be done in this area.

I have not been able to give you more than a sampler of the treats that await you, but I hope I have persuaded you that Calderón will be well served by this Californian Symposium. The revaluation of his work which it undertakes does not find it wanting, but rather, richer and more complex than an earlier generation had supposed. There will be some, perhaps

many, who will distrust and gainsay much that will be
asserted about Calderón's art at the Symposium. This
is as it should be, for scholarship thrives on re-
buttal. It is fitting that in what remains of this
century controversy over the interpretation of
Calderón's work and legacy should be conducted, not
in the essays and polemical writings of those who
know little about it, but in the community of literary
scholars--a part of which is gathered together at this
Symposium.

                              Duke University

Notes

[1] (Madrid: Gredos, 1976), p. 8.

[2] Obras completas, 3ª edición (Madrid: Revista de Occidente, 1953), I, 268.

[3] I cite from the first edition of this work (Madrid: Revista de Occidente, 1950).

[4] "La correlación en la estructura del teatro calderoniano," in Dámaso Alonso & Carlos Bousoño, Seis calas en la expresión literaria española (Madrid: Gredos, 1951), pp. 115-86.

[5] I cite from Poesías completas (Buenos Aires: Espasa-Calpe Argentina, 1940). The unscannable modernized spelling of Manrique's text is Machado's.

[6] "Poética," in Poesía española: Antología (contemporáneos), ed. Gerardo Diego (Madrid: Signo, 1934), p. 152.

[7] Ed. Francisco Fernández Turienzo (Madrid: Ediciones Alcalá, 1971), p. 152.

[8] I cite from the second edition of 1911.

[9] P. 15. A footnote on this term in the second edition, written when the piety of commemoration had worn off, retracts this silly epithet on silly grounds: "Le covirtieron los románticos alemanes, partiendo de una falsa idealización del carácter español y del mismo genio calderoniano. También este punto debe rectificarse. (Nota de esta edición.)"

[10] Historia de la literatura española, 5ª edición (Barcelona: Gili, 1957), III, 362.

[11] Menéndez Pelayo crítico literario (Las palinodias de don Marcelino) (Madrid: Gredos, 1956), p. 99.

[12] Cited from Dámaso Alonso, Menéndez Pelayo crítico literario, p. 100. I do not have ready access to Blanca de los Ríos' book.

[13] The point is clearly demonstrated by a perusal of the titles of Calderón plays listed in Ada M. Coe,

Catálogo bibliográfico y crítico de las comedias anunciadas en los periódicos de Madrid desde 1661 hasta 1819 (Baltimore: The Johns Hopkins Press, 1935).

[14]La poética, ed. Russell P. Sebold (Barcelona: Labor, 1977), p. 404. It is noteworthy that the chapter from which this quotation is taken does not appear in the 1737 edition but in the posthumous one of 1789, when neoclassic dramatic art was as close as it ever would be to being established in Spain.

[15]Juan Pablo Forner, Exequias de la lengua castellana, ed. Pedro Sainz y Rodríguez, Clásicos Castellanos, No. 66 (Madrid: Espasa-Calpe, 1941), p. 121.

[16]Memoria de la Universidad Central al 2º Centenario de don Pedro Calderon de la Barca: se incluyen las composiciones en verso castellano premiadas en el certámen (Madrid: [no publisher indicated: Tipografía de Gregorio Estrada], 1881.

[17](Barcelona: Planeta, 1979). Only the first essay, which gives its title to the book, concerns Calderón. Despite the promising title, the essay is, in the line of Jacques Maritain's adaptation of scholasticism to the modern age, an endorsement of Calderón's Catholic influence on Spanish history, at complete variance with the tradition of Menéndez Pelayo, Unamuno, Machado, and Ortega. Of particular interest to my thesis, in contradiction of the views held by these other intellectuals, is the assertion that "El cierra España de Calderón es el de la eterna aventura viva de una España libertadora, revolucionaria. Aventura que le decadencia histórica, la degeneración viva española, la corrupción--por el costumbrismo--de aquellas virtudes esenciales de lo español, vino convirtiendo en 'cerrazón' espiritual, es decir, en 'cerrazón' antiliberal" (p. 11).

[18]"Los calderonistas de habla inglesa y La vida es sueño: métodos del análisis temático-estructural," Litterae Hispanae et Lusitanae, ed. Hans Flasche (München: Max Hueber Verlag, 1968), pp. 369-413.

[19]"The Father-Son Conflict in the Drama of Calderón," FMLS, 2 (1966), 99-113.

Towards a Psychological Profile of
Pedro Calderón de la Barca

Manuel Durán

Sigmund Freud's famous sentence, "Anatomy is destiny," is, according to many of Freud's critics, too Manichaean an approach to our psychological problems: whether we are born male or female decides everything. Other Manichaean approaches are also possible, and although they seem to satisfy our need for black-and-white definitions, they are equally dangerous. In the realm of literature, they imply a choice between two apparently irreconcilable directions, two systems of values. As in philosophy one is supposed to choose between Plato and Aristotle, in literature we should cast our lot: Tolstoy or Dostoievski? Thomas Mann or Franz Kafka? Albert Camus or Jean-Paul Sartre?

In the field that concerns many of us, the Spanish drama of the Golden Age, the inevitable choice would be, Lope de Vega or Calderón de la Barca?

The Manichaean approach has great merit as a way of enhancing the profiles of a system of values, whether ethical or artistic, by contrasting it with another system which is in many ways its opposite. A great tool for teaching purposes, it outlines and concentrates our attention upon the center of the creative process, the relationship between the parts and the whole, which can be shown to be quite different from the way other writers have organized their work.

In practical terms, and assuming we accept the Manichaean constraint, we should be able to decide, as literary critics, whether on the whole Lope de Vega was the greater writer, or whether Calderón merits being placed on a higher pedestal.

Perhaps we want to go a step beyond the Manichaean choice. Perhaps this choice is unnecessary, perhaps literary criticism and the enjoyment of literature cannot and should not be equated to a horse race with its winner of first place and of second place. Perhaps each writer should be defined on his own terms, that is, related to what he or she wanted to do, to the frontiers and barriers supplied by his generation, his culture, his psychology.

Which brings us to a real obstacle in the case of
Calderón. A work of art, a career in art, is of course
a vast exercise in communication, and this effort is
organized along the lines of a system of values and a
technique of expressing such a system. Again aesthetics
is, of course, at the core of this attempt to express
and communicate. In the case of Calderón, we know much
about his technique, his system of values, and we assume
that the social and historical background that gave
birth to his art was not basically different from Lope's
background. If we want to explain why his art differs
from Lope de Vega's, why he offers us an alternative
to Lope's vision of the world, we are forced into an
analysis of texts, which is always helpful, and moreover into an analysis of the personalities that produced the works. Calderón versus Lope. It is easy to
see that when it comes to psychological analysis, when
we want to define what kind of individual wrote these
great plays, we know all, or almost all, about Lope de
Vega, and nothing, or next to nothing, about Calderón.
As a man, Lope was an exhibitionist, devoid of moral
principles, "beyond good and evil," and definitely not
a gentleman. As a man, Calderón was the opposite,
secretive to the point that we know almost nothing
about his life. While Lope boasts, Calderón conceals.
We must assume Lope lies sometimes. Calderón does not
lie: he remains silent. And he remains always a
gentleman.

Yet Calderón's silence, his omissions, his evasive-
ness about his life, remain a source of concern to all
of us who are interested in his art. Addressing first
the most basic or the easiest question, that of why
Lope was so talkative about his life (letters, mixture
of art and biography in La Dorotea, etc.) while on the
other hand Calderón was so secretive about his life
and art (no basic theory, nothing like the Arte Nuevo
by Lope) we can give only a provisional answer: Lope's
expansive view of life, love, and art is rooted in an
expansive psychology of power, pleasure, and amorality:
Lope is "beyond good and evil." Calderón, on the other
hand, is always mindful of his relationship with the
authorities: God, King, Father, and his temporary
lack of obedience will be overcompensated for both in
his life and in his works. Hence a detailed study of
Calderón's life will give us some clues about his art.

As a brief autobiographical footnote I should like

to add that as a graduate student I took a course on
Cervantes given by a professor, who, in retrospect, I
would judge to be slightly insane. He came to class
garbed in academic robes, which was not in itself too
upsetting. What was far worse was his insistence that
only Cervantes' biography mattered if we wished to
understand Don Quixote and Cervantes' other works.
The pendulum of critical attitudes had moved so fast
after I took this course that three years later I was
told that another famous professor who taught a course
on Cervantes refused to talk about the author of Don
Quixote and exclaimed at the beginning of his course,
"Cervantes? Who was he? Only the text of Don Quixote
matters." A middle course is often the most judicious.

I intend in this paper to make use of Calderón's
biography in order to achieve a better definition of
what I consider one of the basic themes of Calderón's
theater, the relationship between love and duty. This
relationship is crucial to such important plays as La
vida es sueño, El príncipe constante, and all the dramas
of honor. A correct interpretation of Calderón's psychology and system of values may be of help if we want
to understand why this relationship between honor and
duty, on the one hand, and love and passion, on the
other, often ends in frustrating self-denial and even
in the painful necessity of murdering someone dear to
us.

The main obstacle to any critic trying to make use
of Calderón's biography in order to shed light upon his
art is that he soon finds out that we do not have such
a biography. The attempts made by Cotarelo y Mori and
by Frutos Cortés are at best external data, not real
biographies. They tell us when and where he was born,
when he wrote certain works, when he became a priest,
yet they leave Calderón's personality a blank. Since
we do not possess a real biography I intend to make
use of Erik Erikson's principles, as seen for instance
in his book Young Man Luther, and through psychohistory,
in order to reach a preliminary psychological profile
of Calderón. If we can define Calderón as a person,
if we can see him as a man, we shall understand Calderón as an artist much better. I also suspect that
many clues to his personality can be found in his works.
It was an acute observer of men who once remarked: "If
you want to hide something, put it in the most obvious
place." Like Sherlock Holmes, we may conclude that
Calderón hid the most salient aspects of his personality, aspects he was not proud of, in his plays, the

19

most obvious and public of places. In order to confirm my psychological hypotheses about Calderón the man, I shall try to find structural parallels and similar choices and systems of value in his theatre. In order to avoid circularity I shall make use of the method of deconstructive criticism as enunciated in the theoretical and critical works of Paul de Man and Jacques Derrida, thus avoiding the danger of proving something about Calderón's works by an allusion to his life and his psychology, which could be supported only by an allusion to his works. My method, though apparently somewhat complex, is, in reality, very simple: if you want to verify the result of a subtraction you add the resulting sum to the sum above and it should be identical to the first sum: this much we learned in grammar school.

In my attempt at a psychological profile I shall concentrate upon the years 1615-1625. Calderón, born in 1600, is 15 years old at the beginning of this period. My focus will be placed upon Calderón as a young man, long after infancy and childhood, but well before fame, power, and self-consciousness as a public figure. Thus it falls between traditional Freudian emphasis upon the early years--the earlier the better--and the interest of traditional history in the years of public influence.

The crucial event which occurs at the beginning of this period is the death of Calderón's father, a stern bureaucrat, an authoritarian, of strong personality, who in his will calls himself "gran pecadoraço," "a great sinner." Energetically in that same will, he decides what the future of his children will be. Because of the death of Calderón's mother, when the future dramatist was only ten years old, his childhood and adolescence were devoid of the influence of a loving mother. Therefore his father's presence assumed greater importance in his development than it might have. In 1615, on his death bed, the stern father orders young Pedro to become a priest. Narciso Alonso Cortés has published the text of this will (<u>Rev. de Filología Esp.</u>, II, 1915, pages 41-51) in which we read, "A Pedro le mando y ruego que por ningún caso deje sus estudios, sino que los prosiga y acabe, y sea muy buen capellán de quien con tanta liberalidad le dejó con que poder hacerlo." (There was a foundation with an important income left by an aunt to establish a chaplaincy destined to any of the male children of the Calderón family.) Pedro's mother, however, had already pointed out that the most likely candidate to priesthood was the young Pedro: in an autobiographical _romance_ he writes,

> Crecí, y mi señora madre,
> religiosamente astuta,
> como había en otra cosa
> dió en que había de ser cura
>
> (Frutos, p. 12)

which indicates that both his father and his mother were of the same mind: Pedro should become a priest. The young man, however, disobeys, at least for a while, for a long while. As Frutos puts it, "esta materna resolución pesó como un sino sobre la vida calderoniana. Ella hizo que su padre lo encaminase hacia la Universidad. Pero parece que, consciente o inconscientemente, Calderón resistió a su destino . . ." (Frutos, p. 12). The most important aspect of young Pedro's life at that critical moment is his decision to disobey. During the next 10 years his life becomes erratic, unpredictable, aimless. There is no doubt that disobeying the wishes of his father and his mother in such an important matter must have created strong feelings of guilt in a 15-year-old adolescent who was reserved, shy, nervous, and sensitive (as the graphological analysis of his handwriting shows: see Frutos, p. 10) and who was rebelling certainly not out of a lack of religious faith or a lack of respect for his parents. Instead he was facing a deep psychological problem; a sharp, bitter, wounding identity crisis. Who was he, what did he want out of life? He knew he had to search much further before he could bow down and accept his parents' will. While experimenting with his desires and projects, he was bound to increase his feelings of guilt since these wishes and projects would carry him, for a period of ten years in an open way, and for a much longer period in a less clearly defined way, far from the destiny that had been preordained by both his father and his mother. All of this, and much more, had to be hidden from the public view, especially later when he became famous. In any case, his private life had to become a secret life for the simple reason that he could not let other people know a painful secret he himself wanted to forget: in his action as a disobedient son, he had erred and sinned gravely against his parents and against his God. An entire lifetime is not enough to atone for such a sin.

In the meantime his life as a student (and we

should not forget that in his mind his career as a college student was closely linked to his becoming a priest) becomes erratic and unpredictable. Pedro began studying at the University of Alcalá in 1614. Yet in December of 1615 he leaves for Salamanca, and does not return to Madrid until May 1616. In October 1616 he registers again in Alcalá as a student of Canon Law and also in Salamanca but it seems he does not leave Madrid, in fact attends neither University: all the documents and bills containing similar dates place him in Madrid. He is therefore "going through the motions" by pretending to obey his parents' injunctions, and by pretending to continue his studies in preparation to become a priest, while in practice deceiving such expectations and biding his time.

The inner struggle in his heart must have been intense. All his training as a young scholar (with the Jesuits, in Alcalá), was based upon a hierarchical and authoritarian view of the world, an implicit acceptance of authority. His society, his peers, his parents and his grandparents served only to reinforce this notion of implicit acceptance of authority. As a child he seems to have been timid and not too assertive. Yet at age 15 he finds within himself the strength to defy his parents, his society and his God by refusing to prepare for the priesthood. He renounces his ecclesiastical career; he begins to write poetry, he takes part in street brawls and to compete in poetry contests, writes his first play in 1623. However, at the very moment when his name is becoming well known, he disappears from Madrid suddenly. From 1623 to 1625 he does not seem to live in Spain at all (Italy or Flanders, probably both?). What we know about his private life from 1625 on is even less than nothing or next to nothing. His biography is simply a series of titles and publishing dates, with a few special moments: in 1636 he is awarded a great nobiliary reward, the "Hábito de Santiago"; in 1640 he participates in the Catalan campaign; in 1650 he becomes a priest, at last. His rebellion against his parents' wishes thus has lasted for approximately 35 years of his mature life. During this time he has written many of his masterpieces, including La vida es sueño (1635), El príncipe constante (1628) and El médico de su honra (1635). By now the main artistic trends of his work are established, and I must underline that this great artistic production is taking place during a period when Calderón is undergoing a threefold moral crisis. In the first place, with respect to his ecclesiastical career,

he is conscious of having disobeyed his parents. In
the second place, from 1636 on, Calderón is very much
a part of a subtle conspiracy directed by the Count
of Olivares against King Philip IV. The appearances
of this conspiracy are unusually mild and even laud-
able. Olivares builds a beautiful palace for the King
and organizes countless spectacles, plays, ballets,
concerts, in his honor. Calderón cooperates both by
writing and occasionally directing many of these lavish
entertainments. The King approves and commends Calderón in this effort: nothing should be spared in
order to make the Spanish court the most elegant and
artistically creative in the whole of Europe. Yet,
this entire effort was flawed from its very inception.
It was a deliberate and a successful attempt to mes-
merize the King--to distract his attention by turning
his mind away from matters of State so that he,
Olivares, could become, for all practical purposes,
the real ruler, the true King of Spain. Calderón--
certainly not a man lacking in intelligence, perception, or psychological insight--became Olivares'
trusted secretary in this dubious endeavor, one which
we can consider to have been bordering upon treason.
Calderón with his art, helped to make the King forget
his role, his obligations, his duty. There can be no
doubt in our minds that at a certain moment, not far
from the beginning of the scheme in 1636, Calderón
must have been aware of the intent of Olivares' plan
to take over the real power to rule Spain. This would
mean that the true King would be relegated to the
role of spectator of Calderón's plays. Let me emphasize that the King was surrounded by stages, plays
and spectacles: next to his bedchamber there was a
theater stage, the gardens in his palace contained no
less than three areas where these spectacles and plays
could be performed day after day. Wherever we look
during these years we see the handiwork of Calderón.

His private life was or should have been a source
of worry and anguish to a man of his lofty moral
principles. A liaison, an illegitimate child, and
a series of public scandals (the death of Nicolás de
Velasco, the "affaire" of the Trinitarian Convent, in
1628, when Calderón is subjected to house arrest for
a few days) all reveal that the playwright not only
had decided to momentarily disobey his father's order
to become a priest, but they also prove that for the
moment he would assert himself as a free man and as a
sinner. He would rather be a soldier and a knight
than refuse a fair fight, sword in hand: in 1640 he

is wounded in just such a street fight or duel. His title of Knight of the Military Order of Santiago dates from 1637. He fights in the Catalonian campaigns, in 1640 and 1642. In 1642 Calderón seems to tire of military life and his petition to be relieved from his duties is granted. In 1645 his younger brother José died in battle and his elder brother D. Diego died in 1647. These were serious blows to our playwright. It is not impossible to conclude that he may have interpreted in their deaths a warning from Heaven that sinners should repent before it is too late. The basic psychological situation is this: a young man educated by authoritarian parents and whose system of values and sensitivity to hierarchy were reinforced by his Jesuit education has failed, at least for a while, to heed the orders and messages given to him by all the authorities: God, family, society.

The reaction from above, from the Heavens, could be interpreted as being mainly negative: Calderón's brothers have been struck down. When it is the turn of Calderón's only son to die in 1657, at the age of 10, the shock and pain must have compelled him to think once more about the problems of filial obedience, career, destiny, and God's will. Calderón became a priest in 1650, in no way diminishing his production as a playwright. We know nothing about Calderón's mistress. It is permissible to speculate that she may have died while giving birth to their son, or soon afterwards.

Two facts dealing with Calderón's final years deserve some attention. The first is that our dramatist cares a great deal about his work: he points out repeatedly which plays are his and which are imitations or forgeries. The second is that in his final will he seems anxious to emphasize, above all else, his role of priest by willing all his possessions to the Madrid Congregation of Presbyters or priests.

By placing all these facts before us we can conclude the following: just as was the case with the young Luther, Calderón undergoes a slow and painful crisis in his search for his true identity and his role in life. This crisis, however, is not resolved in any dramatic gesture of rebellion but in the eventual acceptance of his father's will. Calderón retreats step by step from his youthful life of "indiscretions," street brawls and sexual transgressions. Since he understands that sooner or later he will

24

become a priest, he adopts the habit of carefully con-
cealing every one of his actions early in life. Later
on this habit will persist even though Calderón does
not have anything to hide. Only his work, especially
his plays, is worthy of his attention: in a way his
plays justify him, since the problem of love versus
duty and honor is carefully discussed in them, and
since in them, duty and honor triumph (on the whole)
over passion: if we want to understand Calderón's
struggle on the road towards priesthood we will have
to look at the plays, and if we want to understand the
basic element behind many of his plays we must think
about Calderón's slow and deliberate withdrawal from
his youthful world of pleasures.

Ultimately, the inner crisis in Calderón's life
was resolved by an act of will, of renunciation: in-
stincts and passions must be repressed and suppressed,
only in this way can salvation be attained. It is no
wonder that the idea of freedom of choice attained
through the inner exercise of willpower plays such an
important role in Calderón's theatre. As James E.
Maraniss puts it,

> The concept of freedom of choice appears in its
> clearest form in the autos sacramentales, some-
> times even as an independent allegorical charac-
> ter such as Libre Albedrío; in the "metaphysical"
> plays, such as underline{El} príncipe constante and underline{La} vida
> underline{es} sueño, it is discussed openly and acted upon
> (Segismundo chooses restraint, Fernando chooses
> martyrdom); and in the honor plays it is implied.
> In Calderón's plays a correct choice brings peace,
> even salvation. Earthly appetites, and the strong
> emotions they arouse, are presented as a kind of
> limitation to Calderón's characters' efforts to
> achieve self-fulfillment. But these limitations
> can be overcome through acts of will; and Cal-
> derón constructs his plays to emphasize the will,
> which, no matter how powerful the obstacles to
> its functioning, always functions and always
> succeeds.

If we remember that many of the plays mentioned above
were written before 1650, that is, before Calderón,
through a painful act of will and renunciation, put
an end to his mundane life and was ordained, we will
realize that in these works Calderón seems to be talk-
ing to himself, showing himself the way, the correct
path. He may also have directed a message to God:

God, the ideal reader, must have understood that Calderón knew exactly what should be done, since he instructed his characters correctly, even if he, Don Pedro, as a man, was taking his time in translating into action, into his private life, what his characters so flawlessly and artistically carried out on the stage. It is impossible, of course, to footnote my intuition which is that throughout his tragic and metaphysical plays Calderón is trying to justify his behavior by alluding to an imminent change in his private life. I think such an intuition can be judged solely on the merits of whether it adds to or subtracts from our understanding and enjoyment of Calderón's theatre.

A tempting corollary (and even more precarious, on logical and positivistic grounds) to the paragraph above could be the following. Let us assume that Calderón's plays are addressed to three audiences: to the general public, to Calderón himself, and to God. The dialogue between Calderón and God which is carried out through the plays written before 1650 could be described briefly in this manner: Calderón argues that he needs more time before reforming and becoming a priest, and that this time should be granted to him, because he knows what must be done, as he indicates in his plays. God may reject such a line of reasoning. Calderón might well retort by saying that there sometimes are tragic and appalling consequences to a blind acceptance of "duty"--which brings me precisely to the point of his plays dealing with marital honor.

The English school of Calderonian criticism in general, and Alexander Parker most cogently, has pointed out that the traditional interpretation of such honor plays may be lacking in depth. No theater is devoid of ambiguities, and the plays by Calderón that offer the most ambiguity are the honor plays. In such plays, the means taken to maintain honor are so self-destructive that one finds it hard to believe that Calderón could retain faith in these methods. I would like to state clearly, without any misunderstanding, that I believe that the ambiguities we have often found in Calderón's honor plays spring from the actual ambiguity in Calderón's acceptance--and rejection--of his father's final message. Calderón was bound at least partially to accept, procrastinate, and reject the will of his father. A theatrical, confused, dreamlike view of the world is in part a result of Calderón's complex perspective--of what he understood was his role in a universe tightly organized by God, Church, and Father. Yet there were many facets of Calderón's personality that could not find a place, a role, a definition, in such a tidy Universe. One way out of such a dilemma was to accept and declare the message that life is an illusion, a dream. Many of Calderón's plays are charged with contradictions and self-defeating paradoxes that distort or destroy any sense of reality. If this world is unreal, we must seek reality elsewhere, in another world. To say that life is a dream is to say that "all the world is a stage," "an assertion that Shakespeare reserved for the melancholy stoic, Jacques." Yet Calderón's despair about this world does not extend into the next; his theatre enhances the glory of God. In many ways Calderón's theatre is the modern transla-tion of Platonic ideas and ideals as defined in some of the Dialogues that the Renaissance put on a pedestal as the quintessence of Classical philosophical thought. Calderón's plays reconcile Plato and the New Testament to an extent that is, in my opinion, much more complete and meaningful than any attempt by Erasmus, Pico della Mirandola, and the numerous Renaissance scholars who attempted this task. We can accept the bitterness that obedience to duty often entails only if we are convinced that suffering and frustration are unreal because only the other world, the Topos Uranos of Plato, the Christian Heaven, is real. Cipriano and Justina, in El mágico prodigioso, overcome temptation and find union only in martyrdom. Only in Heaven will their souls be able to embrace. Even in plays with a happy ending, such as La dama duende, we sense that tension and trouble may persist: Doña Angela's marriage may be only a brief truce; she remains dangerous and unpredictable.

Finally we must conclude that Calderón's plays are based upon three main principles, which structure the characters and guide the action to its climax and conclusion. These principles, like the Trinity, can be said to be subsumed in a unity in which one domi-nant element rallies the other two. The first principle I should like to establish is the need to explain and accept a certain order given to the world by God, an order that permeates the cosmos, nature, and society, and which each individual can ignore or disturb only at his (or her) peril. The second principle is derived from the first. Human passions, and most specifically human love, Eros, must be con-trolled and repressed if it conflicts with the order of the cosmos, nature, society. And the third principle

springs from the other two: such a world exacts painful sacrifices and becomes tense and bleak to the point
that we can fully accept it only within the framework of
the Platonic and Christian tradition that establishes
as unreal the world of appearances that our senses
create in our mind: it is a false image, a distorting
mirror, a shadow moving in the ceiling of a cave that
gives but a pale and confusing image of the sun shining
outside in the real world of Platonic ideas. As James
Maraniss puts it,

> Calderón's theater is the sober celebration of
> order triumphant--a celebration of the order of
> the universe; of the state; of the family; of the
> human personality; and, not the least, of language
> and thought. His plays are conceived in the
> spirit of demonstration; they show the value and
> the vulnerability of the powers of restraint,
> discipline, and renunciation; and they solemnize
> . . . the will and ingenuity necessary to keep
> life's chaotic impulses under control.

"Ce qui se conçoit bien s'exprime clairement."
Boileau's definition of a clear style applies to
Calderón's craftmanship. Because his vision of the
cosmos is both clear and hierarchical, his sentences
can and should be clear, correct, elegant, and
symmetrical, as ladders with which we could climb
out of the chaos and mists of everyday life into the
certainty of the heavenly vision. No sentence in
Calderón's plays is ungrammatical, because these
plays depict a universe that has been organized for
all eternity by God. "God does not play dice with
the cosmos," a sentence that according to tradition
Einstein often wrote on his blackboard, could be a
motto or an epigraph for many of Calderón's plays.

We should also note that the need for order,
logic, cohesion and hierarchy in Calderón's plays--
specifically in Autos sacramentales, but also in the
rest of his production--probably stems from many in-
fluences and forces pulling in the same direction. I
have pointed out the psychological roots of such a
need for a playwright whose personal life was for
many years dominated by an inner struggle between
sensuousness, perhaps passion, and the stern voice
of duty. Yet other forces were at work, and their
impact was probably quite similar.

The seventeenth century is a period of intense

intellectual and political reorganization. The
Renaissance had unleashed many trends that proved to
be chaotic. Everywhere we see a passion for order,
hierarchy and discipline. In the realm of pure science, mathematics and astronomy, we find a Kepler
groping all of his life towards a great goal finally
achieved: the perfect mathematical and physical
description of our solar system. Between Copernicus
and Newton, a perfect bridge built by Tycho-Brahe and
Kepler makes it possible for the first time to understand how the stars move, how the great clock in the
sky ticks the passing of seconds, minutes, millennia.
Philosophy--Spinoza, Descartes, Leibnitz--is ordering
and organizing the world along clear rational lines.
Even language becomes a system of rules and a way of
displaying our logical reasoning: the Jansenists of
Port-Royal discover that grammar is basically very
similar to logic. Far from being a dissenting voice,
Calderón incorporates into his artistic world many
trends that are explicitly or implicitly reshaping the
intellectual map of Europe.

Of course what scientists search for, a clear
pattern found in the stone at our feet and also in the
stars and galaxies far away, is something not impossible for a great poet. He does not need Mendeleiev's tables, atomic theory, Newtonian or Einsteinian
physics because he can marshal Pythagoras, the Four
Elements, the symmetries, contrasts, antitheses, oxy-
morons and metaphors of the high Baroque style. All
of this enables him, as Blake would put it a century
later, to "see Infinity in a grain of sand / and
Eternity in an hour."

The macrocosm is always implicit in man, a microcosm. We are linked to the stars, to the four elements that are the building materials of the cosmos
(as Edward Wilson has carefully explained in an important article). In turn the stars, eternity, infinite
space, can be reflected in the human eyes, in a pond,
and in a bunch of flowers, because in a way which only
poets can see, understand and describe, they are eyes,
lakes, flowers. We note the accurate description of
the stars, "flores nocturnas son," given by Fénix in
El príncipe constante.

If Calderón believed, as I think he did, that
God's signature, and the signs for infinity, eternity,
the stars, and all of cosmic space, could be found in
the human body and the humblest objects (and vice versa

our human ideas, wishes, passions and frailties could
be reflected and amplified by the stars and by infinite
space) then we, Calderón's critics, can be justified
if we look for his thought, his plan, and his artistic
overview of the world, in a small aspect of his works:
two exquisite sonnets that are a form of dialogue
between Fernando and Fénix in El príncipe constante.
If my interpretation is correct, we can see in these
sonnets Calderón's artistic mind at work like a subtle
and clever needle shuttling back and forth between the
infinite and the small, sewing together the fabric of
the world. The first sonnet organizes its images
around a bunch (or is it a galaxy?) of roses. The
second, echoing and answering the first, displays its
lines around a constellation (or is it a bouquet?) of
stars. Fernando, already pledged to a martyr's death,
offers his love to Fénix, inviting her to join him in
sacrifice and a better life in the world beyond this
one. It can be said that with the bouquet of roses
Fernando gives her a reminder of his own mortality:

> Fernando: Estas, que fueron pompa y alegría,
> despertando al albor de la mañana,
> a la tarde serán lástima vana,
> durmiendo en brazos de la noche fría.
> Este matiz, que al cielo desafía,
> iris listado de oro, nieve y grana,
> será escarmiento de la vida humana:
> ¡tanto se emprende en término de un día!
> A florecer las rosas madrugaron,
> y para envejecerse florecieron:
> cuna y sepulcro en un botón hallaron.
> Tales los hombres sus fortunas vieron,
> en un día nacieron y expiraron;
> que pasados los siglos, horas fueron.

And yet Fernando is able to turn these metaphors
of mortality and his awareness of the brevity of
earthly things into a solid reliance upon eternal
values. At the end of the tunnel of death he knows
there is a radiance and a rainbow. This is precisely
why he can afford to be gloomy for an instant. Fénix
answers with another sonnet which deals also with
change, this time heavenly change or the never-ending
spectacle of changes in a night sky lit up by thousands
of stars:

> Fénix: Esos rasgos de luz, esas centellas
> que cobran con amagos superiores
> alimentos del sol en resplandores,

aquello viven que se duelen dellas.
Flores nocturnas son, aunque tan bellas,
efímeras padecen sus ardores;
pues si un día es un siglo de las flores,
una noche es la edad de las estrellas.
De esa, pues, primavera fugitiva
ya nuestro mal, ya nuestro bien se
    infiere:
registro es nuestro, o muera el sol
    o viva.
¿Qué duración habrá que el hombre
    espere,
o qué mudanza habrá, que no reciba
de astro, que cada noche nace y muere?

The first sonnet when placed in its proper context (Fernando's beliefs and purposes) creates a vertical upwards movement, from mortality to immortality, from flowers to the colors and hues of the sky and infinite space. The second sonnet parallels this movement in the opposite direction: the strength flows from the "nocturnal flowers," the stars, down to human destinies which Fénix thinks are written in the stars. The two movements shuttle back and forth, weaving the fabric of the world, defining both space and time: both Fernando's acceptance of mortality and Fénix's fear of it have been expanded and projected in all directions until they reach the utmost recesses of the cosmos.

For only this way, only by leaving behind the narrow limits of the earth and human experience, can Calderón's star-crossed heroes be rewarded for their sacrifice. They lose the person they love but gain the whole world and eternity. Calderón has projected in them the inner secret drama of his own life, his own renunciation of earthly love demanded of him in his father's will.

Borges used to say, "All literature is autobiographical." We all know how much of himself Lope put in his plays and in La Dorotea. In my opinion the same can be said about Calderón. His artistic vision is, we can now see, both complementary to and opposite to Lope's art. Lope is the poet of love. Calderón is the poet who teaches us to renounce frail earthly love and invites us instead to conquer "la inquieta república de estrellas."

Yale University

A New Literary History of Don Pedro Calderón

Robert ter Horst

Literary criticism and literary history pursue antipathetic purposes. Criticism aims to confuse, to reveal the problematical and the complex in a work of art. History, on the other hand, strives to categorize and to clarify. A cardinal sin of criticism is to revel in complexity for its own sake, while oversimplification is literary history's most repulsive trait. On the whole, the vices of criticism seem to me to be less destructive than those of history; but manuals[1] still say such deplorable things about Don Pedro Calderón that I would like, for once, in the manner of Cervantes' Canon of Toledo, to try to improve upon a form of expression that is both indispensable and hateful, to sketch out, then, my understanding of Calderón in terms of literary history.

But first an observation about methodology that applies equally to literary history and to literary criticism. In the case of Calderón, it simply will not do any longer to base general conclusions on a partial reading of the plays. Edwin Honig is wrong to assert that Calderón's "particular gifts quickly emerge on getting to know half a dozen of the plays." Nor is it yet possible to isolate those "thirty or forty comedias and autos" that constitute the "greater part of his best work."[2] Calderón is in fact a largely unknown dramatist. Discussions of his art are usually seriously distorted because of fundamental ignorance and laziness, and because certain kinds of plays, the tragedies of honor, for example, are outrageously overrepresented at the same time that whole rich areas of achievement, such as the mythological and historical plays, pass unnoticed. Among the mythological works one finds La estatua de Prometeo, a drama that rivals La vida es sueño in greatness. Yet it is almost never read or written about, despite Aubrun's excellent edition. The same is true of Calderón's masterpiece of late maturity, El segundo Escipión. In addition, dozens of delicious lighter comedies from the early years remain untouched. Marvels of craftmanship like El escondido y la tapada or Fuego de Dios en el querer bien, which prove Calderón to have been the Noel Coward, the Neil Simon, of the Spanish 1630's, might just as well not exist. The technique of the so-called

33

representative plays, permissible for the purposes of
preliminary reconnaissance, and a technique that,
astonishingly, has persisted from Sloman through Honig
to Maraniss,[3] is no longer tolerable or intellectually
defensible. The responsible critic or historian must
first know what Calderón has written. It is nothing
less than a scandal that many interpreters of Calderón
remain ignorant of vital major areas of his art. We
will not know Calderón better until we read more of
him, most of him, all of him.

Influence

Calderón comes last of the great playwrights of
the Golden Age so that he naturally falls heir to the
drama launched by Lope de Vega and further enriched by
Tirso. But this chronological succession to a wonder-
fully thriving theatre can hardly be called influence,
even though Calderón was a friend of Lope's until 1629
as well as Tirso's youthful contemporary. Collaboration no doubt also improved the young man's craft but
his talent in the larger sense emerges complete and
astonishingly skillful from the first. Amor, honor y
poder, of 1623, is an extremely well-made play, its
only notable flaw an excess of mythological allusion,
natural enough in a 23-year-old poet. However, the
period from 1623 to 1637 is the period of the growth
to greatness of Calderón's formidable gifts. During
those years he appealed successfully to the corrales
as well as to the court audience in the Buen retiro.
In addition he undertook to write the major kinds of
plays that he would practice for the rest of his life,
the light corral-type of comedia, the historical play,
the drama of conversion, the serious play with a
tolerably happy ending, tragedy, the auto sacramental,
the mythological play--a tremendous range for some
fifteen years. In this amazing profusion and variety
not even Lope, for all his prodigiousness, could
accompany or guide Calderón, nor Tirso for all his
ingenuity. Calderón unquestionably learned a great
deal from them, and from others; but it seems necessary
to conclude that no single dramatist did or could
influence Calderón much. His genius was a force, and
later, a law unto itself.

In these formative years there is, nonetheless, a
major literary influence. It is Cervantes, the Cervantes of the Quijote and of the Novelas ejemplares.
The names of other writers do on rare occasion appear
in Calderón plays, that of Mira,[4] for example, in La

dama duende or of Giambattista della Porta in *El astró-logo fingido*.[5] But allusions, direct or indirect, to the author of the *Quijote*, to Don Quijote himself, or to the *Novelas ejemplares*, abound. There are about twenty[6] of them, and they mainly occur in the densely plotted lighter type of play, although there is a reference to Numancia in *El sitio de Bredá* (but not necessarily to *La Numancia*) and to Don Quijote in *Los hijos de la fortuna*.

Unfortunately, Calderón's most significant borrowing from Cervantes is lost, a play apparently titled *Los disparates de don Quijote*. But the great and powerful *No hay cosa como callar* is rather closely modelled on *La fuerza de la sangre*. Moreover, *El astrólogo fingido* shows the *escudero* Otáñez duped into believing that he will be flown home, an unmistakable reprise of the Clavileño episode in the *Quijote*. The fact is that Calderón thought of his early lighter plays of endless intrigue as chivalric novels, and so do a number of his characters.[7] Thus Calderón draws on Cervantes for technique far more than he does on Tirso or Lope. Furthermore, Calderón learned greatly from Cervantes in the matter of the artistic implications of honor, its modes and limits. As explorers of this major, troubling theme, they are far closer than is generally believed, Cervantes less tolerant of infractions, Calderón less ferocious than is thought. But the great lesson in honor that Calderón learned from Cervantes was how to exceed the bounds of honor in art, how to break past its limits, so that from without its confines he could turn back to focus clearly on the phenomenon. Because Cervantes broke out of honor, Calderón was able to define it. The partial presence of Don Quijote in *El alcalde de Zalamea* salutes and bears witness to Cervantes' revolutionary ground-work. However, once Calderón has absorbed what he needs of Cervantes' technique, he proceeds firmly on his own, so that Cervantes' name and works almost completely disappear from the later plays. Indeed, by 1637 Calderón has so decidedly established a theatre of his own, with its uniquely distinctive signs and signature, that he is his own influence, variations on his own theme. In his mature drama, then, there is infinite variety, but very little or none of that "development" which latter-day critics so earnestly seek and so highly prize.

Genetics

To exist and flourish, all drama needs power and
wealth and is naturally drawn to those two public forces
which pose so great a threat to the autonomy of art.
The relationship between the theatre and political and
spiritual might is thus that of moth to flame. Spanish
drama of the Golden Age begins and ends at the then
seat of power, at court, begins in the person and plays
of Juan del Enzina at the ducal court of Alba de Tormes,
ends with Calderón in personal attendance upon Philip
IV, Mariana de Austria, Charles II, and even, post-
humously, upon Philip V.[8] Before Spain had a capital
city, other economic and cultural metropolises drew
drama and dramatists to themselves, Rome attracting
Enzina and Torres Naharro, Valencia Lope de Rueda and
his successors. But after Enzina the cynosure of power
is the king, and the process by means of which Golden-
Age plays approach the sovereign upon whom they depend
and by whom they are at the same time repelled is
strangely slow and laborious. One reason that theatre
had to keep its distance from the king in the corrales
was royal aversion in the case of Philip II, relative
indifference on the part of his son. Even so, powerful courts require spectacle, as Olivares well understood. Kings need to project and see images of themselves in order to believe in and have others believe
in their majesty and might. Drama is another form of
royal portraiture that offers the monarch credibility.
The play is an act of faith in and for the king.
Velázquez and Calderón are even closer than has been
supposed. It is curious, then, to see so conspicuous
a royal presence in the plays of Lope and Tirso while
drama was almost completely absent from court. But
when Olivares built Philip a palace and a theatre,
Spanish drama returned home, to flourish still, but
not long except in the case of Calderón, and to die.
In one external sense, consequently, the history of
Spanish drama of the Golden Age begins with genesis
of the play at court, followed by the migration, once
a certain independence is achieved, away from court to
city. Yet even in the city the drama longs for its
original sponsor, consecrating major roles to his
power and presence, so that Calderón's final transition
from the corral to the Buen Retiro has every appearance
of inevitability.

The highest material and spiritual might is also
for Calderón an essential element in the creative, as
against the social, emergence of dramatic art. His

earliest comedia, Amor, honor, y poder, dynamically
structures itself around a wayward monarch, Edward III
of England, whose extreme sexual passion for Estela,
the daughter of one of his chief nobles, almost destroys
the girl's honor, her brother's life, and their father's
and the whole family's eminent position. Edward is
their fearful antagonist, and they do succeed in over-
coming his violence. Their strengths--amor, honor--
range themselves against his poder.[9] Thus the whole
play comes into being conflictively and negatively, in
opposition to Edward. The king is therefore the prime
factor in the rise of the play, but his opponents are
needed to complete the pattern of struggle. Here and
elsewhere the monarch, temporal or spiritual, is for
Calderón the source of the play.

Absolutism as the origin of theatre appears most
clearly and theoretically in El gran teatro del mundo.
At the beginning of the play, God gazes down upon the
world, admiring its inferior reflection of heaven as
one would gaze upon a picture or portrait that is an
excellent likeness. Aesthetics reveals its primordial
importance for Calderón with the first words of the
apostrophe, "Hermosa compostura," lovely composition.
It is true that the art of building is alluded to with
the term "arquitectura"; but the original notion of a
fine portrait is reinforced with the "sombras y lejos"
of line 3, suggesting the shading and perspective of a
painting. This painting actually comes into view as
God scrutinizes the elemental comminglings that constitute the world. These he calls a "Campaña de elementos,"
campaña in both an artistic and a military sense, at
once a landscape and a theatre of warlike operations.

It would seem that God summons the world into being
motivated by the purest caprice, a desire to project his
power and might. The urge is certainly potent but it
must also be put in the company of the aesthetic impulse,
the "Hermosa compostura," as well as of what might be
called the psychological need to see the divine self
objectively mirrored and represented at a distance,
"sombras y lejos." This distance involves two vital
elements. The two selves, original and reflected, are
the root of that consciousness from which life and art
emerge. When representation takes place, reflection
becomes reflection, unconsciousness conscious mind. In
addition, however, replication, because the original
can never be perfectly reproduced, engenders invidious-
ness and hostility on the part of the lesser. Consciousness thus necessarily causes enmity. Man resents

his flaws as an image and blames God rather than himself for them. But God needs this capricious projection to become more intensely aware of himself, the better to believe in himself. Calderón's divine dramatic consciousness is an act of faith.

In its execution, however, it decidedly resembles the relationship between Philip IV and Olivares. God commands El Mundo to mount a _fiesta_, calling El Mundo his _hechura_, something he has created, of course, but also with the sense of _privado_, or powerful favorite. _Fiesta_ is itself a highly ambivalent term, denoting as much the holiday as the holy day. When one recalls that the performance of _comedias_ ceased in preparation for the Corpus, that El _gran teatro_ del _mundo_ is consciously and technically an _auto sacramental_ alegórico, but that in this _auto_ God calls for a _comedia_, the ambivalence must increase. Yet there can be little doubt that the tone of the work is meant to be festive:

> . . . como siempre ha sido
> lo que más ha alegrado y divertido
> la representación bien aplaudida,
> y es representación la vida humana,
> una comedia sea
> la que hoy el cielo en tu teatro vea.

> (42-47)[10]

Nonetheless, these qualities of _alegría_ and _diversión_ somewhat ill accord with the lives that are lived on stage and with the deaths that are died. On the whole, matters end well, but not for all; and the mood of the play is mainly sombre. _Fiesta_ obviously is an exceedingly complex dramatic concept for Calderón. Yet some of its meaning seems clear. Absolutism breeds the festive impulse. God and the King have to be amused. The play produced for their amusement begins with a desire for relatively light-hearted diversion, and it ends on a relatively happy note. Still, the fundamental matter of the play is surprisingly dark and painful. El _gran teatro_ is really about death, an event which none of us wants to confront and in which none of us really believes for himself. In stating that the basic mood of Calderonian drama is comedic, one must also add that it rarely diverts its attention from man's unhappy condition and destiny. Still, it is important to stress the primacy of the idea of the play with a tolerably acceptable outcome for Calderón's dramaturgy. This is his basic model, and El _gran_

teatro sketches out its theory. It is an _auto_ then,
which expresses the genetic idea for Calderón's secular
comedias. El gran _teatro_ teaches us that absolute
power is the origin of art and consciousness, that
drama reflectively reproduces this consciousness in
a worldly field of strife.

Every Calderón play is therefore in a genetic
sense proximate to God and the king. Those complicated
cape-and-sword _comedias_ set in Madrid, even when the
sovereign makes no appearance in them, depend upon his
closeness, like courtiers spiritually attending upon
him. Not infrequently the _comedias_ openly manifest
their attachment to royalty. Casa con dos puertas
takes place in the immediate vicinity of the gardens
of Aranjuez. In La dama duende we have a brief re-
hearsal of the genesis of drama in the festivities
honoring the baptism of Prince Baltasar. Also, both
Angela and Manuel have business at court. The crisis
of the battle of Fuenterrabía bisects No hay cosa como
callar introducing national concerns into Don Juan's
petty private affairs. But in only one play is the
reigning sovereign personally addressed. A single
apostrophe is not surprising inasmuch as all the plays
are command performances answering the requirements of
absolutism. Yet in El segundo Escipión Calderón does
most movingly speak to poor young Charles II, urging
him to surpass Charles I of Spain in the same way that
Scipio Africanus surpassed his father. Even so, Calderón's adherence to the absolute should not be interpreted as a taste for totalitarianism. The attachment
is complex, involving repulsion as much as it does
attraction. The portrait of the monarch begins with
his flaws; the play takes shape in reaction to his
tyrannies and failings. These are, to be sure, almost
always overcome, just as Velázquez depicts a noble and
kingly Philip IV without omitting the great prognathous
jaw. Ultimately, Calderón's commitment to the king is
neither political nor social. It is a commitment to
the foundations of his art, to the sources of his own
creativity.

Power is the first impulse in the genesis of the
play, but rebellion against the absolute is the second,
equally vital, equally important movement. The idea
of might in Calderón is orthodox--God, King, Religion,
Monarch--but the artistic construct by means of which
we perceive might is hostile, negative, heterodox.
The play is an anti-structure that scales the fortress
walls of established institutions and ideas to merge

39

with them in an ambivalent confusion that has as much the appearance of defeat as it does of victory, no matter from what side it is viewed. In the abstract, however, the process of the play is one that begins with a powerful assertion of orthodoxy which is followed by rebellious counter-assertion, with the end result that protagonist and antagonist merge without losing their respective identities. Calderón has been done a detestable disservice by those who have identified him with only the first element in his usual procedure. Unquestionably he is a very conventional thinker. But Calderón is in no way a "philosophical" dramatist. His ideas are ordinary. For originality one must look to his art. It is a bellicose response to the authoritative persons, ideas, and patterns that rule our lives. Calderón's plays all challenge the Establishment, all take an adverse stance in which they persist until the final ambiguities of victory and defeat. As an artistic formulation in decided contrast to received modes of governing and thinking the play's great function is to defy and to challenge. Our age has consecrated revolution, but Calderón's abhorred it. In that perspective his audacity and originality are increased, and it is a terrible injustice to see him as a pawn of the very institutions which he threatens, artistically if not intellectually. With Calderón conventional thought is orthodox, art heterodox.

The first vibration in the artistic motions of revolt is the rise to consciousness. Since all animation derives from God, the independent exercise of intellection on the part of a creature both confirms the ultimate source of mind and rivals it. To think as Calderonian personages think, with an impassioned totality which has little or nothing to do with systematic philosophy, thus posits a bond between creator and creature and at the same time creates a desire to sever the link between cause and effect. For one cause in Calderón there are always at least two effects, one effect in direct proportion to the cause, the other an inverse function of it. The mind that comes alive is both drawn to and repelled by its origin, loves and hates God, odi et amo. These antithetical emotions, and it is vital to insist that in Calderón mind is always ardent, exist in varying degrees of intensity and express themselves in richly shifting patterns that structure the play.

The point of the rise to consciousness, with all its attendant ardors occurring as mind moves to emotion, is to create a second self in any person involved in the process. It is Scipio Africanus who most concerns Calderón, the son rather than the father, the second being rather than the first. It is in this sense that one must understand all the plays as art's almost invariably successful effort to triumph over nature and time. Of course the first brute creatures and situations are indispensable. They provide the raw material. And Calderón understood and appreciated his raw material as thoroughly as Michelangelo understood those blocks of Carrara marble from which he released his finished figures. But the great tendency of the play is to prepare the birth of the second self in its crucial personages.

The process can be relatively humorous and simple, as when, for example, Don Manuel in La dama duende emerges from the trials in which Angela has complicated him with a broader humanity, one that cares for a whole family and which by its new extensiveness better fits him for the tasks of government that lie in his future. Yet even here the emotional pattern is highly complex, because Manuel's devotion to his comrade-in-arms brings on the hatred and enmity of his friend's brothers and finally those of his friend himself. It assumes a near-tragic intensity in the history of Doña Leonor in No hay cosa como callar. The ordeal of rape by an unknown assailant summons heroic self-control in this admirable woman, and by silence and through suffering she fashions a new and triumphant character that only slightly resembles the conventional dama that she once was. However, in La estatua de Prometeo Calderón has shaped his most complete and most sublime fable of man's metamorphosis into a superior being. There, Prometheus and his brother Epimetheus represent different degrees of the two most basic human propensities, the inclination to nature in Epimetheus, the inclination to culture in Prometheus. Prometheus' first act in his rise to consciousness is to make an image, to carve a splendid statue of Minerva. Image is that middle ground where God and man meet. The statue draws the goddess down to earth, the man up to heaven where, with Minerva's aid, he steals the fire of culture from Apollo. Prometheus' rise to the higher consciousness of religion has, as always, contradictory results. To the extent that the gods are willing to share their possessions, civilization is a blessing, bringing order and contentment to man. On the other hand, even though it was done with Minerva's connivance, Prometheus did steal

41

the divine fire. The creation of the second self by a
man makes of that man an artist who rivals God, who
arrogates divine power to remake himself. Such control,
however commendable its intent, is a usurpation that is
offensive to God as a diminution of his power. Remember
God's affectionate yet somewhat hostile apostrophe to
creation in El gran teatro:

> Hermosa compostura
> de esa varia inferior arquitectura
> que entre sombras y lejos
> a ésta celeste usurpas los reflejos, (1-4)

Consequently, at the same time that the awakened mind
in eager quest of truth ascends to new perception of
harmony, its enterprise affronts the mighty, and dis-
sonance and strife descend to the world, sent down from
Pallas in the form of Pandora. Even so, Calderón's
most vital characters gladly face this danger. They
are all thieves and usurpers, artists, challengers of
divine prerogative. La estatua de Prometeo is their
magnificent fable, also is, in my opinion, Calderón's
greatest play.

Many of its essential features characterize La
vida es sueño. In La vida, however, the loving yet
hostile brothers are joined in one conflictive personality, Segismundo the warrior and the bringer of peace.
His adversary stance challenges the established system
which in Prometeo does not yet exist. He defies God,
as well as by implication his father and his father's
state. Violent though the challenge is, with its
mythic reminiscence of the Titans' assault on Olympus,
in fundamental nature it is intellectual, another ardent
quest for truth: "apurar, cielos, pretendo," "apurar"
revealing the prince's desire for knowledge, his worship of Minerva. Yet the great usurper, tirano in its
Greek etymological sense, of La vida es sueño is King
Basilio, who finds his own mind so all-encompassing
that he dares to assume the divine right to arrange
the future, to order providence, at the same time that
he steals from his son the human right to engage one's
own destiny. It is the scale of his error and of his
arrogance that makes Basilio sublime. He is Promethean.
He struggles with God, would himself be a god, and
fails. God, Basilio, and Segismundo are all artists
in rivalry over the same material, like the three
painters who come to compete in painting Alexander's
portrait in Darlo todo y no dar nada. Orthodoxly God

communicates and seeks to impose his vision in the form
of an image of Segismundo provided by his horoscope.
Basilio cannot accept his own interpretation of that
image, effaces it by banishing his son and trying to
replace him with other heirs. Segismundo quickens to
real psychological and moral existence once he becomes
acquainted with the first picture of himself that the
horoscope paints. Behind and beyond that representation there exists the possibility of another likeness,
and it is this second likeness which, partly by per-
mission and partly by usurpation, Segismundo proceeds
to create. Happily, it is pleasing to both God and
man. Nonetheless, when the civilized portrayal wins
out over and comes to govern its raw and brutal original form, though approving, God must uneasily condone
the creativity of man. Segismundo makes a new image,
does not replicate a given one. He is heterodox. So
is Calderón's art.

Thematics

By thematics I mean a cluster of characteristic
abstractions that identify the basic energies and
motions of a goodly number of Calderón plays. But
before naming any theme, one must assert that no
phenomenon in Calderón occurs singly. His theatre is
quintessentially dualistic. In it there can be no
Prometheus without Epimetheus, no Eros without
Anteros. This fundamental dualism gives every play
its basic structure, one invariably predicated on both
sympathy and strife, exactly as Epimetheus and Prometheus are les frères ennemis. And the two components of each dualism have such nearly equal potency
that it is almost impossible to assign greater significance to one in contrast to the other. Whose claim to
the crown of Poland is stronger, Estrella's or Astolfo's?
However, the order of their appearance is important.
The favored position is later rather than earlier,
second rather than first. The primordial process in
Calderonian drama is entropy, the tendency to degradation, the outflow of vitality into death and nothingness, order and harmony dissolving into chaos and dis-
sonance. All of Calderón's art springs from his initial
vision of inchoateness, of the universe before the
creation. To this nothingness all created things tend
almost irresistibly to return. The tendency is the
first law of nature for Calderón, and his intuition is
not inconsistent with modern thermodynamics. Calderón's
law takes a vast variety of dramatic forms but is

perhaps best formulated in the lament with which La
estatua de Prometeo almost ends:

> ¡Ay de quien vio
> el bien convertido en mal
> y el mal en peor!

(V. Briones, Dramas, p. 2096b)

"El bien" refers to the goodness of the world fresh
upon its creation with God taking pleasure in the
excellent result of his efforts, as in Genesis I, 4:
"Et vidit Deus lucem quod esset bona," 10, 12, 18, 21,
25: "Et vidit Deus quod esset bonum." But no sooner
has the bonum come into being than it is attacked by
degradation, by entropy. Yet not all creatures obey
the first law of nature. Some, a select few, a happy
few, almost always noble or royal, resist it. The
resisters are the principal personnel of Calderonian
drama. Their law of culture and art strives to counter
the law of nature, to bring about an increase of energy
and life in the face of decay and death. Apollo enun-
ciates it as a reciprocal of nature's law:

> ¡Felice quien vio
> el mal convertido en bien
> y el bien en mejor!

(V. Briones, Dramas, p. 2097a)

The key word in both formulations is convertido. Conversion is Calderón's universal theme. All the plays
are in this sense dramas of conversion. But it is of
course the Apollonian response that receives his most
intensive efforts, "el mal convertido en bien." Only
a few plays end tragically, even though tragedy is the
universal law. All the other plays, and even the disastrous ones, are anti-tragic. It is the countertendency
of the vast majority of the plays that makes them
comedic, their aspiration to "el bien" and "el mejor."
Nonetheless, they match their strength against an
almost equally powerful foe, so that tragic tendencies
are about as well represented as the comedic ones.
With Calderón, therefore, we really must abandon all
traditional notions of dramatic genre which posit a
clear and sharp distinction between the comic and the
tragic. Calderón's drama is ageneric, magnificently
and uniquely hybrid. In either mode, however, the
great process is conversion, the first thrust a degradation, the second an exaltation, each incomprehensible
without the other.

In a somewhat narrower technical sense, one quite small group of plays literally deals with conversion, from tepid Christianity to intense, or from a non-Christian set of beliefs to a Christian set. These plays are La devoción de la cruz, El mágico prodigioso, Las cadenas del demonio, El José de las mujeres, La exaltación de la Cruz, Los dos amantes del cielo, La aurora en Copacabana, and El gran príncipe de Fez. All eight are important as avatars of a fundamental dramatic use of energy in Calderón, and in addition to the two already well-known, three others also exhibit great merit, La exaltación de la Cruz, El José de las mujeres, and Los dos amantes del cielo.

Even when one has settled on a universal theme in Calderón, it is, however, not easy and perhaps not even possible to classify the plays. The three trage-dies of course constitute the great exceptions, the rare and horrific situations in which entropy cannot be reversed. To interpret them properly, one must see them as awesome anomalies. In attempting to classify the comedic majority, I would suggest not categories but matières, on the model of the medieval funds of subject matter available both for epic and romance. The matière de Charlemagne, in both its epic and largely Italianate romance phases, is the unifying element in that late group of court plays which A. Julián Valbuena brings together under the rubric of comedias novelescas. I would exclude Auristela y Lisidante and Hado y divisa de Leonido y Marfisa both from the comedias novelescas category and from the Carolingian cycle. Because of its Crusades motif, El conde Lucanor might be admitted to the small Carolingian group, each quite delightful, formed by La puente de Mantible, El jardín de Falerina, Argenis y Poliarco, and El castillo de Lindabris. All these plays, as well as El conde Lucanor, consciously reveal their line of development from medieval and Renaissance sources.

One of Calderón's greatest matières is classical mythology. In adapting myth to drama, Calderón is of course continuing the powerful Greco-Latin tradition which judged myth to be nearly the only suitable sub-ject for tragedy, above all. His plays fashioned from such sources constitute a large and imposing group, some sixteen works spanning 34 years. In roughly chronological order they are El mayor encanto, amor, Los tres mayores prodigios, Amado y aborrecido, El monstruo de los jardines, La fiera, el rayo, y la

piedra, Fortunas de Andrómeda y Perseo, El golfo de
las sirenas, El laurel de Apolo, La púrpura de la rosa,
Eco y Narciso, the great tragic diptych of Apolo y
Climene and El hijo del sol, Faetonte, Fieras afemina
amor, and La estatua de Prometeo. In addition to the
two Apollo plays and Prometeo, which are absolutely
first-rate, La fiera, el rayo, y la piedra and Los
tres mayores prodigios also attain particular excellence.
Eco y Narciso, the only mythological comedia to have
received some critical attention, while very good indeed, is perhaps less rewarding than several of its
companions.

Myth distresses moderns because it so sorely taxes
belief. But just the opposite was true in Calderón's
time. Even though displaced as dogma by Catholic
Christianity, the old stories were not discredited.
They were in fact an alternate and exceedingly attractive opportunity to believe, existing in a kind of
hostile symbiosis with the creed that had superseded
but not obliterated them. Indeed, Christian aversion
to mythology is a measure and guarantee of the large
mythic potential for winning credence, and this very
Calderonian kind of twinning of religion and fable is
probably confirmed by the tendency of myth to weaken
along with faith, for both to become a somewhat weary-
ing ornamentation in the eighteenth century, for both
to trivialize. But not in the seventeenth century.
For a select audience Calderón chose myth because it
was a ready-made hypothesis in art that for the pleasures of the play courtiers were willing to accept
almost without murmur. At the same time, in myth,
aesthetics prevail over dogmatics, so that the artist
is much freer to choose and to alter his material.
Calderón changed and added to his conventional sources,
handbooks of mythology for the most, with a freedom
like that which Michelangelo apparently was given with
the Sistine ceiling. In many ways the results are
comparable, for each is a new cosmogony composed of
old materials, a startlingly fresh vision of the
familiar.

Among the mythological comedias the tragic mass
is more insistent. Fully half of the plays could be
called tragedies. Tradition partly accounts for the
increase in entropy. Calderón could not give Phaeton
another fate. But, like Ovid's, his art transmutes
horrors into tolerable conclusions. However, the
difference between the mythological play and contemporary drama of honor set in Madrid is that revulsive

forces within the honor play just succeed in reversing
the tragic momentum, whereas, in the mythological,
turbulent and terrible content struggles with harmon-
izing form. There, form rather than comicity triumphs.
Spectacle is after all the major mythological mode. In
such spectacle plays sculptural and painterly techniques
metamorphose pagan crudities into high baroque aesthetics. The tragedy is there but artful translation mutes
and deeply embellishes it. The mythological plays thus
take up the universal theme of conversion, although
their dialectic, the great and hostile exchange between
nature and art, is peculiar. The mythological is an
artist's studio for fabricating works of verbo-visual
art from traditional and sometimes revolting materials.
The challenge is to see whether objects of beauty can
be made of them. Like the greatest Renaissance visual
interpreters of the antique, Calderón splendidly succeeds. And his understanding of myth as mediation
between nature and culture, the raw and the cooked,
is strikingly modern, in excellent conformity with
Leví-Strauss' idea of the function of myth among the
South-American Indians he has studied.

Theoretically but not practically, myth sires
Calderón's second major matière, which is honor.
Honor in Calderón is myth made contemporary. The
real plot of Los tres mayores prodigios of 1636 is a
caso de la honra, Deianira's blameless betrayal of
Hercules. In La estatua de Prometeo, however, we have
a complete etiological myth of honor as a form of discord introduced into human sexual relations by Pandora,
who positions Epimetheus and Prometheus relative to
herself on the characteristically Calderonian model of
amado y aborrecido. She loves Prometheus who loathes
her, while Epimetheus adores her, even though she
feels only revulsion for him. Frustration takes Epimetheus to the point where he is perfectly ready to
immolate his brother and the woman he loves and would
have done so if Apollo had not intervened. In order
to deal properly with honor in Calderón, one must
accept it, just as one must accept death. Once the
honor mechanism is engaged, its natural momentum is
a progress to murder unless it is checked. Three
terrible plays demonstrate this truth. Calderón no
more approved or disapproved of honor than he did of
death. In his plays it is entropy, a force of nature.
However, one supreme strategy of his art is to check
and prevail over honor's murderous declension. Each
individual play of honor is a new tactic in continuous
strife. Despite so many narrow victories in the

dramatic skirmish, Calderón rarely lets his audience
lose sight of the essential context of murder. The
cape-and-sword plays usually begin with duelling and
death, usually end with duelling, and with death just
averted. Efforts to show Calderón as morally opposed
to honor diminish and distort the way in which his art
responds to the inevitable.

In addition to being an outward form of determin-
ism, honor has several inward, psychological phases.
As a species of consciousness, as an expression of the
bicameral mind, it has two main components, a sense of
solid and a sense of void, simultaneously. Since
honor uniquely qualifies the noble person, his consciousness in its solid state is an awareness of
possession. The root cognition, common to all humans,
is the awareness of possessing life. And the only way
to achieve this fundamental perception is by realizing
that one can and will lose life. Material consciousness in the commoner takes a spiritual form in the
noble, whose basic and obsessive cognition is that he
has a good name, the having of which puts him at great
risk of losing it. Awareness of the possibility and
the danger of loss is thus the concomitant state of
void that completes the psychological architecture of
honor. I say architecture because honor's most common
symbol is the dwelling house assailed by risk. Its
archetype is Carrizales' fortress home, as Calderón
knows perfectly well when he writes in Act II of El
escondido y la tapada:

> Esta es la casa, sin duda,
> que aquel famoso extremeño
> Carrizales fabricó
> a medida de sus celos.11

or when he chooses a title such as Casa con dos puertas
mala es de guardar. Nor does one need Dr. Freud to be
able to realize that the house is the cultural symbol,
and biological, of the female. And here we have the
second phase of honor. This primarily male preoccupa-
tion depends upon the female. The male provides
possession, the female the risk of loss. Woman completes the psychology of honor, which in Calderón can
best be described by the phrase "tener que perder."
The male principle is "tener," the female "perder."

Honor in Calderón thus psychologically links
female to male with bonds stronger than those of
matrimony. This pairing offers Calderón the

unprecedented dramatic opportunity of studying the male
from the female point of view and the female from the
male. Of course the great innovation is the feminine
perspective, the casa. Calderonian drama of honor dis-
places men from their outer circumstances of action
and draws them into the domestic sphere where words
count more than deeds. Such drama at the same time
expels the woman from her home and thrusts her into
the open male world of acts. The result is that,
while seeing each sex together as lovers, we also see
women and men in an entirely new light, men becoming
possessed of feminine ways, women of masculine ones.
Men speak with seductive eloquence and women triumph
by suffering in heroic silence. The product is a tremendous deepening of human range and potential. Through
honor as a psychological technique, Calderón frees his
men and women from the monism of sexual and cultural
role. One can only wonder that his originality and
audacity have been so little appreciated, but here he
is as profound a pioneer as his predecessor Cervantes,
as well as Cervantes' only true follower in Spain.

Calderón's third main matière is history. A number of plays such as Judas Macabeo, La gran Cenobia,
El mayor monstruo del mundo, Las armas de la hermosura,
El cisma de Inglaterra, are patently historical, that
is, based on well-known accounts of famous people,
mostly rulers. History in Calderón is extremely
elitist. As a form of awareness it is restricted
to the eminent few, royal and noble.

And among those few a small and special group
particularly interests Calderón. It is composed of
those rare eminences who, already on an historical
pinnacle, strive to achieve suprahistorical distinction, to escape time altogether. The link between
such personalities and the creative artist is excep-
tionally close. Indeed, artists usually accompany
them and help them to define and achieve their mission.
Both the artist and the sovereign with suprahistorical
aspirations strive to create from the first historical
self in time a second and less flawed self whose fame
is secure, no longer in time, monumentum perennius.
Thus the basic stance of the historical play is, as
with others, adversary, "Contra el tiempo y el olvido."
And just as the real goal is the perfected self, so
the real enemy is the flaws of the original self.
When the monarch recognizes these flaws, which are
usually sexual, and no longer yields to them, he
suffers a defeat of desire. But the defeat makes

possible a kind of victory that Calderón prizes above
all others, a victory over the ungoverned and lustful
self, the civilized artist countermanding the brute.
Calderón calls this "la más alta victoria" and it was
a commonplace topic of pulpit morality. The phrase
and the process it represents first occur in Amor,
honor, y poder and recur like a musical motif almost
to the end of Calderón's creative existence, in plays
such as Amigo, amante, y leal, Nadie fíe su secreto,
La banda y la flor, and La vida es sueño. The two
greatest developments of the theme are late ones,
Darlo todo y no dar nada and El segundo Escipión.
What gives Calderón's handling of it such distinction
is his identification of a politico-moral lugar común
with the artistic process. Calderón is the first
great Western writer to cast art, if not the artist,
in a heroic mould. He does elevate the artist, too,
portraying Don Juan Roca of El pintor de su deshonra
as a professional painter, having prince Luceyo of
El segundo Escipión pose as a sculptor, giving to
Apeles in Darlo todo y no dar nada the task of depict-
ing Alexander's flaws to him so that Alexander can
correct them, separate himself from Campaspe, and
rise to supreme greatness, secure for all time.

But the most brilliant of all the historical
studies is El segundo Escipión, which fights a wonder-
ful battle against time, within and without. At the
siege of Cartagena, Scipio first emerges in full
historical plenitude, in the full flood of outward-
ness. However, as the siege progresses, the suprahistorical self appears, early, and slowly and pain-
fully. The inner anti-historical consciousness is
out of phase with the historical presence. But in an
extremely complicated configuration of strife, the art
of the inner man grows on the deeds of the outer. The
crisis of the play comes in a pause just before
Scipio's triumph. Then the contemplative personality
overtakes and outstrips the active one. Scipio renounces, and ascends to immortality, the más alta
victoria. On the other hand, the appeal to Charles
II to conform to the model of Scipio was a failure, a
defeat. Even so, in the series, Calderón is himself
the winner of the más alta victoria of them all. He
entered into time to win out over it. The fact that
we now commemorate the three-hundredth anniversary of
his death confirms his triumph, crowns him with laurel.
For he has indeed vanquished oblivion and time.

The University of Arizona

[1] The worst treatment of him may well be that of
J. García López in his Historia de la literatura
española (Barcelona: Editorial Teide, 1959), 290-300.
These eleven pages exhibit such a wealth of error and
misconception that choice becomes perplexed. However,
one example, from p. 292: "En Calderón, el elemento
filosófico cobra una importancia decisiva, pues la
acción aparece a menudo subordinada al pensamiento, y
los personajes llegan a ser a veces meros símbolos de
conceptos abstractos." The best manualistic discussion
of Calderón that I have seen is E. M. Wilson's in
volume 4 of A Literary History of Spain, The Golden
Age: Drama (London: Ernest Benn Limited, 1971), 99-
119. It is, nonetheless, far from being altogether
satisfactory. Wilson, for example, seriously under-
estimates the gravity of cape-and-sword plays such as
La dama duende when, on p. 106, he observes that they
occur "sine periculo vitae." Just the reverse is
the case.

[2] Calderón and the Seizures of Honor (Cambridge:
Harvard University Press, 1972), p. 1.

[3] And continuing nicely in Gwynne Edwards' recent
(1978) study of a handful of Calderón plays.

[4] Act I, 1.28 (A. Julián Valbuena edition in
Clásicos Castellanos): "El Doctor Mira de Mescua."

[5] A. Julián Valbuena ed. Comedias (Madrid: Aguilar,
1973), p. 142a:

> Llegué a Nápoles, adonde
> por mi dicha conocí
> a Porta, de quien la fama
> contaba alabanzas mil.

[6] I will not burden the reader with a list.

[7] Take as an example the exclamation in Act 1 of
Los empeños de un acaso (Valbuena edition of Comedias)
p. 1045a: "es mi amor tan novelero/ que me le
escribió Cervantes." In El alcaide de sí mismo,
Act II, same edition, p. 823a, the connection between
novela and comedia is patent:

> . . . y porque sepas
> la novela más notable
> que en castellanas comedias
> sutil el ingenio traza
> y gustoso representa,
> sabe que estas engañada.

[8]Who selected two Calderón <u>autos</u> for performance during the Corpus of the first year of his reign.

[9]The theme of the play is expressed in the observation in Act I that "hay honor contra el poder."

[10]I apologize for quoting from a textbook; but the Wardropper edition, <u>Teatro Español del Siglo de Oro</u> (New York: Scribner's, 1970), is very fine and has the convenience of numbered lines.

[11]Valbuena <u>Comedias</u>, p. 696a.

Historias de amor y dramas de honor

Cesáreo Bandera

Al hablar del famoso honor calderoniano deben hacerse algunas distinciones. Por ejemplo, no es lo mismo el honor que se exhibe en el Pedro Crespo de El alcalde de Zalamea que el de esos casos de honor que hacían fruncir el ceño a Menéndez Pelayo y que tanto se han debatido en la crítica, en especial los tres famosos, A secreto agravio, secreta venganza, El médico de su honra y El pintor de su deshonra.

Entre el dolor de padre del honrado y orgulloso alcalde, que ve a su hija deshonrada por un advenedizo insolente con el que ella no había tenido la menor relación, y la tortuosa insania que angustia a esos otros maridos que asesinan a escondidas y en silencia, hay una gran diferencia. Estos ocultan su deshonra y su crimen, aquél hace causa pública de su agravio y agarrota legalmente al violador de su hija como lo hubiera hecho con cualquier otro criminal.

También vale la pena recordar aquí ese gesto de humildad del padre que de rodillas suplica al criminal que repare honradamente su ofensa; gesto que emparenta al famoso alcalde con personajes y situaciones de otras obras, como La vida es sueño o La devoción de la cruz; gesto que no encuentra paralelo alguno dentro de las febriles sospechas y maquinaciones de los celosos maridos.

Aquí, sin embargo, hablaremos de estos últimos "casos de honor," aunque convenga no olvidar los contrastes a que acabo de aludir brevemente.

En los tres casos mencionados, la situación dramática puede describirse como sigue: sobre una pareja noble de recién casados a los que, al menos desde fuera, todo parece prometérseles feliz, se cierne la sombra y la persona de un intruso que, de improviso, sin que nadie se lo espere, entra en escena, quién sabe si atraído por esa apariencia de felicidad, envidioso de ella--como dicen los teólogos que acude el diablo a la vista de la dicha humana--e intenta apoderarse del objeto visible de esta dicha, la bella recién casada, entrando así en conflicto con el marido, quien, celoso y honrado a un tiempo, no está dispuesto a aceptar el papel de terzo incómodo y echa la cosa por la tremenda con las consecuencias sangrientas de todos conocidas.

Ahora bien, desde el punto de vista del pretendido intruso el asunto se ve un tanto a la inversa. Pues resulta que en los tres casos es el intruso quien estaba allí primero en su papel de amante. La historia amorosa entre el recién llegado y la recién casada viene de antiguo. Es el recién llegado precisamente el que se queja de haber sido olvidado y de que se haya presentado el marido a robarle una felicidad que él considera suya.

Como se ve, un principio típico de historia de amor. ¿No es así como empieza la mejor de nuestras novelas pastoriles, la Diana de Montemayor? Con la diferencia, claro está, de que en la Arcadia pastoril, la figura del marido, que es el único rival a quien no le está permitido soltar su presa, se difumina hasta casi desaparecer, difuminándose así y quedando como aletargada y latente la rivalidad entre marido y amante. De hecho, aunque todos los pastores aspiran a casarse honradamente con sus pastoras, en ese mundo los maridos no pintan nada.

Lo que aquí me importa destacar es que los famosos casos de honra calderonianos se desarrollan de manera explícita sobre un trasfondo de historia de amor que la obra misma revela como algo que la precede y que le sirve de marco de referencia. De manera que no es que de pronto se le hayan solivian- tado los cascos a la bella recién casada, a la vista de un atractivo tenorio, tal vez cansada de un marido viejo, aburrido o que no le hace caso (como ocurre con tanta frecuencia en la literatura del XIX y XX). Este tipo de explicación sicológica de la infidelidad conyugal le interesa muy poco a Calderón. Se trata más bien, entre otras cosas, de poner de manifiesto y dramatizar lo que en el fondo sabía todo el mundo en esa época, que matrimonio e historia de amor romántica son dos cosas poco menos que imposibles de combinar pacíficamente.

Precisemos aun más, diciendo que la historia de amor que sirve de trasfondo a los famosos casos de honra, es la clásica historia de amor poetizable, objeto literario cuya estructura fundamental se había venido repitiendo cientos de veces desde la antigüedad. A título de ejemplo, pensemos en la fábula que pinta D. Juan Roca, el marido de El pintor de su deshonra,

ía de Hércules y Deyanira con el Centauro. Pero podemos pensar igualmente en las de Píramo y Tisbe,
Tristán e Isolda, Romeo y Julieta o en cualquiera
de las numerosísimas e interminables historias
amorosas de la novela pastoril.

En las quejas, ataques y defensas amorosas de
esos amantes calderonianos cuya tragedia se avecina,
puede leerse una vez más la historia de ese amor que,
como decía un personaje de Shakespeare "never did run
smooth." Pues si no es la forzada ausencia, es la
diferencia de edad o de clase o la oposición paterna
o cualquier otra más o menos previsible o imprevisible
circunstancia que perennemente obstaculizará la
ansiada felicidad de la pareja. Tan perenne e inevitable es el obstáculo que más bien parece, como
decía el mismo personaje de Shakespeare, "an edict
in destiny."

Pero si falta cualquiera de esos obstáculos en
apariencia externos a la relación amorosa misma, no
por eso tienen la felicidad más a mano los amantes,
pues ellos mismos se encargan de crear obstáculos
entre sí, desacordándose mutuamente. Cunado uno suplica el otro desdeña y viceversa. Y además--cosa
curiosa--podemos estar casi seguros de que, si no
aparecen obstáculos externos, el desacuerdo amatorio
girará en torno a la presencia, real o imaginada, de
un tercero, un rival o bien de ella o bien de él. No
hay cosa tan exquisitamente frágil como la pacífica
felicidad de los amantes. Con razón decía un gracioso
calderoniano, el de La niña de Gómez Arias,

> ¡Oh, cuánto deseo
> de saber cuándo se alegran
> dos enamorados tengo! (Jor. I)

Hasta la sin par Doña Mencía de El médico de su
honra, la más íntegra y admirable de esas malhadadas
esposas, en los breves momentos de amoroso deliquio
con su marido al principio de la obra, se muestra
inquieta y celosa de este último.

A veces los mismos interesados meditan sobre esta
especie de destino fatal, como la Doña Leonor de A
secreto agravio:

> ¡Oh, cuántos han amado de esta suerte!
> ¡Oh, cuántos han querido
> recibiendo por gracia los agravios!

Deste error no han podido
librarse los más doctos, los más sabios;
que la mujer más cuerda,
de haber amado, amada no se acuerda.
Cuando Don Luis me amaba,
pareció que a Don Luis aborrecía;
cuando sin culpa estaba,
pareció que temía,
y ya (¡qué loco extremo!)
ni amo querida, ni culpada temo. (Jor. III)

Y cuántos otros pasajes se encontrarían en cualquier rastreo por la producción dramática de Calderón! Por ejemplo, ya que hemos mencionado ese "edict in destiny" del personaje de Shakespeare, pensemos en la niña de Gómez Arias, Dorotea, que quiere "pedirle residencia a los astros" para que respondan de ese destino por el que,

al que aborrezco yo
me ha de amar, y porque a mí
me ha de aborrecer aquél
a quien el alma di! (Jor. III)

De una u otra forma, el obstáculo está ahí siempre. Si no ¿qué sería de tales historias, como historias, o sea como algo que interesa novelar o teatralizar? Es el obstáculo el que mantiene vivo el deseo y la atención del lector o espectador. Como es bien sabido, cuando la mítica o clásica tragedia de amor se aburguesa y se convierte en comedia con final feliz, el típico "se casaron y vivieron felices" es precisamente el final de la historia. Con estas o parecidas palabras se nos indica implícitamente que, de ahí en adelante, la cosa carece por completo de interés. Tal vez por eso le extrañara tanto al cura del Quijote que en la historia de amor del "Curioso impertinente," Anselmo y Camila estuvieran casados. Extrañeza del cura y profunda ironía de Cervantes.

Ya lo había dicho Isolda en esa tal vez la más apasionante historia de amor de la tradición occidental: el legendario jardín que cantan los poetas, donde los amantes gozan de perpetua felicidad, se encuentra rodeado de un impenetrable muro de aire, o sea de nada. De nada--añadiremos nosotros--ajeno a la relación amorosa misma. Y ni qué decir tiene que ni Isolda ni Tristán ni ningún otro amante cantado por los poetas ha entrado jamás en ese jardín, aunque todos han

creído que hacia él caminaban o que lo tenían al
alcance de la mano.

La importancia teórica de este deseo poetizable
para la comprensión de ese fenómeno histórico y pro-
fundamente humano que llamamos hoy literatura, es
algo que he tratado de poner de manifiesto en otras
ocasiones. Me limito aquí simplemente a algunas consideraciones generales sobre el tema.

Si el obstáculo está ahí siempre, si surge tan
pronto como surge el deseo amoroso como posibilidad
poetizable en la propia conciencia de los amantes, y
si no queremos seguir culpando del obstáculo a las
estrellas o al destino, tendremos que admitir que
estamos en presencia de un deseo contradictorio, que
se adhiere a todo aquello que se le opone o lo antago-
niza; un deseo, por tanto, que se vuelve contra sí
mismo, que duda o sospecha de sí mismo, revelando una
radical inseguridad en el sujeto. Dentro de este
deseo anida desde un primer momento la presencia y
el sentimiento de un deseo reflejo o simétrico que se
le opone.

La historia de amor nace ya conflictiva. Cada
historia en particular podrá ocultar o revelar con
mayor o menor éxito este carácter conflictivo del
deseo, pero la consideración de una tras otra y de
todas entre sí no deja lugar a dudas. El poeta no
hace sino desarrollar la lógica interna de ese deseo,
cuando coloca en escena al rival de carne y hueso, el
pretendido intruso que viene a turbar una felicidad
tan atrayente como ilusoria. Huelga decir, por otra
parte, que no todos los poetas sino sólo los más
grandes saben que el rival no surge por ningún acci-
dente de fortuna o mera coincidencia de circunstancias.

Puede ser accidental, claro está, que la rivalidad se centre en Juan en lugar de Pedro. De hecho,
desde el punto de vista de este deseo poetizable, es
siempre accidental que el rival sea éste o aquél.
Pero esta accidentalidad con respecto a la identidad
personal del rival se corresponde estrechamente con
la necesidad interna de una estructura sicológica en
la que la negación antagonista del deseo tiene siempre
un papel. Accidentalidad y necesidad son aquí como
las dos caras de un mismo fenómeno.

Permítaseme repetir, resumiendo: un deseo que
enajena, que se somete, aun rebelándose, a su propia

contradicción, es decir a cualquier deseo ajeno que, imitándolo, lo contradiga. Pues bien, sobre este trasfondo, enmarcado por esta problemática sempiterna de la historia de amor, sitúa Calderón la famosa y tiránica ley del honor que angustia a los maridos de las tres obras mencionadas.

Oigamos una vez más cómo se plantea el pintor, D. Juan Roca, quizás el más sensato de estos insensatos maridos, el problema de su honor, mejor dicho de su deshonor:

> ¡Válgame Dios!, ¡qué de cosas
> debe en el mundo de haber
> fáciles de suceder
> y de creer dificultosas!
> Porque ¿quién creerá de mí
> que siendo, ¡ay de mí!, quien soy
> en aqueste estado estoy?
> Mas ¿quién no lo creerá así,
> pues todos la escrupulosa
> condición del honor ven?
> ¡Mal haya el primero, amén,
> que hizo ley tan rigurosa!
> Poco del honor sabía
> el legislador tirano,
> que puso en ajena mano
> mi opinión y no en la mía,
> ....
> ¿El honor que nace mío,
> esclavo de otro? Eso no
> ¡Y que me condene yo
> por el ajeno albedrío! (Jor. III)

El honor, ese honor que el alcalde Pedro Crespo había definido como patrimonio exclusivo del alma, es decir ese honor que define y es expresión de la integridad individual e intransferible de la persona y que, como vimos, no está reñido con la humildad, es el que ahora brilla, como suele decirse, por su ausencia. No es tanto el sentimiento del honor, cuanto el sentimiento del honor perdido el que atenaza y exaspera a estos maridos.

Ahora bien, después de oir esa denuncia vehemente de la tiránica ley del honor en boca de los maridos, hay que preguntarse por qué terminan siempre por someterse a los dictados de esa ley que les roba el albedrío. ¿Es que son débiles de carácter? Mal se compagina semejante debilidad con la inflexible determinación que los caracteriza. ¿Es que ese sometimiento que los lleva al crimen, es forzado y los exime de responsabilidad, algo así como un "perdona, querida, pero no tengo más remedio que matarte porque hay una ley social que me obliga a ello"? Semejante cobardía tampoco es compatible con el tipo de personaje que Calderón nos presenta aquí.

El caso es que estos maridos colaboran activamente, motu proprio, y de manera apasionada, a que se cumpla esa ley social. Es entonces la "ley" de esa colaboración íntima que hace que se cumpla una ley que les roba el albedrío y los somete a la voluntad de otro, la que interesa tener en cuenta. Pues es la primera de estas leyes, homólogas en su estructura y que caminan hacia un mismo fin, la que hace que se cumpla la segunda. Sin la primera, sin esa colaboración activa del sujeto en su propia desgracia, la otra, la tiránica ley del honor, no tendría ningún efecto, no sería ni siquiera "ley" y la tiranía social caería por su propia base. La respuesta de Calderón a esta pregunta, aunque riquísima en sentido, es perfectamente simple: los celos.

Ese mismo D. Juan Roca que denuncia la contradicción insalvable de una ley que se llama del honor y que sitúa a la persona fuera de sí, es el que poco después de las palabras citadas, describirá el cuadro que acaba de pintar sobre la fábula de Hércules y Deyanira, alegoría de su propia situación, de la manera siguiente:

> Como está la ira
> en su entereza pintada,
> al ver que se lleva hurtada
> el Centauro a Deyanira;
> y con tan vivos anhelos
> tras él va, que juzgo yo
> que nadie le vea que no
> diga: "Este hombre tiene celos."
> Fuera de la tabla está,
> y aun estuviera más fuera
> si en la tabla no estuviera
> el Centauro tras quien va.[1] (Jor. III)

La misma respuesta, y aun más explícita si cabe, encontramos en el Don Lope de A secreto agravio y en el Don Gutierre de El médico. El cómplice, pues, de esa ley tiránica del honor son los celos, el deseo celoso. ¿A quién le puede, entonces, extrañar que

estos maridos intenten a toda costa ocultar ese deseo
celoso que de manera íntima e inconfesable los hace
cómplices de su propia deshonra? Esta es la gran
diferencia entre su situación y la de un Pedro Crespo.
En este último no existe tal deseo.

¿"Celoso, yo"?--le dirá Don Gutierre a su mujer
Doña Mencía--

> ¿Sabes tú lo que son celos?
> Que yo no se qué son ¡viven los cielos!
> Porque si lo supiera,
> y celos llegar pudiera
> a tener . . . ¿qué son celos?
> Atomos, ilusiones y desvelos,
> no más que de una esclava, una criada,
> por sombra imaginada,
> con hechos inhumanos
> a pedazos sacara con mis manos
> el corazón, y luego,
> envuelto en sangre, desatado en fuego,
> el corazón comiera
> a bocados, la sangre me bebiera,
> el alma le sacara,
> y el alma, ¡vive Dios!, despedezara,
> si capaz de dolor el alma fuera.   (Jor. III)

Poco después el honrado Don Gutierre desangrará
a su mujer hasta la muerte.

Y si hay celos, es ahí donde se producen las más
secretas e inconfesables complicidades. Complicidades
que no se le pasan por alto a la mirada atentísima y
profunda de Calderón, quien a través de las circunstancias y motivaciones immediatas de la intriga, ve
un panorama mucho más amplio. ¿Qué quiere decir, por
ejemplo, esa típica escena de El médico, en la que de
manera a todas luces deliberada y minuciosa se nos
presenta al celoso marido, Don Gutierre, asaltando su
propia casa a escondidas y de noche, poco después de
que hayamos visto al rival, Don Enrique, hacer exacta-
mente lo mismo, ambos temerosos, "con pasos de
ladrones"?

¿Y qué decir de las sorprendentes coincidencias
y paralelismos entre Don Luis y Don Juan, rival el
primero, íntimo amigo el segundo de Don Lope, el
marido de A secreto agravio? No hay que cambiar
mucho para que el rival se confunda con el amigo y
viceversa. De hecho, como se recordará, en uno de

los momentos claves en la intriga de la obra, Don Lope
está a punto de batirse a muerte con Don Juan, el
amigo, que acaba de sustituir, a oscuras, al rival,
en tanto que, a continuación, ofrece su ayuda a éste
y le facilita salir de su propia casa a escondidas.
Es más, podríamos preguntarnos qué necesidad tenía
Calderón de incluir entre los papeles del drama el de
ese amigo a quien el marido acoge y oculta en su casa
y cuya función en términos puramente literales no
parece ser otra que la de poner a este último sobre
aviso de la presencia del rival. Literalmente hab-
lando, esta función es por completo superflua, pues
Don Lope ha visto por sí mismo al rival rondando la
calle y se ha hecho sus cábalas al respecto. ¿Qué
pinta ahí, como suele decirse, ese amigo que de súbito
aparece en escena disfrazado, como aparecerá momentos
después el rival, también disfrazado? ¿Y no es ya
demasiada coincidencia de nombres que al rival se le
haya confundido con un homónimo del amigo, un tal Don
Juan que había muerto en Flandes? Por más dispuestos
a admitir que estemos, la existencia de un gusto
especial, barroco, por las coincidencias y paralelismos, sería absurdo pensar que a Calderón se le pasan
por alto estas cosas al parecer innecesarias.

Pero si aún dudamos, ¿qué decir, entonces, de esa
otra escena, tal vez la más dramática de El Pintor de
su deshonra (o sea de su propia deshonra, título que
ya lo dice todo), en la que el marido, en medio de la
confusión del incendio en una noche de máscaras, en
la que es poco menos que imposible distinguir al amigo
del enemigo, entrega a su propia esposa inconsciente
en brazos del rival? Demasiadas coincidencias para
ser simplemente coincidencias.

No matan estos maridos por honor sino por ocultar
su deshonor, que es algo muy distinto. Por ocultar a
los ojos de los demás y a su propia conciencia esa
vulnerabilidad esencial de la persona, hija de la ira
y del deseo y causa a la vez de éstos, que el sujeto
descubre dentro de sí mismo, como una vergüenza inconfesable, al ser mirado por los ojos y el deseo de
otro, mirada esta que exaspera y que fascina a un
mismo tiempo. Cada uno de estos maridos podría decir,
como el violento y fascinado Segismundo de La vida es
sueño,

> Pues la muerte te daré
> porque no sepas que sé
> que sabes flaquezas mías.

La compleja y polifacética problemática del deseo enlaza unas obras con otras. Aquí sólo podemos sugerir brevemente estos enlaces, aunque el asunto requiera un tratamiento mucho más amplio.

En Calderón la violencia es siempre la otra cara del deseo y viceversa. No de todo deseo, por supuesto. Sería absurdo negar la posibilidad real de una "intención sincera," como diría Cervantes, por frágil que esta intención o deseo del bien pueda ser de hecho. Hablo aquí--repitámoslo una vez más--de ese deseo en él que se gesta el vivo interés o la fascinación que ejerce la obra literaria; el deseo que se alimenta, por así decir, del obstáculo; que se adhiere con mirada "hidrópica" a la representación o imaginación de su propia desgracia. Ese deseo o ventana al exterior que, como dice el Clarín de La vida es sueño,

> sin rogar
> a un ministro de boletas,
> un hombre se trae consigo;
> pues para todas las fiestas,
> despojado y despejado
> se asoma a su desvergüenza.

Es decir que a efectos de la relación intersubjetiva o interindividual que la violencia de la representación dramática pone de manifiesto, lo mismo da que hablemos de celos, de honor ultrajado o de la fascinación que mantiene al espectador "asomado" a su propia desvergüenza, a su deshonor. Lo cual quiere decir que estamos en presencia de una estructura de relación mucho más fundamental que cualquiera de estos fenómenos por separado, pues es la base de todos ellos y ninguno de ellos la define o agota por completo. A esta estructura fundamental de relación (y es importante subrayar el carácter relacional de la misma, pues no se trata ni de un principio trascendente ni de un instinto) se la ha llamado deseo mimético. Mimético en su misma esencia, es decir que en el desear inevitablemente imita y en el imitar inevitablemente desea. Estructura, por tanto, que socava desde un primer momento la independencia y la autosuficiencia del sujeto; que es de hecho incompatible con éstas. En esta estructura deseante y mimética, nos dice Calderón, se encuentra la raíz del deshonor, de los celos y del atractivo de la creación literaria misma; atractivo que a su vez guía y espolea la imaginación creadora del poeta. Pese a todos nuestros analíticos himnos de alabanza (a los cuales me uno yo entusiásti-

camente), Calderón sabe que entre imaginación y culpa
--para usar las palabras que él mismo usa en el auto,
La viña del Señor--existe una estrechísima relación.
(Cabría hablar aquí, por ejemplo, del sentido de esa
imposibilidad que encuentra el pintor, Don Juan Roca,
de retratar, es decir de imaginar pictóricamente, la
belleza serena, la inocencia, de su mujer, en tanto
que puede pintar con maravilloso realismo el celoso
estar fuera de sí del mitológico y literario
Hércules).

Por otra parte, esta convergencia de la imaginación creadora del poeta y de los tortuosos caminos del
honor ultrajado y de los celos no debe ser motivo de
escándalo para nadie. Al fin y al cabo no es nada
nuevo decir que, para Calderón, la condición humana
es una condición crepuscular, convergencia de luz y
de tiniebla. De manera que, en términos puramente
humanos, nada, por luminoso que sea, puede reclamar
para sí una inocencia de raíz, pues la raíz, que es
la que le interesa y la que investiga Calderón, lo es
tanto de la luz como de la oscuridad.

State University of New York/Buffalo

Notas

[1] Obsérvese que el estar fuera de sí es estar
donde está el rival. Al mismo tiempo ese "fuera de
la tabla está" indica el realismo representativo de
la figura.

Ironic Views of Marriage in Calderón

Hannah E. Bergman

The typical *comedia* typically ends with a wedding. In fact, when the characters of a *comedia* pair off to take their marriage vows, the audience knows that the play is over--one of the theatrical conventions that Calderón enjoys poking fun at:

> Ya sabrán vuesas mercedes
> que en el punto que se casan
> las damas de la comedia
> es señal de que se acaba.[1]

It follows that *comedias* in which couples already married appear are far less frequent, although a few examples come readily to mind. Some of Calderón's best-known plays, in fact, depict husbands and wives: *El médico de su honra*, *A secreto agravio, secreta venganza*, *El pintor de su deshonra*. Although, as I have argued elsewhere, these so-called "honor plays" might perhaps be more accurately described as "horror plays," and are certainly in no sense typical of Calderón's *oeuvre*, their very notoriety establishes him in the popular mind as a man with a rather jaundiced view of matrimony. It has already been noted that even in comedies which end in wedding bells, the hero's servant argues forcefully in favor of continued bachelorhood.[2] Usually overlooked, however, is a group of plays in which the *gracioso* is the married man.

Most of these plays are fairly late and correspond chronologically to that large group of *entremeses* which derive their humor principally from a quarrelling married couple. Since *entremeses* so often carry actors' names in the cast, we know that such characters were popularized by the comedy team of Juan Rana (Cosme Pérez) and Bernarda Ramírez, working together roughly 1649-1662.[3] Calderón wrote parts especially for Juan Rana in full-length plays as well as in *entremeses*, and very probably for Bernarda also.[4] What I propose to examine here, however, is not so much how a comic turn successful in interludes was transferred to three-act plays to add humor but rather how the dramatist integrated the motif into the thematic structure of more ambitious works, and to what extent it may provide further evidence

65

concerning his attitude towards marriage.

The earliest play among those to be considered is
El purgatorio de San Patricio (1628-1636). As in the
other five dramas, the play's gracioso is not a
sophisticated urban lackey but a country bumpkin
(Juan Rana's specialty, although we cannot be sure
that he originated this particular role). His wife,
also a villana, is an episodic character whom we see
only twice. Her big scene comes near the middle of
Act I and is quite like an entremés, as much in the
comic elements and their treatment as in the fact that
it is almost entirely unrelated to anything else in
the play. We meet Llocía when General Filipo, having
recuperated from a shipwreck that washed him up near
their cabin, is taking leave of her with a few gallant
words and a hearty embrace. Paulín espies them and
asks the audience what to do:

> ¿Qué me toca hacer aquí?
> Matarlos? Sí; yo lo hiciera,
> Si una cosa no temiera,
> Y es, que ella me mate á mí.[5]

He again seeks counsel a few lines later when Filipo
gives Llocía a valuable good-bye present:

> ¿Y aqui qué me toca hacer?
> Pero si marido soy,
> Y sortija miro dar,
> Lo que me toca es callar. (loc. cit.)

This, of course, is the typical reaction of an
entremés-husband. After another embrace Filipo goes
offstage, and now Paulín proposes to thrash his wife
for dallying with "that soldier," but she manages to
talk him out of it. On learning Filipo's true rank
Paulín begs his pardon and invites him to take Llocía
away, to please them both. With Filipo gone, attention shifts to Patricio, whom Llocía also finds quite
attractive, for himself and to spite her husband:

> . . . en queriéndome zelar,
> Me tengo de enamorar
> De todo el género humano. (I, 57 a)

Nothing comes of this, and Llocía's only further intervention is to open the door for Ludovico as he carries
Paulín off in the second act. We are reminded of her
briefly in the last act when Paulín, returning to

Ireland after many adventures with the evil Ludovico, decides to abandon a master who is pursued by supernatural apparitions, for "fantasma por fantasma, / Bástame mi matrimonio" (I, 68 b).

Insofar that Filipo is, however briefly, one point of the comic triangle Paulín-Llocía-Filipo, and is also Ludovico's rival for the princess Polonia, there is a tenuous relationship between the "entremés" of the first act and one of the other elements of the play. This is, however, but one thread of the complex main action, certainly not the one most viewers are likely to remember, and Llocía's role is so limited that probably all Calderón had in mind was to provide a little comic relief in this violent, terrorific play.

In the other plays the graciosa is a character in her own right, with a larger and more complex role. Calderón uses a comic love triangle to offset a serious rivalry among the major characters in several works, but this is not the only way gracioso couples function in these plays. Thematic and structural links between the comic subplot and the main action are strengthened, and in some cases very carefully worked out. The remaining plays were all written at least 15 to 20 years later than El purgatorio.

In El golfo de las sirenas (Jan. 1657) the rustic pair Alfeo/Celfa play an extensive part, especially in the loa and mojiganga which must be seen as integral elements of the work as a whole. It is up to them to take us from La Zarzuela--scene of the loa--to Trinacria, and later on, from Trinacria back again to La Zarzuela. In the central section, Celfa and Alfeo inform Ulises about the idiosyncrasies of Scila and Caribdis, and the two peasants are made to suffer the punishments these divinities had intended for Ulises: Celfa is locked up in a tower, and Alfeo is thrown into the sea.

Discord between the couple is established at the beginning and emphasized throughout the play. Their first speeches are filled with insults and quarrelling; when Ulises presses Alfeo into service as pilot, Celfa is delighted at the prospect that perhaps he will never return. For his part, Alfeo feels that if they are going to throw him into the sea as an imposter, they should have thrown her in first. Although as it turns out, Alfeo is the one who, unwillingly and unknowingly, saves Celfa from the tower, the

67

couple is not reconciled; as husband and wife recognize each other, she rejects her freedom if it is to come from him, as he rejects the thought of freeing her.

The part of Alfeo is one of those written expressly for Juan Rana, whose own name appears repeatedly in the text (552 b, 554 b, 556 b).

El golfo de las sirenas is not among the plays in which two married couples, one comic and one noble, are placed in systematic opposition. Calderón's public surely knew, as we do, that Ulises is also a married man, but in this play the author makes absolutely no reference to that circumstance, weaving his main action entirely around the rivalry between Scila and Caribdis as they try to seduce him and bring about his downfall.

In the powerful tragedy of the rise and fall of Semiramis, La hija del aire (1650?) Calderón also avoids showing his protagonist as married, but the concept of matrimony is never very far away. In Part One the dramatist, altering his source, presents Menón not as husband but as suitor, ending the play as Semiramis is about to be married to Nino; in Part Two she is already a widow, suspected of having murdered the king. The negative view of marriage implied in the main story is graphically shown in Part One with the gracioso couple. When they first appear in the crowd of villagers who welcome King Nino to Ascalon, Chato is disparaging his wife Sirene as fickle and physically disgusting, while for her part she threatens to beat him up as soon as they get home. With the quartering in their house of one of the soldiers of the king's escort, a triangle develops which recalls that of El purgatorio. Chato, seeing Floro embrace his wife, debates on a proper course of behavior, but instead of asking the audience for advice, he launched forth in a remarkable parody of those anguished soliloquies of an honor-haunted husband for which Calderón is so famous:

> Ya estamos solos, honor:
> ¿Qué hemos de hacer? --¿Qué sé yo,
> Si el mundo bajo me hizo
> De barro tan quebradizo,
> Y de bronce ó mármol no,
> ¿Qué hay que esperar, si me ven
> Quebrar al primero tri?

68

> --¿Eso dices, honor? --Sí.
> --¡Juro á ños, que dices bien!
> ¿Qué pie o brazo me ha quebrado
> Su abrazo? ¿de qué me asusto?
> Fuera que el sentir el gusto
> Del prójimo es gran pecado.[6]

Act II finds them living with Semiramis and Menón on the outskirts of Nineve, still quarrelling. Fragmentary phrases of their argument are overheard by Semiramis, whose misapplication of them to herself gives the scene the important function of foretelling her fate; on the surface, however, it portrays Chato's indignation about the triangle. What irritates him more than the soldier's continued attentions to Sirene is Floro's punctuality at mealtimes. He ends the scene invoking the assistance of an appropriate divinity:

> Vulcano, á ti me encomiendo,
> Dímelo tú, pues que tú
> Eres Dios, que entiendes desto.   (II, 72 a)

As the triangle of the main action comes to the fore and is resolved with Nino tyrannically forcing Menón to renounce Semiramis, the triangle of the graciosos dissolves; abandoned by Floro, Sirene comes to seek Chato, but he sends her away.[7] The parallelism between the ridiculous Chato and the tragic Menón is by no means perfect, but Calderón invites us to associate the two men near the midpoint of the play, where Chato observes Menón resisting the efforts of Arsidas, acting for Nino, to take Semiramis away and comments that while Arsidas must be Menón's "soldado," at least he's not coming for dinner. A thoughtful reader may find a more significant parallel if he equates Chato's inaction on seeing Floro embrace Sirene (both in Act I and in Act II) with blindness, foreshadowing the literal blindness of Menón at the end of the play. It is Chato who must guide the eyeless Menón in the final scene.

Of all the plays considered here, La hija del aire is the only one to offer some sort of explanation for the discontent that may afflict a marriage even before any real or imagined infidelity takes place. Although the context is comic, there is a serious undertone. Outsiders, says Chato, may see a woman devoutly on her way to church and think her saintly, never dreaming of the foul temper she displays

at home. At her window or on the street, neatly
combed and dressed, she is beautiful, but at home,
unkempt, unshod, what a different story! That's the
trouble, concludes Chato:

> Que tú mirándola estás
> Como una muger no más,
> Y yo como mi muger. (II, 65 b)

The court audience for which Calderón dramatized
the story of Venus and Adonis in La purpura de la rosa
(1660) did not need to be reminded that this is a tale
of adultery--adultery in the second degree, as it
were. Except for a brief exchange (II, 171 b) questioning that Amor could be "de Marte . . . bastardo
hijo," and a passing reference to "Monseñor Vulcano,"
the play presents Venus as an erring wife trying to
keep Marte from learning about her new love, and Marte
as a cross between jealous lover and wronged husband.
On the level of the graciosos one element of the ambiguity is eliminated: Chato and Celfa are clearly
married to each other from the outset, although their
relationship is anything but affectionate. As husband,
Chato objects to Celfa's friendship with one of the
soldiers who attend Marte. But soon the shoe is on
the other foot: the magic mirror which reveals to
Marte that Venus is enjoying the company of Adonis
also shows the soldier Chato and Celfa, their earlier
animosity gone, gathering flowers together. He finds
it quite intolerable that a woman should betray her
lover with her own husband! Despite the fact that
Calderón, with his customary irony, had already had
the soldier notify the audience that "Si a Celfa
quiero bien, / Es sólo el rato que importa / A la
maraña" (II, 172 a), his jealousy is developed as a
burlesque counterpoint to the fury of Marte. Even
he is astonished to see himself as jealous as though
he were the husband ("zelos maridales," II, 174 a).
In the climactic scene, as Marte prepares his vengeance against Adonis, the three graciosos are brought
together. It is the soldier who acts as the offended
party, berating Celfa for her deception; to her dis-
may, unlike his master, he vents his fury not on his
rival but on her, with a sound thrashing. Seeing
Chato stand by without defending her, Celfa passes
on the beating to Chato, so that as we last see this
couple they are once again in discord, just as when
we first met them.

There is a direct textual relationship between

this play and one of Calderón's _entremeses_, _El dragon-cillo_. In both works the soldier is not really a soldier "porque no es sino dragón" (II, 169 a),[8] and in both cases the _gracioso_-husband not only misinter-prets "dragón" to mean 'dragon' but also associates that concept with his wife as "serpiente" (_Púrpura_, 176 a; _Dragoncillo_, loc. cit.). The "dragón" of the interlude, however, is not the wife's lover, and this particular _entremés_, modelled on _La cueva de Salamanca_ by Cervantes, has less resemblance to the quarrelsome couples of the plays we are examining than many other interludes.

The rather close integration of the comic subplot with the serious main action noted in _La púrpura de la rosa_ is carried even further in _Celos aun del aire matan_ (Dec. 1660), where there are married couples on both levels. The triangle formed by the principals has a tragic outcome, while that of the servants is grotesque. I do not mean to suggest a mechanical parallelism between the two actions. On the peasant level two _graciosos_ compete for the favors of Floreta, but there is no corresponding rivalry between the masters whom these servants attend. At no time do Eróstrato and Céfalo enter into conflict; in fact, only for brief moments do the two appear on stage at the same time. On the other hand, the comedians have a number of good scenes together, especially those in which Clarín courts Floreta literally in front of her husband Rústico, unrecognizable because the goddess has transformed him into an animal. His comments on this courtship, perfectly intelligible to the audience, are interpreted by the other characters as barking or growling. Even when it appears that an adultery may be consummated, the tone of the scenes remains light, in _entremés_ style. But the unhappy Pocris is tortured by jealousy on learning that the absences of her hus-band Céfalo are due to his fascination with Aura, al-though she knows that the latter has been transformed into air. Where we have madness, death, and transfor-mation for Eróstrato, Céfalo, and Pocris, the world of the _graciosos_, briefly convulsed by Olympian inter-vention, goes back to its normal course: Rústico recovers his human shape and is reunited with his Floreta, leaving Clarín out in the cold. Although obviously the grotesque transformation of Rústico echoes that of Aura at the beginning and foreshadows that of Céfalo at the end, and gives rise to some very funny scenes, the fact that he is presented as a hus-band and not as a simple suitor to Floreta emphasizes the contrast between a plebeian (but in this case, not mismatched) couple, where not even the strongest provocation inspires real jealousy, and the noble pair which in spite of the tenderest declarations of love cannot resist the threat of imaginary jealousy, jealousy of air itself.[9]

As my final example I should like to draw attention to a play in which erotic jealousy or its absence is not a factor in the contrast between two couples. Throughout La Aurora en Copacabana (1652?),[10] a work in which the gracioso comes to play a significant, and unusual, role as antagonist of the hero, the pair of commoners Glauca/Tucapel is placed in systematic opposition to the noble couple, not because their social sphere is humble but because their lack of harmony and affection are so contrary to the conventionally idealized love of the protagonists. Even before the action of the play has really begun the tone that will characterize their relationship is established:

> Yup. ¡Que siempre habéis de reñir!
> Los dos. ¿Pues quién sin reñir se huelga?

(II, 443 b)

If the hero, believing her threatened by a monster, bravely puts his lady behind him to protect her from the danger, the gracioso is in favor of sending his wife on ahead. When the graciosa learns that the only loss the Indians have suffered in their first encounter with the Spaniards has been the capture of her husband, she describes the event as her good fortune, and only regard for social proprieties brings her to make a belated little show of sorrow. Meanwhile, Yupangui and Guacolda struggle desperately to achieve their love in spite of powerful hostile forces. In the first act the poet has counterposed the reactions of the two couples first against a physical danger and then in the moment of separation; in the second act he contrasts them as they endure absence, and in the moment of reunion. It is Glauca who underlines the different meaning which absence has for the two women:

> Glau. De dos extremos no sé
>   Cual venga á ser el mayor,
>   Tu temor, ó mi temor.
>
> Guac. Cómo?

```
Glau.                Como en ambas fue
             Una la pena cruel
             Y contraria; pues si no
             Sabes de Yupangui, yo
             Tampoco de Tucapel.
             Y en tormento tan esquivo,
             Que el mío es mayor, es cierto;
             Pues tú temes que esté muerto,
             Y yo temo que esté vivo. (II, 460 b)
```

Guacolda is scandalized at these words: "Eso dices?"
Not yet married, she does not know how such things
change after the wedding.

```
Glau.                Si supieras
             Tú lo que un marido ha sido
             A todas horas marido,
             Eso y mucho más dijeras. (loc. cit.)
```

For his part Tucapel, who was anxious to get home just
"por hacerme el gusto / De hacer el disgusto á Glauca"
(II, 454 b), does not even bother to greet his wife on
entering. He has spent years as a prisoner of the
Spaniards, he has witnessed the siege of Cuzco and
the miraculous apparition of Our Lady, he has been
transported to his village through the air by diaboli-
cal arts--but he comes in shouting for his supper as
though he were returning from a normal day's work in
the fields. On the other hand, the reunion of the
protagonists is painted in the most tender and moving
terms.

In Acts I and II Calderón uses the graciosos to
create a double contrast: noble couple against peasant
couple, and lovers whose passion has not yet been consummated against a husband and wife bored with each
other after many years together. Both of these differences, however, disappear in the third act. After
Peru has been conquered and its inhabitants converted
to Christianity, social differences among the Indians
have been erased; Yupangui and Guacolda, previously
rich nobles, have lost their possessions and now live
humbly. Although they have been married for many
years, they continue in perfect happiness: for them
the poet has penned his most beautiful expressions of
conjugal love. But the sweet harmony that reigns
between the protagonists finds no echo among their
servants. Glauca has only a small role in this act;
her main intervention is in the scene in which she

favors her spouse with expressions such as "mi mayor /
Quebradero de cabeza" and "bestia en dos pies," denying him entry into the house as long as he refuses to
accept baptism. Misfortune has not softened Tucapel
either, for he is spurred to seek out his wife only
by harsh necessity, whose "cara de hereja" is "tan
mala, que es menor daño / el ver la tuya que el verla"
(II, 469 a). Despite the fact that the play ends with
the conversion of Tucapel (that is, his re-entry into
the community), no reconciliation is shown on stage
between the mismatched servant pair, from beginning
to end in studied and total contrast to their masters.

As I have attempted to show, not all the husbands
in Calderón's plays conform to the stereotype of the
"marido calderoniano," yet the view of marriage remains generally bleak. The poet himself, as we know,
never married. Would it not be legitimate to draw
further conclusions about his personal attitude
towards matrimony from the prominence given to negative aspects of the institution in plays largely
written, I believe, within ten years after his
definitive renunciation of it for entry into the
priesthood?

Lehman College and Graduate Center
City University of New York

[1] Saber del mal y del bien; see my study "Auto-Definition of the Comedia de capa y espada" (Hispanófila Especial, Núm. 1, 1974), 11-13, for additional examples.

[2] H. W. Hilborn, "The Calderonian gracioso and Marriage," BCom, III, No. 2 (Nov., 1951), 2-3.

[3] One example would be Calderón's El desafío de Juan Rana, which in its earliest edition (Tardes apacibles de gustoso entretenimiento..., Madrid, 1663) gives their names, although these are omitted in the Hartzenbusch version (BAE, XIV). Cosme and Bernarda appear also in Calderón's El toreador; Juan Rana poeta and El retrato de Juan Rana, both by Solís, and Moreto's El retrato vivo, among others. In Los Juan Rana (Jardín ameno de varias flores..., Madrid, 1684) Bernarda and two other actresses boast that each has played his wife. Juan Rana as alcalde plays a bit part in Lope de Vega's Lo que ha de ser (1624); this seems to be his first appearance. In the entremeses of the 1630's Juan Rana's partner was often Jaime Salvador, who acted as his "straight man." Cosme Pérez became completely identified with the Juan Rana character.

[4] Cosme created the part of Espinel in Bien vengas, mal, si vienes solo (ca. 1634?); it is quite possible that the gracioso role of La dama duende (1629) was written for him. As Juan Rana he appeared in El golfo de las sirenas (1657), Fortunas de Andrómeda y Perseo (1653) and Fieras afemina amor (1670).

[5] Calderón, Comedias, ed. J. J. Keil, 4 vols. (Leipsique, 1827-1830), I, 55 b. Future citations to this edition in text, indicating volume and page.

[6] II, 66 a; I have altered the punctuation to clarify the "dialogue" nature of the speech.

[7] By the beginning of La hija del aire Part Two Chato, like Semiramis, has been widowed.

[8] Cf. BAE, XIV, 616 a.

[9] The burlesque play Céfalo y Pocris, which parodies the scene of the death of Pocris, does not use

the *graciosos* in the same fashion nor present them as married. Since this entire play burlesques sentimental ideals, it does not require the special techniques described here.

[10] In my view, it is reasonable to associate composition of the play with the inauguration of a shrine to Our Lady of Copacabana in Madrid in 1652. Joan Mary Hill, S.M.D. de N., adduces other evidence pointing to this year in addition to the dedication of the chapel ("Calderón's *La aurora en Copacabana*: A Figural Interpretation," diss. U. Kentucky, 1976, p. 253 and passim). Other dates that have been suggested are "Nov. 1650-Sept. 1651" (Valbuena Briones), "Nov. 1649" (Lohmann Villena), "ca. 1661" (Hilborn), and "1651" (Pagés Larraya). The play was not published until 1672.

Eros moralizado en las comedias
mitológicas de Calderón

A. Valbuena-Briones

El tema del amor como tentación sensual, que se
aparta del entendimiento trascendente del concepto del
amor neoplatónico, infunde y da sentido a tres comedias
mitológicas de Calderón. El mayor encanto, amor,[1] El
monstruo de los jardines[2] y Fieras afemina amor[3] tratan
episodios de la vida fantástica de tres héroes griegos,
Ulises, Aquiles y Hércules, según la adaptación latina,
y corresponden a dos momentos de la carrera literaria
calderoniana. La primera comedia citada pertenece al
período de "vigorosa inspiración" de Calderón, y las
otras dos al de "esplendor fastuoso."[4]

Las doctrinas neoplatónicas del renacimiento
habían difundido el motivo filosófico del peligro de
"que la razón se deje vencer de la sensualidad,"[5] de
abolengo clásico. El personaje Octaviano Fregoso
explica, en El cortesano, de Castiglione, que, si el
individuo por gozar de la hermosura "se deja guiar por
el sentido, da de ojos en grandes errores."[6] El
famoso manual de caballeros, sigue la teoría expuesta
por Marsilio Ficino en el Convivium Platonis Commentarium, escrito hacia 1475, e incluido en la publica-
ción de las Opera, de Platón, circa 1485. Ficino en
la "Oratio Secunda" del Convivio presenta la doctrina
platónica de los dos tipos de amor, debido a la doble
naturaleza de Venus, en la que establece la diferencia
entre el amor intelectual (Venus Urania) y el amor de
los sentidos (Venus Pandemos), y propone, por boca de
Pausanias, las censuras ante el caso de que el ser
humano prefiera la belleza del cuerpo a la del alma.[7]
Calderón utilizó esta filosofía como meollo de los
episodios míticos que llevó a escena, pues observó su
valor dramático y la desarrolló por medio de ilus-
traciones poéticas.

Según los platónicos, "amor no es otra cosa, sino
un deseo de gozar lo que es hermoso,"[8] pero con el
entendimiento de que, cuando se aprecia la hermosura
en los humanos, ésta "es un lustre o bien, que mana
de la bondad divina,"[9] resplandor que se extiende y
derrama sobre todas las cosas creadas "como luz del
sol."[10] Calderón ilustra esta doctrina con emblemas
dramáticos,[11] basados en la tradición clásica de los

77

mitos. El uso de esta tradición poética para explicar
la moralidad cristiana en las costumbres de la época
había sido defendido en los colegios jesuitas, según
apuntó Seznec en un conocido libro.12 Con estos antecedentes no es de extrañar que Lope de Vega en la
aprobación, al Teatro de los dioses de la gentilidad,
de Baltasar de Victoria, defendiera la postura de que
las fábulas clásicas encerrasen doctrinas filosóficas
que atañen a la pintura, a la poesía y a la astro-
logía, y que en el estudio de esas bellezas se en-
cuentren "cosas sagradas," que sirven a los propósitos
de la fe y la moralidad.13 Calderón, que sigue
atentamente las recomendaciones de Lope, aceptaría
la interpretación alegórica de las fábulas latinas,
defendida por los mitólogos, a la vez que por los
tratadistas neoplatónicos, de la época.

Especial mención merece la Philosophía secreta,
de Juan Pérez de Moya, por la influencia que tuvo en
el barroco.14 El matemático Pérez de Moya, ya en
edad avanzada, dedicó sus estudios a la mitología
clásica y expuso con claridad y detalle su valor
alegórico:

Toda fabula--dice--se funda en un razonamiento
de cosas fingidas y aparentes, inventadas por
los poetas y los sabios, para debajo de una
honesta recreación de apacibles cuentos, dichos
con alguna semejanza de verdad, inducir a los
lectores a muchas veces leer y saber su escondida
moralidad y provechosa doctrina.15

En el capítulo II del libro primero de esta obra, se
establecen hasta cinco modos en el análisis de la
fábula. Además del sentido literal y del físico o
natural, se pueden considerar, según el autor, varios
aspectos referentes a fines teológicos, morales y
propiamente alegóricos.

En los famosos Diálogos de amor, de León Hebreo,
de los que el inca Garcilaso de la Vega hizo una
traducción al español, bastante difundida, se expone
la interpretación alegórica de las fábulas:

Los poetas antiguos--dice León Hebreo--que
enredaron en sus poesías, no una sola, sino
muchas intenciones, las cuales llamaron
sentidos 16

En el cuidadoso examen crítico que sigue sobre la

interpretación filosófico--literaria, León Hebreo acepta los varios modos alegóricos indicados por Boccaccio.

Se puede ver, por lo dicho hasta aquí, que Calderón pertenece a un período cultural que acepta la tradición, originaria en la baja Edad Media, de la interpretación alegórica de los mitos. Esta actitud no es aceptable para los mitólogos contemporáneos. Los estudios de antropología de las ciencias de los pueblos primitivos han llevado al descubrimiento de que los mitos forman parte de una tradición oral que revelaba el origen del mundo y el poder de las fuerzas naturales mediante historias de significación religiosa, mantenidas en rituales sagrados, y que poseen verdades sociológicas.17 Calderón recoge, empero, la idea de que los mitos son historias inventadas o fábulas que contienen o pueden ilustrar una alegoría moral y la aplica a su arte dramático. Esta corriente la había iniciado en el siglo XIV el benedictino Pierre Bersuire en el libro décimoquinto de su obra <u>Reductorium Morale</u>, que se divulgó bajo el título de <u>Ovidio moralizado</u>. Fue continuada por Giovanni Boccaccio en la <u>Genealogia deorum</u>, Venecia, 1472, otro libro que tuvo numerosas reimpresiones, refundiciones y traducciones; y fue difundida y estudiada por Pérez de Moya y Victoria en el mundo hispánico.18 El dramaturgo acude al cuerpo de los mitos clásicos, especialmente en el período de "fastuoso esplendor," e ilustra con ellos las doctrinas neoplatónicas y la filosofía del camino de la vida, expuesta brillantemente en <u>La vida es sueño</u>.19 Calderón es primordialmente creador. El mito clásico le atrae por lo que tiene de asombroso y temerario, por lo terrible y lo extraño de la historia. Quizá pueda parecer poco verosímil, pero ¿qué importa esto si de fábula se trata?20 Se permite cambiar y transformar aquellos aspectos del episodio en cuestión, que cree convenientes para su arte; además, amplifica y desarrolla aquellos otros que corresponden con su intención psicológica o escenográfica. Entre los diecisiete dramas mitológicos y zarzuelas de este autor, se han escogido tres obras que tratan el tema del peligro del amor sensual y que ilustran el valor del dominio de las pasiones. Cada uno tiene su independencia en cuanto al tratamiento del mito, pero poseen en común el tema, al que hemos denominado <u>eros moralizado</u>; y en cada uno de ellos el héroe es apartado de sus hazañas, y con ello de su auténtico destino, al admitir la pasión amorosa, caída que sirve de vituperio en sus anales. Los episodios en cuestión son los amores de Ulises y Circe, los de Aquiles y Deidamia, y los de Hércules y Yole. El de Ulises se narra en La Odisea, de Homero,[21] y en Las Metamorfosis, de Ovidio;[22] el de Aquiles en el Ars amatoria,[23] y en Las Metamorfosis, de Ovidio.[24] y en la Bibliotheca sive deorum origine, de Apolodoro;[25] y el de Hércules, con la advertencia de que Calderón integra en la historia de Yole, la servidumbre del héroe a Onfale,[26] en la Bibliotheca, de Apolodoro,[27] y en Deipnosophistae de Athenaeus.[28]

Calderón concentra la historia de Ulises y Circe, según la tradición ovidiana, en el acto primero, pero la modifica con diversos elementos para transformarla en un gran espectáculo barroco. La descripción que el profesor Shergold hace de la disposición del escenario manifiesta claramente el gusto intensificado de recursos escenográficos, utilizados en el parque del Buen Retiro.[29] La información está tomada en parte de una carta--memorandum de Cosme Lotti[30] y en parte de las acotaciones de la pieza de Calderón, el cual siguió varias de las proposiciones del ingeniero-escenógrafo italiano.

El segundo acto constituye una amplificación de los versos "annua nos illic tenuit mora, multaque praesens tempore tam longo vidi . . . ."[31] Calderón, en su versión--invención creadora, ha añadido nuevos personajes como Arsidas, el príncipe de Trinacria--este es un país fantástico que coincide con Sicilia--que se presenta como un amante desdeñado por Circe; como la pareja Flérida y Lisidas, versión barroca de los innamorati de la comedia italiana; así como también los juegos histriónicos de Lebrel y Clarín, perspective irónica del tema principal. Estas nuevas figuras sirven para desarrollar, en una situación más compleja, la pasión de Circe y Ulises, arte de fingimientos y disimulos, en donde no falta una academia de amor, y que culmina en la hermosa declaración de Ulises bajo el concepto de una garza perseguida por halcones, emblema calderoniano que ha estudiado Sloman.[32]

El acto tercero de El mayor encanto, amor es el mejor realizado. Parte de la situación paradójica de que sean ahora los griegos, que Ulises había salvado de sus transformaciones zoomórficas, los que traten de sacarle de la molicie y estupor en que se encuentra, dominado por el amor de Circe. Se valen para ello de una estrategia musical. Hacen sonar una salva con cajas y estruendo militar para sacar de su letargo al héroe griego; pero la astuta maga contrarresta los efectos con otra música, esta vez apacible y que halaga el gusto sensorial, lo que inclina a Ulises para que se confiese esclavo del amor. La situación se complica con el levantamiento de los soldados, dirigidos por Arsidas y Lisidas, celosos del trato halagüeño que reciben los griegos en la isla, pero son dispersos por las fuerzas sobrenaturales de Circe que fingen en el aire ejércitos fantásticos que socorren a sus ninfas. Antistes, como último recurso para llamar a la razón a su jefe, coloca las armas de Aquiles junto a su lecho, y bajo el influjo de éstas emerge la sombra del hijo de Tetis, el cual increpa a Ulises por su afeminamiento. Esto trae consigo la peripecia de la obra, pues el descuidado héroe decide la partida de la isla entre terremotos y erupción de volcanes que subrayan la ira de Circe burlada.

La obra comienza con una tempestad, que simboliza el caos de la naturaleza ante las fuerzas de la fatalidad, cuando éstas se imponen momentáneamente, desafiando la providencia divina. Se presenta el emblema dramático, de origen gongorino, del extranjero que arriba a tierras extrañas. En este caso son los marineros griegos que desembarcan en un lugar, cuyos pobladores han perdido la libertad o ejercicio del libre albedrío al haber sido transformados, dadas las inclinaciones sensuales, en plantas--vida vegetativa-- o en animales--vida instintiva sin elección--por los encantos de Circe.

La maga, dueña de la isla, "es--dice Pérez de Moya--aquella pasión natural que llaman amor deshonesto, que las más veces transforma a los más sabios y de mayor juicio en animales fierísimos y llenos de furor, y algunas veces los vuelve más insensibles que piedras, acerca de la honra y la reputación."[33] Los compañeros de Ulises, convertidos en fieras vienen a representar "las potencias del alma que conspiran con los afectos del cuerpo y no obedecen a la razón."[34] Ulises simboliza, empero, la fuerza del espíritu que deja a la razón elegir libremente lo que es bueno para él. Fácilmente, pero con la intervención de la Providencia, bajo la imagen simbólica del ramo de flores, puede dominar las primeras y más bajas tentaciones, pero la victoria definitiva sobre la belleza sensual, encarnada por Circe misma, no la logra sin una larga lucha interior

que se dramatiza a lo largo de los dos últimos actos,
y en la que cae durante un período en la esclavitud
del "mayor encanto" o amor.[35]

Calderón, aunque acepta la alegoría moral que da
sentido y dirección a la pieza, adorna el asunto con
procedimientos escenográficos para atraer y admirar
al público, y, además, amplifica extensamente el episodio mítico con recursos dramáticos en los que se
manifiestan los cambios de decisiones y la lucha interior de Ulises, los cuales ilustran, como indicó
Séneca, en la Epistula LXXXVIII,[36] los peligros a los
que se halla expuesto el hombre. Por otra parte,
muchos elementos estructurales son típicos del género
cómico y tienen como único objetivo el de entretener
con lo que cumple con la máxima "delectando pariterque
monendo."

Nuestro autor en El monstruo de los jardines
lleva a escena el tópico de Aquiles entre las hijas
de Lycomedes. Este tuvo especial repercusión en el
arte barroco. Pedro Pablo Rubens, que pintó una
buena colección de cuadros sobre la historia de
Aquiles,[37] immortalizó la situación dramática del
Aquiles desenmascarado en un soberbio óleo "Aquiles
descubierto entre las hijas de Lycomedes" realizado
hacia 1617,[38] y que se conserva en el Museo del Prado.
El episodio de Aquiles en Scyros lo había relatado con
bastante detalle Estacio en la Aquileida,[39] Boccaccio
en la Genealogia[40] y Natale Conti en Mythologiae sive
explicationis libri decem.[41] Baltasar de Victoria lo
trata a su vez con cierta extensión en su Teatro;[42]
y explica también cómo fue descubierto.[43]

Los elementos estructurales de El monstruo...
guardan relación con los de El mayor encanto, amor;
sin embargo, se ha dado más profundidad filosófica
a la alegoría en esta ocasión, así como también se ha
desarrollado con más sabiduría técnica los cambios de
decisión, debidos a las estrategias musicales, de
objetos funcionales y orales.

La secuencia elemental comienza con una tormenta
que anuncia la desarmonía interior de Aquiles. Como
consecuencia de la tempestad, el barco de Lisidoro ha
naufragado, y este personaje, que es príncipe del
Epiro, llega gongorinamente a una extraña tierra.
Se trata de una isla, en donde ocurren portentos y
en la que hay un templo dedicado a la veneración de
los dioses Venus y Marte. Este islote, situado

enfrente del promontorio de Gnido, es el lugar en donde la diosa Tetis ha escondido a su hijo Aquiles en una cueva para evitar el horóscopo que anuncia su temprana muerte en la guerra de Troya. Las quejas del desafortunado muchacho "¡Ay mísero de mí! ¡Ay infelice!" son una réplica de aquellas otras en las que Segismundo expresaba su resentimiento por su falta de libertad. Ulises ha llegado a Gnido y con la ayuda de Polemio, el monarca de este reino, va a consultar el oráculo del templo en la isla para que les revele el lugar en el que está escondido Aquiles. El héroe al oir el canto armonioso de la princesa Deidamia y sus damas se ve movido a salir de su encierro y al verla queda prendado de su hermosura.

En este primer acto se observa una nueva versión del mito de la caverna con el que Platón ilustra su teoría epistemológica en La República.[44] M. F. Sciacca vio la relación estructural entre el mito famoso y la torre de Segismundo.[45] Calderón presenta ahora una nueva variante. La persona reducida en la cueva o sea Aquiles viene a simbolizar la vida inauténtica en un mundo de sombras y falsas apariencias dirigido por el hado, que no permite contemplar el mundo inteligible de la meditación racional. En la teoría neoplatónica el oído y la vista sirven para despertar el ansia de la hermosura que conduce, si se persevera en él, a la contemplación y conocimiento de la armonía cósmica. La voz y la música de Deidamia hacen que Aquiles salga de su estupor y sueño, y la contemplación de la doncella le incita a incorporarse al mundo intelectual. Según Ficino hay una triple belleza: la del sonido que se percibe por el oído, la del cuerpo, por los ojos; y la del alma, por la mente.[46] Este es el camino cognoscitivo de Aquiles; pero este joven inexperto, habiendo llegado al grado de la belleza corpórea, confunde el reflejo de la armonía de la creación con la belleza misma y equivocadamente tratará de poseer el bien material sin atender a la meditación trascendente; otra vez, el autor trata el tópico del amor sensual que oscurece el entendimiento del protagonista, hasta que, finalmente, el griego sabe salir del laberíntico dilema mediante el ejercicio del libre albedrío.

En el acto segundo, Tetis inventa un medio para que Aquiles, que ha determinado salir de su encierro para admirar la belleza de Deidamia, pueda, según ella cree, hacerlo sin poner en peligro la vida. Aquiles se presenta en la corte de Polemio como

Astrea, una prima a la que apenas se conocía y cuya
venida se esperaba. Se alberga con las mujeres de
palacio y despierta en Deidamia la curiosidad por un
amante encubierto que la procura misteriosamente en
los jardines, y que no es otro que él mismo. Séneca
había dicho que "seamos advertidos" y que se eluda
"el ciego amor del deleite,"[47] pues vencido el freno
de la razón todo es caer sin detenerse hasta quedar
tendido.[48] Tetis ayuda paradójicamente al hado al
permitir que su hijo habite en el palacio de Polemio,
ofendiendo el honor de los que le hospedan.

En el acto tercero, Aquiles ha conquistado a
Deidamia y los amantes se tratan durante el día como
primas, pero durante la noche Aquiles viste sus ropas
varoniles y goza de la compañía de su amada trans-
formándose en el fantasmal "monstruo de los jardines,"
que aparece y desaparece sin dejar rastro. En esta
jornada ocurre la situación dramática pintada por
Rubens y registrada por los mitólogos. Sin embargo,
el dramaturgo amplifica y escalona el episodio en un
sabio titubeo psicológico con los cambios emocionales
de Aquiles que se resiste a abandonar el goce de su
enamorada, así como a enfrentarse con su destino.
Calderón hace que el mercader de joyas sea un criado
de Lidoro, mientras el astuto Ulises observa cuidados-
amente la reacción de la falsa doncella que prefiere
el sombrero y las armas a las joyas que se ofrecen.
Ulises vuelve a sorprender a Aquiles, pues tocan caja
y un clarín, acentos guerreros que conmueven al héroe
de los pies veloces y que le hacen dar voces en favor
del imperio griego; en ambos casos la supuesta Astrea
hace la deshecha atribuyendo la conducta a instintos
amazónicos propios de su personalidad. Ulises que
está ya seguro de la identidad de la falsa doncella
le susurra cuando esta desprevenido: "Guárdate,
Aquiles; que te dan muerte."[49] Otra vez, el personaje
descubre su identidad por la reacción violenta, pero
todavía insiste en darse por desentendido y mantenerse
en el disfraz; las palabras despectivas de Ulises le
deciden a cambiar el atuendo femenil y le promete
unirse a sus tropas. Nuevamente los ruegos de
Deidamia le llevan a retractarse, en una escena de
contrastadas emociones, en la que los sentimientos
del protagonista son agitados por músicas guerreras
y cadencias de amor, que alternan en un juego paralel-
ístico; ello prolonga el titubeo psicológico hasta la
llegada de su rival, Lidoro, pretendiente oficial de
Deidamia, con el que Aquiles se enfrenta olvidando
los fingimientos y dándose a conocer en público.

Tetis llega entonces con oportunidad para salvarle de
la ira del rey Polemio. La diosa se percata de que la
protección con que le había resguardado había servido
para aumentar la inclinación fatal, pues sólo se puede
vencer el destino adverso cuando el ser humano se
enfrenta con él.

La fiesta dramática Fieras afemina amor se representó en el Real Coliseo del Buen Retiro para celebrar
el cumpleaños de Doña Mariana de Austria,[50] y de ella
se hizo una lujosa edición suelta, estudiada por
Wilson.[51] En esta obra de gran aparato escenográfico,[52] Calderón intensifica los elementos estructurales
de variado origen, subordinados a la figura de
Hércules y al tema del eros moralizado. El dramaturgo se ha esmerado en la armonización de la ensambla-
dura de tan diversas micro-estructuras, a la vez que
ha logrado brillantemente que la función paradigmática
sea consecuente con las líneas generales de pensamiento que se han observado en las piezas anteriores,
aunque en este caso haya una mayor riqueza de motivos
y símbolos.

En Fieras afemina amor se tratan con diversa extensión algunos de los trabajos que Hércules realizó
bajo el servicio a Euristeo. La muerte del león de
Nemea,[53] con el que empieza la pieza mitológica,
tiene una breve consideración, pero el episodio de
la entrada en el jardín de las Hespérides[54] posee,
por el contrario, una explayación a lo largo de la
obra y está estrechamente trabado con el tema principal. La ascensión al monte Parnaso, en donde
Hércules obtiene el caballo alado, con el que vence
al dragón que guarda las manzanas de oro, parece una
adaptación original de la historia de Belerofón a las
hazañas del héroe tirino. La lucha con Anteo, hijo
de Cibele, la narra Pérez de Moya,[55] el cual da como
fuente de información a Pomponio Mela.[56] Igualmente
el episodio de Onfale atribuido a Yole está tomado
del relato de Pérez de Moya.[57] Puede decirse que la
línea del leit-motiv de la pieza mitológica es una
adaptación del texto de la Philosophia Secreta.[58]

La caracterización de Hércules sigue en líneas
generales la tradición mítica. Se trata de un héroe
varonil, de aspecto impresionante y terrible, poco
hábil en materias cortesanas, y, a veces cercano a
lo grotesco, que lleva a cabo hazañas muy difíciles
de realizar gracias a la fuerza, la habilidad y el
valor.

La situación paradójica de este esforzado campeón
en el episodio mencionado surge como consecuencia de
la relación odio-amor mantenida con Yole, la que
termina con el momento infamante de la proclamación
de su afeminamiento. La causa de la mancha de su
fama estriba en haber desdeñado y despreciado el poder
del amor y con ello haber ofendido a los dioses Venus
y Cupido, los cuales preparan el castigo de su vanidad.

La obra está organizada sobre dos ideas contrarias,
la del valor varonil versus el encanto del amor sensual.
La primera se desarrolla en el juego alegórico mediante los trabajos y hazañas del protagonista que tiene
su climax--que coincide con el major aparato esceno-
gráfico--en la lucha con el dragón que guarda el
jardín de las Hespérides. La segunda empieza a
sobresalir cuando Yole finge admiración por el héroe
vencedor que acaba de dar muerte a Anteo, a pesar de
la ayuda de la diosa Cibele. Las Hespérides simbolizan
los halagos sensuales de la corte, o sea la hermosura
material, el canto grato a los sentidos y el ingenio
en el discurso. Yole prefiere las fuerzas materiales
y busca el descrédito de la virtud y la dedicación
ennoblecedora que Hércules representa con sus hazañas.
La acción se sitúa en Libia, en el reino africano de
Euristio, lugar apropiado para la tentación de los
sentidos que va a ocasionar la caída del héroe griego.
Al campeón le ayuda Apolo, cuyas musas cantan los
hechos del esforzado guerrero, pero pierde su apoyo
cuando utiliza a Pegaso para vencer al dragón que
guardaba las manzanas de oro. Al llevar a cabo esta
hazaña le mueve el deseo oscuro de cautivar a Yole
que se había refugiado en el jardín, y desvela como
resultado de ello un encubierto apetito erótico que
siente hacia la bella princesa. Los falsos halagos
de Yole transforman al tosco guerrero en la figura
cómica de la que se burla la corte, castigo de su
flaqueza humana.

En los tres ejemplos estudiados se ha observado
el cuidadosa tratamiento del tema eros moralizado. El
amor sensual se presenta como un peligro y los que
caen en él lo hacen por ignorancia, al no comprender
el sentido profundo de la belleza, que eleva el
espíritu humano hacia el entendimiento de la armonía
y la meditación trascendente, cuando evita la perver-
sión vergonzosa de la servidumbre al goce material.

University of Delaware

[1] Se representó el 25 de junio de 1636. N.D. Shergold, "The First Performance of Calderón's El mayor encanto, amor," Bulletin of Hispanic Studies, XXXV, 1958, págs. 22-27.

[2] Se estrenó el otoño de 1667 en Sevilla. Hugo A. Rennert, "Notes on the Chronology of the Spanish Drama," Modern Language Review, II, julio 1907, págs. 331-341.

[3] Se estrenó en el enero de 1670. Kurt y Roswitha Reichenberger, Bibliographisches Hundbuch des Calderón - Forschung, Tomo I, Verlag Thiele und Schwarz, Kassel, 1979, pág. 1849.

[4] Para esta nomenclatura puede consultarse mi estudio "La motivación personal y estética en la elaboración de las comedias de Calderón," Cuadernos para Investigación de la Literatura Hispánica, Fundación Universitaria Española, Seminario "Menéndez Pelayo," nos 2-3, Madrid, 1980, págs. 225-235.

[5] Baldesar Castiglione, Il Cortegiano, anotado e ilustrado por Vittorio Cian, Lib. 4o (Firenze: Sanson, 1908), pág. 365. Trad. de Juan Boscan.

[6] Ibidem, pág. 410.

[7] In Convivium Platonis Commentarium, Oratio Secunda, cap. VII, Omnia Opera, vol. II (Basilea: 1561), págs. 1320-1363.

[8] "Amor non è altro che un certo desiderio di fruir la belleza," ed. cit. de Il Cortegiano, pág. 408.

[9] Ibidem, pág. 409.

[10] Ibidem.

[11] Se aplica el término de emblema dramático a cierta situación de la acción, alegórica, que se repite en la obra del dramaturgo.

[12] Este crítico dice al respecto: "The teaching of Fable is justified. It is exalted for its edifying value as well; it too, aims at 'the greater glory of God.' Mythology in fact, say the Fathers, is not a

jumble of absurd or shocking tales, it is a body of
moral precepts, cunningly hidden under the mask of
fiction 'as the stone hidden in the fruit.' In this
light, there is in mythology nothing to alarm the most
delicate conscience." Jean Seznec, The Survival of
the Pagan Gods, 2ª ed. revisada (New York: Pantheon
Books, 1953), pág. 275. La edición original es
francesa (La survivance des dieux antiques, Studies
of the Warburg Institute, vol. XI, London, 1940).

13. "Aprobación," de Lope de Vega, fechada el
2 de septiembre de 1619, Teatro de los dioses de la
gentilidad, de Baltasar de Victoria, vol. I, Salamanca,
1620.

[14]La primera edición está hecha en Madrid, 1585.
A esta siguieron la de Zaragoza, 1599; la de Alcalá,
de 1611; las de Madrid, de 1628 y 1673.

[15]Véase la edición de Eduardo Gómez de Baquero,
colección Los clásicos olvidados, Nueva Biblioteca de
Autores Espanoles, vol. VI, dos tomos, Madrid, 1928,
lib. I, cap. I, pág. 7.

[16]La traduzión del Indio de los tres Diálogos de
Amor, de León Hebreo, Madrid, en casa de Pedro Madri-
gal, 1590. Hemos utilizado la edición crítica de
Eduardo Juliá Martínez, en dos tomos (Madrid, 1949),
por la que citamos. Vol. I, págs. 179-80.

[17]Sobre la interpretación del mito pueden con-
sultarse: B. Malinowski, Magic, Science and Religion
(New York: Doubleday, 1955); Mircea Eliade, Myth and
Reality, trad. de Willard R. Trask (New York: Harper
& Row, 1963); Claude Lévi-Strauss, The Savage Mind
(Chicago: Univ. of Chicago Press, 1966; la edición
original es francesa, 1962); del mismo autor, The
Raw and the Cooked, trad. de J. y D. Weightman (New
York: Harper & Row, 1969; la edición original francesa
es de 1964); G. S. Kirk, Myth: Its Meaning and
Function in Ancient and Other Cultures (Berkeley:
Univ. of California Press, 1970). También es util
la introducción de H. J. Rose, Mitología griega, trad.
de Juan Godo Costa (Barcelona: Labor, 1970). La
edición original es A Handbook of Great Mythology
(London: Methuen and Co., 1958).

[18]Véase, a este respecto, el libro citado de
Seznec.

[20]Fundamental como estudio de introducción a las comedias mitológicas es el capítulo XI de <u>Calderón</u>, de A. Valbuena Prat, Juventud, 1941, págs. 169-183. Muy útil también, en la línea interpretativa de Valbuena Prat es el artículo de W. G. Chapman, "Las comedias mitológicas de Calderón," <u>Revista</u> de <u>Literatura</u>, V, nº 4 (Madrid, 1954), págs. 35-69.

[20]En el acto II de <u>El</u> <u>monstruo</u> <u>de</u> <u>los</u> <u>jardines</u>, se halla un interesante pasaje que revela el tratamiento que Calderón hace de la fábula. Es parte de una conversación entre Tetis y Aquiles:

Tetis. "Pues ya que a su extremo llega
tu pasión, llegue a tu extremo
la mía también, y sea
un asombro de otro asombro
reparo infeliz.

Aquiles. ¿Qué intentas?

Tetis. Que tú sepas tu peligro,
y yo poner medio sepa
con que tu a Deidamia asistas
y yo seguro te tenga.

Aquiles. Pues ¿qué aguardas?

Tetis. Temo que
no verosímil parezca.

Aquiles. Al amor todo le es fácil.

Tetis. ¿Si es terrible?

Aquiles. No lo temas.

Tetis. ¿Si es temerario?

Aquiles. ¿Qué obsta?

Tetis. ¿Si es extraño?

Aquiles. Que lo sea.

Tetis. Y ¿si acaso...

Aquiles. Di.

Tetis.   peligra
          en términos de novela?

Aquiles.   ¿Qué importará, si es mi vida
           fábula, que lo parezca?"

(Dramas, Aguilar, Madrid, 1966, pág. 1998, I.)

[21] Lib. X, vv. 135-574; XII, 8-150.

[22] Lib. XIV, vv. 242-310.

[23] Lib. I, vv. 681-704.

[24] Lib. XIII, vv. 162-173.

[25] Lib. III, 13.8.

[26] Bibliotheca, lib. II, 7.8; Las Heroídas, de
Ovidio, lib. IX, v. 54 y ss.

[27] Lib. II, VII, 7.

[28] Lib. XI, 461, y XIII, 560.

[29] "The stage on the lake represents the island of
Circe, and is to be raised seven feet above the water,
with a curving ramp or staircase leading up to it. It
is to have a parapet of rough stones, adorned with
coral, pearls, and shells, and with waterfalls and
other similar things. In the middle of the island
there is to be a high mountain with precipices and
caves, surrounded by a dark, thick wood with tall
trees, some of which have human faces, with green
and tangled branches growing from their heads and
arms. On the branches hang various trophies of hunt-
ing and wars. The stage is lit with artificial light-
ing, and this is able to grow brighter when required
to do so." N. D. Shergold, A History of the Spanish
Stage (Oxford: Clarendon Press, 1967), pág. 280.

[30] C. Pellicer, Tratado histórico sobre el origen
de la comedia y el histrionismo en España, vol. II,
pags. 146-166.

[31] "Permanecimos en aquél país un año, y durante
ese largo período vi muchas cosas," la trad. es
nuestra. Ovidio, Las metamorfosis, lib, XIV, vv.
308-9.

[32]A. E. Sloman, "Calderón and Falconry: a note on dramatic language," Romance Philology, 1953, págs. 299-304.

[33]Philosophia Secreta, ed. cit., vol. II, pág. 219.

[34]Ibidem.

[35]Baltasar de Victoria hace referencia al tratar este episodio mitológico al emblema LXXVI de Andrea Alciato, Emblemata cum commentariis (Padua, 1621), pags. 336-340.

[36]L. A. Séneca, Obras completas, trad. de Lorenzo Riber (Madrid: Aguilar, 1943), pág. 560.

[37]Véase la parte X, "The Achilles Series," de Egbert Haverkamp Begemann, en el Corpus Rubenianum Ludwig Burchard (Bruselas: Phaidon, 1975).

[38]Edward Dillon, Rubens (London: Methuen and Co., 1909), pág. 131.

[39]Lib. IV, vv. 819-960, ed. de Paul M. Clogan (Leiden: E. J. Brill, 1968).

[40]Ob. cit., lib. XII, cap. LII.

[41]Lib. IX, cap. XII, Venecia, 1567.

[42]"Y como su madre Thetis le auía pronosticado que auía de morir en Troya . . . se fue a la isla de Cyros, que es una de las Cicladas en casa del rey Lycomedes. . . . Entró en áuito de donzella y, como era hermoso y de poca edad, fue fácil engañar al Rey y a todos los de su casa." Teatro de los dioses de la gentilidad, vol. I, Lib. I, cap. XII.

[43]"Por algunos indicios y secretas relaciones supo Ulises cómo Achiles estaua en hábito trocado en casa del rey Licomedes; fuesse allá usando de un particular estrategema, y fue que se fingió bohonero o tendero, llevó variedad de joyas y de galas, de las que entonces usauan las damas, fuesse al quarto dellas a preguntar si querían algo de aquella mercadería; començó a descoger las mercadurías y las damas echar mano de lo que más les agradaua. Ulises tenía avisados a sus compañeros que con cierta señal

91

tocassen al arma, y como en aquel punto tocassen, sospechando que eran enemigos, como vio Achiles el arco y las saetas, que auía puesto Ulises entre las demás mercaderías, de industria quitó los vestidos mugeriles para salir al rebato." Ibidem, pág. 73.

[44]Lib. VII, 514a - 521b.

[45]"Verdad y sueño de La Vida es sueño de Calderón de la Barca," Clavileño, II (1950).

[46]Convivium, ed. cit., "Prima Oratio," cap. IV, "De Utilitate amoris," págs. 1322-3.

[47]De vita beata, XIV, 2. Trad. de Lorenzo Riber.

[48]Epistula XCIV, 63. Trad. de Lorenzo Riber.

[49]El monstruo de los jardines, Aguilar, pág. 2019 I.

[50]El cumpleaños de doña Mariana fue el 22 de diciembre. No era raro que se retrasara la celebración de los aniversarios mediante el estreno de una obra dramática, especialmente si esta requería una elaborada preparación de tramoyas, como ocurrió en este caso.

[51]E. M. Wilson, "La edición príncipe de Fieras afemina amor de Pedro Calderón de la Barca," Revista de Biblioteca, Archivo y Museo, año 24, nº70 (Madrid, 1961), págs. 7-28.

[52]N. D. Shergold, A History of the Spanish Stage, "Court Plays of the Reign of Charles II (1665-1700)," cap. 12, obra cit., págs. 351-353.

[53]Apolodoro, Bibliotheca, lib. II, V, I; Diodoro Siculo, Bibliotheca historica, IV, II.

[54]Apolodoro, ibidem, lib. II, v. 11.

[55]Philosophia Secreta, ed. cit., tomo II, lib. IV, cap. VIII, págs. 113-115.

[56]De situ orbis, lib. I, cap. 5.

[57]Philosophia Secreta, tomo II, lib. IV, cap. XXII, pág. 138-9.

[58]He aquí la parte principal del texto: "(Yole)
codiciosa de la venganza, con maravillosa y constante
astucia, con amor fingido encubrió su corazón, y con
disimulación trajo a Hércules a amarla en tanto grado,
que no sólo le hizo desnudar de sus ásperos vestidos
y que se vistiese otros muelles y mujeriles, mas
ponerse sortijas y anillos en los dedos y untarse
con ungüentos preciosos, y peinarse y aun tocarse
cofias, y otras cosas de mujeres; y como aun con
todas estas cosas no le pareciese haber satisfecho
su ira, después de haberle traído a tanta blandura,
se hizo que asentado como mujer en el suelo hilase
con sus dueñas y contase las patrañas de sus trabajos.
Parecióle a esta mujer su mayor honra haber afeminado
a un hombre tan robusto y valiente que haberle muerto
con cuchillo o ponzoña." Philosophia Secreta, págs.
138-9.

La vida es sueño and the

Labyrinth of Illusion

Everett W. Hesse

I

On rereading La vida es sueño recently, I was
struck by the confusion that permeates the play. I
decided to search for the cause of the chaos and
found it to be the dispersion of illusion throughout
the drama. By illusion I mean a false impression,
whether based on fancy or on wishful thinking or on
a false perception because of one's self-deceit or
the deceit caused by another. This false perception
causes a misinterpretation of the actual nature of
the causative agent. The term illusion then as I
will use it embraces deception including self-deception or delusion, misconception, false belief and a
distorted conception. The amount of illusion in the
play is so widespread that in its intricacy and per-
plexity it may be conceived as a labyrinth.

Some of the confusion arises from the several
meanings of the play's title. It may carry its "face
value" meaning that life is a dream, i.e., that life
is only a figment of the imagination, a fiction, and
that real life begins only after death in the next
world. It can also mean that events, fortunate and
unfortunate, pass rapidly as though in a dream and
do not endure. Life is like a dream also in the sense
that it is so chaotic that it becomes almost impossible
to distinguish between fact and fiction, dreaming and
waking, and truth and a lie.

The action that takes place before the curtain
rises also contributes toward the confusion. Astolfo
has deceived Rosaura by seducing and then abandoning
her to pay court to another woman (Estrella); he is
motivated by his ambition to gain the throne through
a loveless marriage to Estrella who detects Astolfo's
perfidy, since he still wears Rosaura's picture
around his neck. Clotaldo has deceived Violante,
Rosaura's mother, by seducing and then abandoning her.

I will explore the ramifications of illusion as
it appears in the speech and actions of the several
main characters: Basilio, Rosaura, Astolfo, Clotaldo
and Segismundo and in their relationship to one another.

II

First I will consider the question of illusion with reference to Basilio and his relation to his son. Segismundo's birth under extraordinary circumstances marked by an earthquake, violent storms and an eclipse of the sun signaled not only the arrival of a new prince but also the demise of his mother. Such cataclysmic events impelled Basilio to consult the prince's horoscope. Since it portended a rule of tyranny not only for other people but also for the king himself, who would be humiliated and conquered, Basilio sought a way out of the predicament by imprisoning Segismundo. As time passed, he began to wonder if he had pursued the right course of action by taking away the prince's human and divine right to govern. Basilio had undoubtedly considered his action just since it was motivated by idealistic intentions. Unfortunately, however, he had failed to perceive the negative impact incarceration would have on his young son. There was nothing morally wrong in his decision to spare his people the rule of a future tyrant. His morally wrong action was to play the part of a tyrant himself by denying his son the tender loving care that the child needed in his formative years. With these serious doubts in mind, Basilio decides to put the imprisoned Segismundo to a test to see if he is fit to rule. The test is to be carried out in part as a deception, or as an illusion of truth. Now truth is a body of real events, things and facts. It may apply to an ideal abstraction conforming to a universal or generalized reality or it may represent a quality of statement, acts or feelings of adhering to reality and avoiding error or falsehood, as we shall see later. First, the prince is to be kept in ignorance regarding his identity as the future king. But at the beginning of Act II, Basilio changes his mind and decides that Segismundo is to be informed of his royal identity. Second, if the prince fails the test, he is to be returned to prison with the explanation that his experience at court was all a dream. This will constitute a deliberate falsehood designed to prevent the prince from falling into a spell of depression and disconsolation, and also to disabuse his mind of the idea that he is the crown prince. This leads Basilio to formulate the postulate, ". . . en el mundo, Clotaldo, / todos los que viven sueñan" (1148-49),[1] which passes for a truism. It is a philosophical statement to express a way of looking at life, and may not be considered as truth.

Basilio then relegates the task of disillusioning his son to Clotaldo, the boy's surrogate father, tutor and jailer, with the exhortation, "le saca con la verdad" (1160). But the "truth" that Basilio has in mind is to be slanted in such a way as to guard against the prince's possible disconsolateness in the event that he fail the test. Basilio, who had initiated a plan of action without first considering the effect of his scheme on his son's personality and behavior, thus becomes a victim of self-deception. The incipient evidence of Basilio's misguided policy appears when the king seeks to embrace his son. This outward sign of love, however, comes too late. Its effect is negated by Segismundo's outrageous act of defenestration and his complete rejection of paternal love at this point in the play. Here Segismundo begins the process of condemnation of his father's idea of child rearing, accusing him of debasing his dignity as a human being and treating him like an animal. Angered by his son's recriminations, Basilio attempts to modify the prince's behavior with an hypothesis implying a possible deception, ". . . quizá estás soñando, / aunque ves que estás despierto" (1530-31).

Segismundo refuses to accept this explanation, for it is obvious to him that, "no sueño, pues toco y creo / lo que he sido y lo que soy" (1534-35). So the prospect of convincing his son to alter his conduct by means of the illusion that he may be dreaming fails. When Clotaldo later attempts to impose the same illusion of a dream as a reality, it again arouses the prince's ire and provokes a threat, "veré, dándote muerte, / si es sueño o si es verdad" (1682-83).

I will next consider Rosaura's deception and that found in her relationship with Clotaldo. Rosaura's male attire does not deceive Segismundo who falls in love with her beauty, her voice and her humanity. The masquerade was an illusion but her beauty and the accompanying feelings of compassion for the prince were all of reality for Segismundo.[2] There was no illusion about the bond of empathy which united these two wretched companions of misfortune.

The illusion produced by her masculine disguise, however, traps Clotaldo who is deluded into thinking that Rosaura may be his "son" when she displays the sword given her by her mother. He recognizes it, and after hearing her explanation, he is overwhelmed by what it portends, "aún no sé si determinarme / si tales sucesos son / ilusiones o verdades" (296-98). He finally reaches the conclusion, "éste es mi hijo" (413). But in his present state of mental confusion he recoils from his initial reaction when his love for his offspring conflicts with his loyalty to his king. Furthermore, he reasons that a man who has been dishonored is himself without honor and so asserts, "no es mi hijo, no es mi hijo / ni tiene mi noble sangre" (443-44). Then he begins to reconsider, convincing himself by his reasoning that, what else would a noble person do but pursue a wrongdoer and bring him to justice? Therefore, he considers "him" truly as his son, "mi hijo es, mi sangre tiene, / pues tiene valor tan grande" (455-56).

Clotaldo weighs the possibility that the king may decree death for his offspring for having entered forbidden territory. Therefore, he decides in favor of a partial deception, that is, of withholding the truth of his identity from her; if she dies, it will be "sin saber que soy su padre" (468).[3] With the later discovery of Rosaura's feminine identity, Clotaldo is now totally bewildered, "¿qué confuso laberinto / es éste, donde no puede hallar la razón el hilo? / ... / yo vasallo, ella mujer?" (975-77, 980).

The illusion of some secret affection and esteem which she feels toward Clotaldo leads her to insinuate something about herself which has not been revealed, "si no soy lo que parezco / y Astolfo a casarse vino / con Estrella, sí podrá / agraviarme . . ." (970-73).

Instructed by her father to take service as a lady-in-waiting to Estrella, Rosaura assumes the identity of Astrea. Estrella, who trusts Astrea implicitly, has requested her to obtain the picture of another woman that Astolfo wears. When Rosaura confronts him, Astolfo addresses her as "Rosaura," but she plays her role to the hilt, thus reciprocating the deception he played on her in the pre-stage action, "¿Yo Rosaura? Hase engañado / Vuestra Alteza si me tiene / por otra dama; que yo / soy Astrea . . ." (1888-91). Astolfo is not deceived by the illusion of her new identity, "aunque más esfuerzos hagas, / ¡oh, qué mal, Rosaura, puedes / disimular!" (1912-14). He recognizes her voice and comments that "tan destemplado instrumento / que ajustar y medir quiere / la falsedad de quien dice, / con la verdad de quien siente" (1918-21). Taking a leaf from her book,

Astolfo carries the deception forward. Since she has come in search of her picture, he counters with the proposal of an illusion, which is to return the original lifelikeness of herself to Estrella, i.e., to go present herself as a living portrait (1932-35).

Angered by his delaying tactics, Rosaura invokes the ingenuity of love to aid her in recovering her portrait. The ruse she employs is to invent a story, a deception that contains some elements of truth: as she was waiting for Astolfo, she remembered a picture she had in her pocket. She was looking at it when it fell to the floor. Astolfo, who had just arrived to hand over a picture of another woman, picked it up and refused to return it to her. Thus the one he has is hers. Estrella wrenches the picture from Astolfo and, after checking it, delivers it to Rosaura who departs hastily. Rosaura's act of deception serves several purposes. First, she recovers her picture, and second, it drives a wedge between Astolfo and Estrella since Astolfo cannot deliver the "other" picture, and third, it alienates Astolfo and Estrella, which is exactly what Rosaura had hoped to accomplish.

Astolfo has not only seduced Rosaura but has abandoned her in favor of his cousin Estrella whom he hopes to marry and by a marriage to ascend the throne. In gongoristic terms he greets Estrella with courtly flatter. He refers to her eyes as "rayos," and "cometas." The birds are "trompetas" and the fountains "cajas." The birds are then described in a catachresis as "clarines de pluma" and the trumpets as "aves de metal" (483-84). Estrella's discerning eye penetrates the deception, perceiving a contradiction between the "finezas tan cortesanas" and the "acciones humanas" (496; 498). She calls his flattery a "baja acción" worthy only of a beast, a vile act that she tags as "madre de engaño y traición" (507). Estrella has noted that Astolfo wears around his neck the picture of another woman, which convinces her of his deceitful intentions.

Later in Act Two, the scene between Astolfo and Estrella is resumed. That Astolfo still loves Rosaura is implied in his action of wearing her picture. But in order to pacify Estrella, he removes it with a striking observation about human behavior in relation to love and fidelity, "perdone, Rosaura hermosa, / este agravio, porque ausentes, / no se guardan más fe que ésta / los hombres y las mujeres" (1774-77).

The most extensive diffusion of the labyrinth of illusion occurs in the main action and more specifically in Segismundo's mind. It is occasioned by the partial truths or illusion of truth that Basilio and Clotaldo have told him, by the rapid change from prison to palace, by the failure of the educational program in which he was placed and by the lack of parental affection. Segismundo, who conceives of himself as ". . . una fiera de los hombres / y un hombre de las fieras" (211-12), and a "monstruo humano" (209), labors under the delusion that he should have more freedom than that enjoyed by animals and inanimate objects since he has a free will, a better instinct and a soul. But after Clotaldo points out that prison bars have been a deterrent to his cruelty and vaulting pride, Segismundo momentarily glimpses a flash of truth, ". . . ¡ah cielos, / qué bien hacéis en quitarme / la libertad! . . ." (329-31).

Before Segismundo was drugged and brought to the palace, Clotaldo described to Basilio how he prepared the lad mentally to accept the responsibility of kingship by appealing to an illusion of the glory of royalty with a reference to the eagle which flies in the ethereal regions of the skies. There was no further need to stimulate the call to majesty, for Segismundo's vaulting ambition and pride were in the ascendancy, "porque en efecto, la sangre / le incita, mueve y alienta / a cosas grandes" (1052-54). This appeal to Segismundo's pride is diametrically opposed to the attitude of humility which the king hopes to find in his son. Little did either the king or Clotaldo realize the deleterious effect that the latter's suggestion would exert on the behavior of the young prince.

After Segismundo, drugged in his prison cell, awakes from the soporific, he can hardly believe his eyes, for the opulence of the court contrasts sharply with the dark and miserable emptiness of the dungeon. He knows it cannot be a dream as that would be a deception, "decir que es sueño es engaño: / bien sé que despierto estoy" (1236-37). After Clotaldo has informed him of his true identity and the reason for his incarceration, Segismundo goes on the rampage and mistreats his neighbors. According to Basilio's concept of right and wrong conduct, Segismundo's comportment falls into the latter category, and is therefore an illusion rather than a reality. Hence, Basilio now warns him "que seas humilde y blando, / porque quizá

estás soñaňdo, / aunque ves que estás despierto"
(1529-31). This identification of what Segismundo
knows to be true with a dream-world of fantasy and
illusion prompts the prince to defend his position
tenaciously though angrily, "¿que quizá soñando estoy,
aunque despierto me veo? / No sueño, / pues toco y
creo / lo que he sido y lo que soy" (1532-35). The
statement made by Basilio (1530-31) and repeated by
Clotaldo (1679) together with his re-awakening in
prison have left such an indelible imprint on Segismundo's psyche that he is now almost ready to accept
the premise as a truism. His remark "¡qué de cosas
he soñado!" (2087) prompts Clotaldo to inquire about
what he dreamed. Segismundo is not quite prepared to
accept the proposition that his experience was a dream,
"supuesto que sueño fue, / no diré lo que soñé, / lo
que vi, Clotaldo, sí" (2109-11). Then he relates not
what he dreamed (the unreal), but what he saw (the
real). Only his love for a woman was true since
everything else ended, but his love for her did not
end. Following Clotaldo's admonition, ". . . que aún
en sueños / no se pierde el hacer bien" (2146-47), is
Segismundo ready to believe the postulate that "la
vida es sueño" when he affirms, "es verdad . . ."
(2148).

The disillusion Segismundo suffers when Rosaura
informs him of the reality of his court experience
only serves to increase his confusion, "luego fue verdad, no sueño" (2934). He finds the copy so similar
to the original that it is almost impossible to distinguish one from the other. He talks himself into
believing that hurting one's neighbor is evil (the
dream) and accepts the "obrar bien," the good (the
reality) to treat others as he would himself. This
is what Kierkegaard might call the "great leap into
faith."

III

Basilio became the victim of a self deception
when he thought he could spare his country the rule
of a tyrant predicted by the horoscope by imprisoning
his infant son. He was so intent on insuring freedom
for his people that he forgot about freedom and human
rights for his son until his conscience began to
trouble him. His intention of avoiding tyranny for
his people was good but his plan to incarcerate an
infant son was ill-conceived. His withholding of
information regarding Segismundo's true identity and

his barbaric cruelty toward his son caused confusion, frustration, anger and violence.

The visual deception occasioned by Rosaura's several disguises leads finally to the clearing of her honor and the return of her erstwhile lover Astolfo. But her masculine attire does not deceive Segismundo, who falls in love with her. Clotaldo was deceived at first and refused to recognize her as his offspring until his reason convinced him of the rightness of her mission. Garbed as Astrea, Rosaura fails to deceive Astolfo who recognizes her voice. By a deception she succeeds in recovering her portrait and in driving a wedge between Estrella and Astolfo.

Verbal deception plays a significant role throughout the play. Estrella is not deceived by the flattering metaphors Astolfo selects to court her. She has detected the note of infidelity in his wearing of another woman's picture.

Basilio and Clotaldo try to manipulate Segismundo's behavior by a threat in the guise of a truism. At first Segismundo resents the lie but with its repetition he finally comes to talk himself into accepting it as truth or the illusion of truth since he finds it increasingly difficult to distinguish between illusion and reality.

This metaphysical drama also implies a social message which transcends the epistemological issues, ". . . sea verdad o sueño, / obrar bien es lo que importa" (2423-24). We can conclude that it makes no difference whether we deceive ourselves or others provided that our intentions are good. Or, to state it another way, the end justifies the means

San Diego State University

Notes

[1] Edition consulted: Calderón, <u>La vida es sueño</u>. Edición de Everett W. Hesse (Salamanca: Almar, 1978).

[2]
    sólo a una mujer amaba . . .
    que fue verdad, creo yo.   (2134-35)

[3] This has a parallel in Basilio's decision to keep his identity a secret from his son, "sin que él sepa que es mi hijo" (797), which he later retracts (1113-14).

Menón y el determinismo trágico

en La hija del aire

Susana Hernández Araico

"Incomprensible y escandalosa" llama Ruiz Ramón
la poca atención que se le ha dedicado a La hija del
aire[1] en el pasado. Pues a pesar de ser encomiada
por varios críticos como la obra maestra de Calderón,[2]
permanece relativamente ignorada. Al celebrarse el
tricentenario de la muerte de Calderón de la Barca,
apremia entonces rendir homenaje a su arte dramático
en esta obra.

Sus dos partes trazan en conjunto el desarrollo
trágico de Semíramis, una reina legendaria de Babi-
lonia, bellísima y prodigiosa.[3] La Segunda parte,
cuyo autor posiblemente no haya sido Calderón,[4] presenta el afán de Semíramis por mantenerse en el poder
con su fuerza militar, un disfraz y otras estratagemas
que la conducen a una muerte patética.[5] Por otro
lado, la Primera parte exhibe la construcción incon-
fundible de Calderón con una prisionera desesperada
por su libertad, renuente al encierro que evitaría su
horóscopo nefasto. En esta parte, Semíramis sale de
su prisión tenebrosa, confiada en su libre albedrío.
Mas su mismo enclaustramiento le acucia esa ambición
que la impulsa a casarse con el rey Nino para obtener
poder.[6] Se encamina así a cumplir la profecía de que
ha de convertir a un monarca en tirano, matarlo y
luego morir ella despeñada. Pero la tragedia de
Semíramis no se lleva a cabo en la Primera parte;
sólo se plantea.

Según su horóscopo, el rey Nino parece el blanco
de su fuerza destructiva. Sin embargo, este personaje
no representa una figura propiamente trágica.[7] Su
transformación en tirano resulta lamentable en términos morales; dramáticamente, carece en sí de impacto
conmovedor, igual que su asesinato anunciado en la
Primera parte y sólo mencionado después en la Segunda.
La tiranía de Nino, pervertido por su apasionamiento
con Semíramis, repercute principalmente en su general
Menón. Sobre él recae un determinismo dual--pre-
ordenado según el vaticinio de Venus y arbitrario de
acuerdo con la fortuna. Unicamente él encarna el
valor trágico de la Primera parte y le da sentido de

obra terminada, independiente de la Segunda.

De los personajes en torno a la protagonista, Menón sobresale por su propia sustancia dramática y su contribución al desarrollo de la acción.[8] Es la primera persona que habla en la obra dando orden de que el cortejo real pare cerca del escondite de Semíramis. Por Menón sale después ella de su prisión, y por él se entera Nino de la hermosura avasalladora de la heroína. Estas acciones encarrilan la tragedia que sólo Menón encarna al final de la Primera parte. Suscitando terror y lástima, su trayecto dramático representa un cambio de gran éxito a frustración hasta intenso sufrimiento. Físicamente deshecho, todavía demuestra bondad al final aplaudiendo el triunfo matrimonial de Semíramis con Nino. De repente se siente poseído y en medio de un eclipse tempestuoso, repite el vaticinio de Venus sobre la protagonista.[9] En esta posesión final culmina el ofuscamiento de la razón que acarrea la catástrofe de Menón. Aparentemente impulsada por el hado y la fortuna, su tragedia se advierte desde la primera jornada en el simbolismo ambivalente del sol y la invocación de estas fuerzas deterministas.

Un interludio musical al principio de la primera jornada introduce la imagen ambigua del sol. Menón se muestra general fiel y servidor ordenando un saludo de tambores y trompetas para el rey Nino con quien regresa de una campaña victoriosa. Lisías, gobernador de Ascalón, la provincia donde Menón para las tropas, ordena que "a aquellas salvas de Marte / sucedan las de Amor."[10] Esta canción suave que sigue al saludo militar constituye el tema simbólico de la obra y, en particular, de la tragedia de Menón:

> A tanta admiración
> suspenso queda en su carrera el sol (33-34;
> 71-72).

En un nivel literal, el estribillo expresa la gran admiración que causa el cortejo de Nino--hasta el mismo sol se detiene a verlo. Simbólicamente, alude a la infanta Irene cuya hermosura se equipara con la grandeza del rey. Además el sol, "suspenso" de "tanta admiración," prefigura el enamoramiento del rey con la bella Semíramis que se halla encerrada muy cerca. Igualmente simboliza el ofuscamiento de la razón que padecerán Nino, Semíramis y, sobre todo, Menón; pues para él va a significar una ceguera física que le suspende la luz del día cuando el rey le manda sacar los ojos.[11]

La música exacerba la frustración de Semíramis encerrada. Edwards ha señalado que la yuxtaposición del triunfo del rey Nino y las quejas desesperadas de la protagonista no dejan duda sobre la identidad del rey que su vaticinio amenaza.[12] Pero la presencia del símbolo del sol en su prisión infeliz también enfoca desde un principio sobre Menón la amenaza del hado.

Para apaciguar a la Semíramis desesperada, su guardián Tiresias le explica el motivo del festejo y le aconseja que se recluya de nuevo:

> Sosiégate, y vuelve, vuelve
> a la estancia que te dio
> por cuna y sepulcro el Cielo;
> que me está dando temor
> pensar que el sol te ve, y que
> sabe enamorarse el sol (107-12).

Tiresias primero alude al sol en contraste con la prisión oscura de Semíramis; también se refiere simbólicamente al monarca victorioso. Una vez reforzado el simbolismo real del sol, la primera parte del vaticinio que Semíramis rememora esquematiza su impacto catastrófico sobre el favorito del rey:

> . . . Venus . . . anunció
> . . . .
> . . . que por mí habría
> en <u>cuanto</u> <u>ilumina</u> <u>el</u> <u>sol</u>,
> tragedias, muertes, insultos,
> ira, llanto y confusión.
> . . . .
>   Que a un Rey
> glorioso le haría mi amor
> tirano y que al fin vendría
> a darle la muerte yo (132-42; subrayado mío)

El pronóstico de Venus claramente anuncia aquí la destrucción de Nino y más adelante de Semíramis también (149-51). Pero, por medio de la imagen del sol que se refiere al rey, amenaza primero a Menón. Según el vaticinio de Venus, Semíramis ejercerá su influencia desastrosa, en primer lugar, donde el sol esparce sus rayos--simbólicamente sobre quien el rey favorece, es decir, Menón. El peligra más que ningún otro personaje en torno al rey porque su victoria militar lo ha

colocado en la cumbre de la fortuna.[13] La caída
trágica de Menón parece mobilizarse por un determinismo
dual--preordenado en la profecía de Venus e imprevisto
en el acaso arbitrario.

El acecho de la casualidad fatal se nota cuando
el rey le promete constante apoyo a su general. De
nuevo surge la imagen del sol al expresar confianza
ambos personajes en la extensión permanente del poder
real. La amenaza anterior del vaticinio de Venus convierte ahora la ambivalencia del lenguaje simbólico
en presagio de cambio de fortuna para Menón:

> Nino: Tú, Menón, . . . valiente
> los sagrados laureles de mi frente
> tanto has facilitado,
> que a ti el mirarme de ellos coronado
> confesaré que debo.
> . . . de Ascalón eres ya dueño,
> aunque triunfo pequeño
> a tus grandes servicios.
> . . . .
> . . . yo con la divina y soberana
> beldad de Irene, mi gallarda hermana,
> . . . .
> ir a Nínive quiero:
> en ella, pues, te espero
> para partir contigo
> mi cetro y mi corona. El sol testigo
> será de una privanza
> a quien nunca se siga la mudanza.
>
> Menón: Invictísimo joven, cuya frente
> no sólo de los rayos del Oriente
> inmortal se corona,
> pero de zona trascendiendo en zona,
> de hemisferio pasando en hemisferio,
> hasta el ocaso extenderá su imperio . . .
>
> Nino: Dame, Menón, tus brazos,
> y cree que aquestos lazos
> nudo serán tan fuerte
> que sólo le desate . . .
>
> Menón: ¿Quién?
>
> Nino: La muerte (247-307).

Por medio del simbolismo ambivalente del sol, este
intercambio prefigura la desgracia de Menón.

Refiriéndose a la belleza de su hermana, el rey sin
querer predice su cambio hacia el general. En la rima
de "privanza" con "mudanza" resuena esta vuelta de
fortuna que amenaza a Menón a pesar del constante
agradecimiento que Nino le promete. El oriente y el
ocaso con que Menón a su vez alude al vasto dominio
del rey también atribuye la brevedad de un día a sus
mercedes. El ocaso además insinúa la ceguera y la
muerte que de hecho resulta para Menón con el fin del
favor real. El rey pretende asegurarle su apoyo para
toda la vida; pero al mismo tiempo advierte que ha de
acarrearle la muerte a su favorito.

Esta ironía trágica en el diálogo surge immedia-
tamente después que Nino premia a Menón con la provincia que hasta ahora Lisías ha gobernado. Indica
que la merced del rey marca la cumbre de la fortuna
para Menón y a la vez encierra la semilla de su desgracia. Efectivamente, el general va a caer bajo el
poder destructivo de Semíramis debido a su nuevo
dominio sobre Ascalón y el resentimiento de Lisías
que conlleva.

Menón mismo sugiere la corta duración de su
buenaventura cuando lo felicita la hermana del rey.
El símbolo ambivalente del sol surge de nuevo al
final de este diálogo amoroso y presagia otra vez la
desdicha de Menón:

Irene: De mil contentos llena,
           no a dar, a recibir la norabuena
           me ofrezco yo, Menón, porque a ninguna
           persona toca más vuestra fortuna.

Menón: En eso no hacéis nada,
           que sois en ella muy interesada;
           pues cuanto yo valiere,
           no es más que un corto don que darme
                      quiere
           el Cielo, porque tenga
           un sacrificio más que se prevenga
           llegar con mudo ejemplo
           al no piadoso umbral de vuestro templo.

Irene: Haced breve esta ausencia.

Menón: Feliz fuera
           amante, que adorar un sol se atreve,
           si él a la ausencia hacer pudiera
                      breve (307-28).

Al llamar su fortuna un "corto don" del "Cielo,"
Menón expresa su conciencia sobre la posible brevedad
de su suerte. Enamorado, se declara víctima ejemplar
del amor; y de hecho lo será según el vaticinio de
Venus y los propósitos morales de Calderón. Lament-
ando su separación del "sol," o sea, la bella princesa,
irónicamente Menón advierte que su deslealtad hacia
ella por su próximo apasionamiento con Semíramis
significará una oscuridad infeliz para él.

Como Lisías va a guiarlo al escondite de Semíramis, su presencia en la escena amenaza la felicidad
de Menón con la infanta. El resentimiento del gobernador en un aparte (329-32) transforma su felicitación
y oferta de servicio a Menón en hipocresía peligrosa
(333-36; 364). Pero el idealismo político del general
(340-43) le impide prevenirse contra Lisías; y confía
del todo en él al asumir el poder sobre Ascalón. En
privado, Menón se muestra aprensivo ante su nuevo
puesto y teme la mutabilidad de la fortuna:[14]

> Viento, llévale a Irene estos suspiros;
> y tú, diosa Fortuna,
> condicional imagen de la luna,
> estate un punto queda;
> diviértela tú, Amor, para su rueda,
> para que sean testigos
> los cielos que una vez han sido amigos (364-
> 70).

Muy consciente del impulso giratorio de la fortuna,
Menón quisiera--aunque no confía--que el dios Amor lo
apoye en su éxito político así como en su felicidad
con Irene. Irónicamente, el abuso de su poder en
Ascalón, a instancias de Lisías, lo induce a traicion-
arla con Semíramis. Y su apasionamiento con esta mujer
protegida por Venus lo acarrea a la desgracia. Amor
entonces no va a detener la rueda de Fortuna para
Menón--al contrario.

Incumbe reafirmar aquí que su caída de la fortuna
y la amenaza contra él en el vaticinio de Venus se
cumplen sólo debido a la intervención de Lisías. Existe
entre el general y el gobernador una rivalidad tácita
en el amor aparte de su competencia por las mercedes
del rey. De las seis veces que Lisías ha hablado, la
cuarta se dirige a Irene mientras se congracia con
Nino; la alaba como "de tanto humano sol divina
aurora" (222). En contraste, Menón no demuestra en
público ninguna afición a Irene mientras que hace

alarde de su devoción al rey. Cuando el general y el gobernador aparecieron primero en escena para dar la bienvenida al cortejo real, Menón ordenó una salva marcial a la cual Lisías contrapuso la portentosa canción de amor, "A tanta admiración / suspenso queda . . . el sol" (33-34; 71-72). Menón se ha mostrado descuidado del amor mientras Lisías alaba a Irene y casualmente anuncia el apasionamiento irracional del general con Semíramis.

Después de su apóstrofe a Fortuna, la siguiente vez que aparece Menón, se nota que Lisías lo ha entusiasmado a buscar el escondite de Semíramis donde Amor lo atrapará. Las palabras del general a Lisías le hacen eco a aquella canción de la primera escena y denotan el ofuscamiento de la razón de Menón:

> De todas cuantas grandezas
> desta provincia me has dicho,
> ésta que buscando vengo
> solamente es la que admiro.
> . . . .
> vuelve otra vez a contarlo,
> que quiero otra vez oírlo,
> porque se informe mejor
> mi ardimiento de tu aviso (607-10; 615-19;
> subrayado mío).

Apasionadamente, Menón se apresura a encontrar la prisión de Semíramis porque Lisías se la ha descrito como gran maravilla y misterio. El gobernador vuelve a incitar la curiosidad y valentía de Menón describiéndole un lugar fantástico y temible. Luego es imposible que su advertencia de no profanar esa zona desanime al general.

La conciencia anterior de Menón sobre la brevedad de la fortuna no le sirve de nada para ejercer su nuevo dominio con más circunspección. Debería moderar su búsqueda ansiosa; pero—como la canción de la primera escena anuncia—se entrega a una admiración que le suspende la razón. Por eso dice:

> Dar un corazón, Lisías,
> a admiraciones, rendido
> a los hechos de los dioses,
> más tiene de sacrificio
> que de irreverencia; ven
> . . . .
> no temas pues vas conmigo (661-65; 668;
> subrayado mío).

Menón se considera aquí víctima de una fuerza superior.
Se declara sumiso a un determinismo preordenado para
justificar su incapacidad de refrenar su valentía
impetuosa.

El determinismo dual que recae sobre Menón se
intensifica cerca del escondite de Semíramis con un
caso de cledonomancia y una profecía explícita. Por
casualidad la prisionera se queja de tal manera que
parece dirigirse al general:

> ¡Oh monstruo de la fortuna!
> ¿Dónde vas sin luz ni aviso?
> Si el fin es morir, porqué (sic)
> andas rodeando el camino? (711-14)

Este lamento de Semíramis fortuitamente amonesta a
Menón por su arrojo irracional. La evasión inútil
de la muerte que se refiere al encierro de Semíramis
resulta para Menón un recordatorio de su caída inevitable; pues primero se la ha identificado con la
fortuna. Y se reafirma esta identificación cuando
Semíramis coincide en responder, "Contigo / contigo,
fortuna, hablo" (718-19), después de preguntarse
Menón, "¿Con quién hablará?" (718) El representa la
fortuna; y como por coincidencia, Semíramis se queja
de su mala suerte, el siguiente reto de la prisionera
contra la fortuna transforma la cledonomancia en un
pronóstico de derrota trágica para Menón:

> Pero no me has de vencer;
> que yo, con valiente brío,
> sabré quebrarte los ojos (721-23).

Esta amenaza constituye un desafío profético contra
ese atrevimiento que ha elevado al general a la
cumbre de la fortuna. Advierte el apasionamiento
ciego que Semíramis le causa; también predice la
ceguera física con que Nino lo castiga por su renuente
apego a esta mujer que el rey va a desear para sí mismo.

La profecía parece tener un efecto inmediato sobre
Menón. Sólo con el tono amenazante de esta mujer, su
impetuosidad da lugar a una pasión amorosa que lo
priva de la luz de la razón. Y exclama:

> Sin luz quedaron los míos
> al oírlo; . . . .
> . . . .

112

                    ¡Qué frenesî!,   ¡qué locura!
                    ¡Qué letargo!,   ¡oh qué delirio! (724-25;
                                                        729-30)

Este apasionamiento irracional de Menón verifica el
simbolismo de la suspensión del sol en la canción
amorosa al principio de la obra. También denota el
rendimiento total de su voluntad a fuerzas fuera de
su control. Pues si antes ha dicho que se sacrifica
a "los hechos de los dioses" (663), ahora se declara
"ministro" de sus "leyes" (740-45). Y las únicas in-
vocadas en esta primera jornada son el vaticinio de
Venus y la rueda de Fortuna. Sin darse cuenta que
operan en su contra, Menón asume la responsabilidad
de ejecutar un decreto predeterminado y otro
arbitrario.

    El simbolismo ambivalente del sol sugiere su
iniciativa en cumplir el pronóstico de Venus--que
amenaza destruirlo a él--cuando saca a Semíramis de
su prisión. Menón le dice que salga "a ver el sol"
(777); en efecto la está animando a que conozca al
rey antes de enterarse del peligro que esta mujer
representa para el monarca.[15] Una vez que Semíramis
le explica la profecía de Venus, Menón no piensa que
pueda repercutir en su puesto de favorito del rey.[16]
Y sacándola de su escondite, asume la responsabilidad
de su propia caída de la fortuna. Por eso al concluir
la jornada, Lisías le advierte, "No labres tu muerte
tú mismo;" (1013-14)

    Obsesionado con Semíramis, Menón--al comenzar la
segunda jornada--quisiera esconderla de nuevo para
que "ni el sol la viera" (1088). Agradecida con él,
ella a duras penas (1234-49) promete "vivir del sol
ignorada" (1207) cuando Menón se va a la corte. Por
un lado, el general recela que el rey la conozca; por
otro, su lealtad al monarca lo conduce a enterarlo de
la belleza de Semíramis (1432-34). En cuanto a la
infanta, Menón no ha recapacitado en lo mínimo sobre
el amor de Irene;[17] y no le importa herirla alabando
enfrente de ella la hermosura de Semíramis con minu-
ciosos detalles (1519-1650). Así Menón despierta en
Nino una curiosidad apasionante por ver a esa gran
belleza (1651-57). Aunque el rey promete vencerse y
no ver a Semíramis por respeto al amor de Menón por
ella, la siguiente vez que aparece es a caballo des-
bocado, en el monte donde estaba escondida Semíramis
originalmente (1795-96; ver 733). Lo que parece un
caso fortuito en la caída del caballo del rey cerca

                            113

de Semíramis se debe a que Menón lo ha provocado a buscarla.[18] Obsesionado con su belleza, el mismo general es culpable de que Nino se apasione por ella y lo rebaje a él a la nada para no competir por el amor de Semíramis con su favorito.

El resto de la Primera parte de La hija del aire desarrolla la tragedia de Menón trazada magistralmente en la primera jornada con el simbolismo ambiguo del sol y el determinismo dual del hado y la fortuna.[19] Valiéndose del sol para referirse simultáneamente al rey y a la belleza femenina o a la razón, Calderón convierte una imagen tradicional en un símbolo dinámico cargado de tensión poética que abarca a los personajes principales. En particular, el símbolo refleja el conflicto que Menón experimenta al nublarse su razón y anteponer devoción por la belleza femenina al servicio leal del rey. Los elementos deterministas a su vez cumplen una función irónica de gran fuerza dramática. Calderón se vale de ellos para sugerir la predisposición trágica de los personajes y, sobre todo, para subrayar la responsabilidad de Menón por su propia tragedia. Al final suscita lástima; ciego y miserable, todavía capaz de felicitar a Semíramis antes de sentirse poseído y repetirle su vaticinio, parece sufrir un castigo desproporcionado. Pero su ceguera coincide con la seriedad de su miopía espiritual. En la Primera parte de La hija del aire, Calderón enfoca en Menón su visión triste sobre la imperfección trágica de la humanidad, inconsciente de posibilidades del mal.

California State Polytechnic University, Pomona

[1]Historia del teatro español (Desde sus orígenes hasta 1900) (Madrid: Alianza Editorial, 1967), I, 328.

[2]Gwynne Edwards, en la introducción a su edición de La hija del aire (London: Tamesis Books Ltd., 1970), xvi, cita una carta de Goethe. Además véase: José Bergamín, Mangas y capirotes (Espana en su laberinto teatral del XVII) (Madrid, 1933), p. 187; A. Valbuena Prat, Calderón, su personalidad, su arte dramático, su estilo y sus obras (Barcelona, 1941), p. 128, e Historia del teatro español (Barcelona, 1956), p. 404; A. A. Parker, "Towards a Definition of Calderonian Tragedy," Bulletin of Hispanic Studies, 39 (1962), 226; Ruiz Ramón, p. 328.

[3]Edwards, pp. xxiii-xxix.

[4]Constance Rose, "Who Wrote the Segunda parte of El hija del aire?" Revue Belge de Philosophie et d'Histoire, 54 (1976), 797-822.

[5]Para un análisis de la tragedia de Semíramis como mujer, véase mi ensayo, "La Semíramis calderoniana como compendio de estereotipos femeninos," presentado en la National Hispanic Feminist Conference, San José, 29 de marzo, 1980. Se publicará próximamente en una antología con otras dieciocho ponencias de esta convención.

[6]Para el carácter contraproducente de la prevención del horóscopo en otros personajes como Semíramis y Segismundo, véase mi tesis doctoral, "El concepto de ironía en la tragicomedia calderoniana," Diss. UCLA 1976, pp. 170-98.

[7]Edwards, en su artículo "Calderón's La hija del aire and the Classical Type of Tragedy," Bulletin of Hispanic Studies, 64 (1967), 177-81, opina que la Primera parte representa la tragedia de ambos Nino y Menón.

[8]Ruiz Ramón (pp. 319-20) observa que los personajes en torno a Semíramis son mucho más indispensables que los que rodean a Segismundo. Para la importancia del papel del gracioso en las dos partes de La hija del aire, véase el cuarto capítulo de mi tesis "El contraste irónico del gracioso (especialmente en La hija del aire," pp. 87-113.

[9]Esta escena que se menciona al principio de la Segunda parte (II: 117-30) no sólo eslabona las dos partes sino que también sirve de arranque para la Segunda. Pues Semíramis se propone comprobar entonces que esos "admirables portentos" fueron señales de un futuro favorable (II: 321-88).

[10]Versos 7 y 8 en la edición de Edwards. Todas las siguientes citas de la obra son de dicha edición. A partir de ésta, el número de los versos se incluirá en el texto.

[11]Edwards, "Calderón's La hija del aire...," pp. 166-67, interpreta este estribillo sólo en términos positivos, como símbolo de la felicidad de Nino, Menón e Irene.

[12]"Calderón's La hija del aire...," p. 167.

[13]Según Séneca, la fortuna ataca sólo a los fuertes (Véase A. Valbuena Briones, "El senequismo en el teatro de Calderón," Papeles de Son Armadans, 31 (1963), 249-70). Boccaccio refuerza esta idea en su De Casibus (Véase mi tesis, pp. 136-41). Howard R. Patch, "The Tradition of the Goddess Fortuna in Medieval Philosophy and Literature," Smith College Studies in Modern Languages, 3, no. 4 (julio 1922), 210-11, observa que "it is a trait of her character [Fortuna's] to delight in humiliating the exalted." Respecto a Calderón, es importante notar que este concepto de Fortuna coincide con la tradición judeocristiana de la Biblia, donde Dios derrota a los poderosos (Véase el "Magníficat" de María, Lucas 1:52).

[14]Edwards, "Calderón's La hija del aire...," p. 164, dice que Menón demuestra demasiada confianza en la fortuna en este apóstrofe.

[15]El sol, en relación a la prisión de Semíramis, se refiere desde un principio al rey en la advertencia de Tiresias (107-12). A. Valbuena Briones, "La palabra 'sol' en los textos calderonianos," Perspectiva crítica de los dramas de Calderón (Madrid: Rialp, 1965), p. 61, ha interpretado esta invitación de Menón como oferta de la luz de la razón que sin duda Semíramis anhela (1003-06). Hay que recordar que, en torno a su escondite, todo denota oscuridad, confusión y apasionamiento; así que la protagonista no puede ver el sol ahí. Además, Menón, compenetrado de esta zona,

no se halla en condiciones de ofrecerle una vida razonable. La prueba está en que, al principio de la segunda jornada, Menón la ha llevado de un monte cavernoso a otro florido y asoleado (1015-48) que no deja de ser prisión para Semíramis (1239-56).

[16] Es interesante notar que, a Menón, Semíramis no le repite la profecía de la misma manera que la explica la primera vez (132-42); así que Menón no se ve amenazado por su proximidad al regio sol que Nino representa.

[17] Al comenzar la segunda jornada, es evidente que, para Menón Semíramis ha suplantado a Irene por completo. El general alaba a aquélla con la palabra "sol" (1020) que ha utilizado para halagar a Irene (327); y también le dice a Semíramis, "Cuya luz ardiente, pura, / vence al rosicler del día" (1021-22). Este "rosicler" que Semíramis supera en la estimación de Menón es la "aurora" que se ha identificado antes con Irene (222).

[18] Para el apasionamiento irracional que se asocia con la caída del caballo, véase A. Valbuena Briones, "El simbolismo en el teatro de Calderón," Romanische Forschungen, 74 (1962), 65-66.

[19] Más referencias al determinismo dual se encuentran en los siguientes versos: 2775-92, 2854-56, 3271-75, 3312-13.

Funciones dramáticas del hado en

La cisma de Inglaterra

Francisco Ruiz-Ramón

Como las otras "tragedias de error" calderonianas,
entre las cuales pueden citarse El mayor monstruo del
mundo, Los cabellos de Absalón, o La hija del aire, la
acción de La cisma de Inglaterra está construida con
la precisión técnica de un delicado aparato de relo-
jería en el que cada uno de los mecanismos está inden-
tado en los otros moviéndolos a la vez que es movido
por ellos, produciendo un ritmo cada vez más acelerado,
imposible de detener o de alterar. Cuando llegamos a
su desdado final, muertos Volseo, Ana Bolena y la
reina Catalina, se nos impone el sentido trágico de
una acción dramática cuyo curso es el resultado, paso
a paso, de un fatal encadenamiento de actos individuales, de elecciones personales que, fundados en el
error, libremente asumido, producen en cada instancia,
así como globalmente, justo los efectos contrarios a
los buscados. Los dos resortes maestros en la construcción de la acción y de su significado, fuentes,
a la vez, de su sentido final, son, desde la primera
a la última escena, el Hado y la ironía trágica. Con
extraordinaria maestría técnica--de técnica dramática
--Calderón acude para estructurar la acción y su
snetido trágico a dos de los elementos esenciales de
la Poética aristotélica, o "partes sustanciales,"[1]
como los denominaba el Pinciano: peripecia y agnición
o anagnórisis.

He dividido esta ponencia en dos partes: en la
primera, ofrezco unas consideraciones de carácter
general sobre la poética de la tragedia calderoniana;
en la segunda, aplico esas consideraciones al análisis,
limitado a unos cuantos puntos muy concretos, de La
cisma de Inglaterra.

1

Los que he denominado tragedias de error calderonianas presentan un elemento estructural común, el
Hado,[2] cuyas formas de explicitación dramática son el
horóscopo, la profecía o el sueño. Mediante éstos
queda establecido desde el principio el orden de la
acción dramática, la cual consiste en el desarrollo,

por medio de las peripecias, del Hado anunciado.
Predicado desde el inicio, generalmente en la primera
o primeras escenas, lo que va a suceder, el dramaturgo concentra su trabajo de construcción dramática
en el cómo va a suceder. Ese desplazamiento del acento
estructural del qué al cómo aproxima la dramaturgía
calderoniana a la dramaturgía típica de la tragedia
griega clásica, en donde también, como es bien sabido,
el acento estructural recae en el cómo, y no en el qué,
el cual, dados los materiales con los que operaba el
trágico griego, era conocido por el espectador. Lo
realmente importante, desde el punto de vista de construcción del drama, era el sistema de relaciones
dialécticas que el dramaturgo establecía entre el qué
y el cómo, y, naturalmente, saltando al plano séman-
tico, las significaciones últimas que de esas relaciones dimanaban.

Covarrubias en su Tesoro escribía del Hado: "En
rigor no es otro que la voluntad de Dios, y lo que
está determinado en su eternidad, latine fatum."
Prescindiendo aquí de la interpretación o acomodación
cristiana del Fatum, lo que define a éste podemos
deducirlo sin esfuerzo de otras definiciones posteriores, donde, como es lógico, sigue apareciendo la
connotación cristiana, pero de donde no se ha eliminado
su nota fundamental. Así, por ejemplo, en el
Diccionario de Autoridades encontramos estas dos
acepciones: 1. "Orden inevitable de las cosas; pero
considerado bien, no es otra cosa que la voluntad de
Dios, y lo que está determinado sucederá a cada uno."
2. "Orden de las causas naturales, que son regidas por
Dios Nuestro Señor."

Y en la última edición del Diccionario de la Real
Academía encontramos, entre otras, estas tres acepciones: 1. "Divinidad o fuerza desconocida que, según
los gentiles, obraba irresistiblemente sobre las demás
divinidades y sobre los hombres y sucesos." 2. "Encadenamiento fatal de los sucesos...5. Serie y orden de
causas tan encadenadas unas con otras, que necesariamente producen su efecto." Lo que me interesa que
retengamos es esa constante noción en el fatum de
"orden inevitable" y de "encadenamiento fatal," no
porque Calderón piense o crea en la inevitabilidad o
la fatalidad del Hado, lo cual sería a todas luces
absurdo, por antihistórico, pensarlo, sino porque esa
doble connotación constante en la noción del fatum o
hado está presente, con valor de elemento estructurante,
en la construcción de la acción dramática de todas las

tragedias de error calderonianas. En este sentido, de composición no de significado, el Hado es el más básico y más importante elemento de la estructura dramática típica del Calderón trágico.

El Hado, en tanto que elemento estructurante de la acción, produce dos efectos casi automáticos: circularidad y suspense. Se parte del punto A, anunciado en el horóscopo, la profecía o el sueño, formas de explicitación o manifestación dramáticas del Hado, como ya indiqué antes, para volver al punto A. Al mismo tiempo que el Hado produce este efecto de circularidad de la acción, produce también, como todo augurio literario, el efecto estético de concentrar la acción en un punto del futuro, con el consiguiente incremento del suspense, a la vez que, en estrecha correlación con la circularidad, hace más apretada y tensa la estructura. Mediante la explicitación del Hado la dirección del destino, y consecuentemente de la acción, es dada o sugerida de antemano, creando así la expectación de cómo aquél se cumplirá.[3]

Otra de las consecuencias inmediatas de la presencia del Hado como elemento estructural es la de producir, casi automáticamente, el carácter bipolar de la acción dramática. En efecto, el conflicto se estructura mediante la relación de oposición entre necesidad y libertad, siendo así los personajes responsables del curso de la acción, la cual depende de la interpretación que cada uno de ellos da al contenido del Hado, interpretación estribada, en cada instancia concreta, en el correspondiente sistema de bipolaridades que define al personaje, el cual está dirigido por una fuerza rectora--ambición, soberbia, pasión amorosa--que le imprime carácter, constituyéndose en fuerza generadora de todas sus acciones, a la vez que en fuente del error de juicio que conducirá al cumplimiento del Hado.

Por virtud de esa doble oposición--necesidad/libertad y razón/pasión--que el Hado introduce en el plano de la acción y en el plano de los caracteres, el dramaturgo introduce también, con extraordinaria economía dramática, el sentido de la trascendencia como raíz de la visión trágica de la condición humana, libre pero limitada por su propia menesterosidad, que el drama da a ver.

Las acciones individuales, disparadas en distintas y conflictivas direcciones, a partir del momento clave de la elección que cada personaje hace, como consecuencia de su particular interpretación del Hado, son configuradas dramáticamente mediante peripecias múltiples, dialécticamente entrelazadas, formando un proceso único que aboca en el desenlace trágico. Cada personaje, disparado hacia una meta A, llega necesariamente, por la lógica misma de la acción emprendida, a no-A, meta ya incluída desde el principio en el contenido del Hado. Llegado a ese momento final de la peripecia, se produce, por parte del personaje, la agnición, la cual no es sino el descubrimiento de la irreversibilidad de la meta no-A, a la que así mismo se condujo pensando evitarla.[4]

Si el Hado es, en el plano de la estructura, el principio unificante de las peripecias, en el plano de la significación lo es la ironía trágica, que se constituye en fundamento semántico de la unidad de acción, pues en virtud de ella cada peripecia es factor y función del sistema global de significación de la acción trágica.

2

En *La cisma de Inglaterra* el Hado se manifiesta no mediante una sola, sino mediante las tres formas de explicitación normales en Calderón: el sueño (Enrique VIII), el horóscopo (Volseo) y la profecía de Pasquín (Ana Bolena). Consideramos brevemente cada una de ellas por separado, antes de atender a las relaciones entre las tres.

La cisma comienza con el sueño de Enrique, que el espectador ve físicamente encarnada en el espacio escénico, teatralizado en un brevísimo diálogo entre el Rey y el fantasma--"sombra" le llama Enrique--que sólo dice una frase--"Yo tengo de borrar cuanto tú escribes"--y desaparece.[5]

En un estudio sobre el sueño en la tragedia griega Lenning establece la siguiente clasificación que vale la pena retener: los sueños se manifiestan a) bajo una forma exterior o b) bajo una forma interior. En a) un ser aparece en el sueño a fin de dar al durmiente una orden o una advertencia. En b) el durmiente ve escenas en las que aparecen uno o varios personajes o incluso un objeto simbólico que se revela a sus ojos. En esta categoría entran

las alucinaciones o las visiones proféticas. En ambos
casos un "más allá" que se manifiesta en el sueño se
inserta en el mundo de los vivientes. Este sueño
requiere una interpretación simbólica más o menos
complicada. La "aparición" produce o es la expresión
de un estado de angustia o de miedo.[6]

En La cisma se combinan las dos formas y se
expresa la reacción de horror del durmiente. Cuando
Enrique, en la escena que sigue a la del sueño, se
lo cuenta al Cardenal Volseo, lo hace an estos términos inequívocos respecto a su estado de ánimo:

> . . . Oye, que aquí empieza
> el horror de más espanto,
> el prodigio de más fuerza,
> que entre las sombras del sueño
> imágenes dío a la idea.
> Escribiendo estaba, pues
> (en el sacramento era
> del matrimonio, ¡ay de mí!)
> y cargada la cabeza,
> entorpecido el ingenio
> de un pesado sueño, apenas
> a su fuerza me rendí,
> cuando vi entrar por la puerta
> una mujer... Aquí el alma
> dentro de mí mismo tiembla,
> barba y cabello se eriza,
> toda la sangre se hiela,
> late el corazón, la voz
> falta, enmudece la lengua. (I, 92-110)

Toda una serie de signos de indicio--"señas," las
llama Enrique--sugieren que el horror y la angustia,
horror y angustia reiterados en distintos momentos
posteriores del drama, que la aparición provoca, son,
a la vez, expresión de un estado de ánimo, de una disposición subconsciente, anterior al sueño y al
comienzo de la acción dramática, disposición que el
sueño objetiva. El sueño de Enrique es así, a la vez,
explicitación del Hado: alguien borrará lo que el rey
escriba, es decir, cambiará la dirección y el sentido
de su vocación y de su quehacer o misión como monarca;
pero ese alguien y el Hado anunciado responde a un
estado o disposición subconsciente vigente, aunque en
estado de latencia, en el personaje desde el arranque
del drama. De ahí el significado de ese preciso verso
antes citado: "imágenes dío a la idea."

123

Lo ominoso del sueño se intensifica todavía más, y de manera más precisa y explícita, con la segunda serie de signos, cuyo valor simbólico ya fue estudiado por Alexander A. Parker,[7] concentrados en torno al episodio de las cartas trocadas: colocar por error-- palabra clave repetida dos veces--la carta de Lutero sobre la cabeza y la del Papa a los pies.

La interpretación que Enrique elige dar al sueño y al episodio de las cartas trocadas, supone ya la interferencia de Volseo. El sentido oculto de esa interferencia nos lleva a la segunda manifestación del Hado: el horóscopo relativo a Volseo.

En el monólogo que sigue a la escena anterior dice Volseo, tras subrayar la ambición y la lisonja como resortes de su conducta:

> Un astrólogo me dijo
> que al Rey sirviese; que así
> tan alto lugar tendría
> que excediese a mi deseo.

(Un breve paréntesis: aquí está ya presente la ironía trágica--Volseo pondrá fin a su vida colgándose--que como hilo rector enhebra todas las peripecias dándoles unidad de sentido.)

> Hasta aquí, Tomás Volseo,
> no cumplió la astrología
> su prometido lugar;
> pues aunque tan alto estoy,
> mientras que Papa no soy,
> me queda que desear.
> Díjome que una mujer
> sería mi destrucción.   (I, 613-632)

Siendo así que no sólo las palabras antecitadas, sino también su actitud y su modo de actuar y el comentario de otros personajes (Tomás Boleno o los soldados y pretendientes en corte) destacan como rasgos definitorios del Cardenal su vanidad, su soberbia y su arrogancia (I, 419), sólo la Reina Catalina se atreve a echárselas en cara. Circun- stancia que produce el primer enfrentamiento entre ambos, cuyas consecuencias son de capital importancia. Plenamente justificado por la acción dramática el enfado de la Reina, a quien Volseo arrogantemente le ha negado la entrada al cuarto del Rey, Volseo no establece--pero sí el público--la relación de causa

a efecto entre su propia conducta y el enojo de
Catalina. Cegado por su soberbia, comete el error
de interpretar falsamente el horóscopo del astrólogo,
identificando a Catalina con la mujer que sería su
perdición. La peripecia que arranca de su soberbia
y su error tendrá consecuencias trágicas para él y
para el resto de los personajes. Calderón, con extraordinaria maestría técnica enlaza férreamente hybris,
hamartia, peripecia, agnición e ironía trágica en
todas las acciones subsiguientes. Esta errónea interpretación del horóscopo nos lleva a la tercera forma
de explicitación del Hado: la profecía de Pasquín.

El gracioso Pasquín, perteneciente a esa interesante familia de figuras del donaire de las grandes
tragedias calderonianas--el Clarín de La vida es sueño,
el Chato de La hija del aire, el Polidoro de El mayor
monstruo del mundo, el Coquín de El médico de su honra
--es, de todos ellos, el más cercano por su condición
y por su función al de los bufones de Shakespeare. En
La cisma, entreverado de loco y de vidente ("Soy
ciego y alumbro a oscuras," dice de sí mismo, I, 430),
monomaníaco de la "astróloga ciencia," profetiza a
Ana Bolena "el hado que la previene // el Cielo y el
fin que tiene // reservado a su hermosura":

> Lo primero que saca
> la profecía que véis,
> es que vos, Ana, tenéis
> cara de gran bellaca.
> Y aunque vuestro amor aplaca
> con rigor y con desdén
> la hermosura que en vos ven,
> muy hermosa y muy ufana
> venís a palacio, Ana.
> ¡Plegue a Dios que sea por bien!
> Y así será, pues espero
> que en él seréis muy amada,
> muy querida y respetada;
> tanto, que ya os considero
> con aplauso lisonjero
> subir, merecer, privar,
> hasta poderos alzar
> con todo el imperio inglés,
> viniendo a morir después
> en el más alto lugar. (III, 2779-2784)

A Ana Bolena la ejecutarán cuando ocupe el más alto
lugar: el de esposa del rey Enrique VIII. Pero, del
mismo modo que Enrique y que Volseo, interpreta el

contenido de la profecía desde el punto de vista que mejor cuadra con sus deseos y con su particular sistema de intereses, ambos estribados en la psicología profunda del personaje, que sus palabras, reacciones, y acciones van revelando sutilmente. El error de interpretación en que cada uno de ellos incurre, y que determina el curso de su conducta, es consecuencia del influjo de cada personaje sobre los otros, disparado cada uno de ellos hacia la consecución de sus propias metas mediante la manipulación, siempre consciente, de las vidas ajenas, utilizadas como medios instrumentales para la obtención y la satisfacción del fin particular perseguido.

En su papel de <u>tentador</u>, Volseo, motor de la tragedia, para satisfacer su ambición y su deseo de venganza moverá los hilos de las pasiones de Ana y de Enrique, poniendo en marcha su "plan diabólico" para eliminar a Catalina y encumbrar a Ana Bolena. Los mecanismos de la "máquina trágica" puesta en movimiento por las relaciones resultantes del complejo nudo de las pasiones definitorias de los tres personajes unidos por el Hado funcionan con ritmo cada vez más acelerado, reflejado en el ritmo de la acción y en la concentración del tiempo trágico, hasta que cada uno de los tres personajes es conducido por sus propias acciones libres al momento crítico de la <u>agnición</u>, verdadera situación límite en la que descubre que ya no puede volver atrás y se cumple la toma de conciencia de la irreversibilidad del proceso trágico. Llegados a ese punto, ya anunciado por el Hado, el mal no tiene remedio. La puerta está cerrada y la restitución la juzgan imposible. No hay salida: Volseo se suicida, Ana es ejecutada y Enrique mira desoladamente hacia el futuro de división del reino que él mismo ha suscitado:

> ¡Qué mal hice! ¡Qué mal hice!
> Mas si no tengo remedio
> ¿de qué sirve arrepentirme?
> ¿De qué sirven desengaños
> y deseos? ¿De qué sirven
> si está cerrada la puerta? (III, 510)

La tragedia se cierra con la escena de la jura de la Infanta, presente el cadáver de Ana Bolena, donde la gala y el esplendor de ornamentos y clarines contrastan con la desolada actitud del Rey. El final

126

de la tragedia de unas vidas humanas es el comienzo
de la tragedia histórica de un pueblo dividido por
el cisma.

Tenía plena razón el profesor Alexander A. Parker
cuando en la conclusión de su citado artículo de 1948
consideraba La cisma de Inglaterra como una obra
maestra.

Purdue University

Notas

[1] López Pinciano, _Philosophia antigua poética_ (Madrid, 1953), 3 vols. ed. Alfredo Carballo Picazo. La cita en II, p. 25.

[2] En este trabajo sólo me ocupo de la función estructural del Hado, no de sus significaciones.

[3] Ver al respecto el estudio de Mgens Brönsted "The Transformations of the Concept of Fate in Literature," en _Fatalistic Beliefs in Religion, Folklore and Literature_ (Stockholm, 1967), p. 175.

[4] Ver F. L. Lucas, _Tragedy: Serious Drama in Relation to Aristotle's "Poetics"_ (New York, revised edition, 1962).

[5] Pedro Calderón de la Barca, _La cisma de Inglaterra_ (3) (Madrid: Castalia, 1981), Acto I, verso 6. Ed. F. Ruiz-Ramón. A partir de ahora citaré siempre de esta edición, indicando entre paréntesis el Acto en números romanos y la página en numeros arábigos.

[6] R. Lenning, _Traum und Sinnestraüschung bei Aeschylos, Sophocles, Europides_, Diss., Tubingen, Berlin, 1969, Tomo la cita de Guy Rachet, _La tragédie grecque_ (Paris: Payot, 1973), p. 178.

[7] Alexander A. Parker, "Henry VIII in Shakespeare and Calderón; An Appreciation of _La Cisma de Inglaterra_," _MLR_, XLIII (1948), pp. 327-352.

The Other Side of the Metaphor: An Approach to

La devoción de la cruz

Edward H. Friedman

When a literary work is interpreted symbolically, its internal logic and principles of causality may be deemed subordinate to the abstract system which conveys the textual message. The significance of the effect, rather than the probability of the cause, provides both the point of departure and the point of reference for interpretation. Tirso de Molina's El condenado por desconfiado, for example, achieves its force through exaggerated cases: the repentant criminal gains salvation, while the doubting anchorite is condemned to hell. To emphasize the possibility of a last-minute conversion, Tirso creates an antithetical structure in which roles and destinies are ultimately reversed. The conceptual center of the play is the progression toward salvation, and within this perspective the actions take on an abstract significance. The spectator need not rationalize the specific nature of the demon who appears before Paulo nor justify the incongruity of Enrico's brutality with his filial devotion, because these aspects of the plot figure only as means toward a doctrinal end. The story of Enrico is similar to that of Eusebio in Calderón's La devoción de la cruz, except that Eusebio's confession comes after his death, and his devotion takes the form of adoration of the Cross. As in Tirso's play, one can establish a pattern of incongruity, made more complex by Calderón's vacillation between the codified social system of this world and inexplicable events of extramundane origin. What distinguishes the fantastic elements of El condenado por desconfiado from those of La devoción de la cruz is the extrinsic value of the supernatural in the first work and its intrinsic value in the second. In El condenado por desconfiado, the historically feasible literal level moves toward a symbolic level; in La devoción de la cruz, on the other hand, the production of meaning stems from the interaction between several metaphorical formulas. Calderón's particular use of symbols and symbolic events immediately orients the work to a figurative plane, which then finds its literal correlative and unifying element in linguistic irony.

In a traditional framework, the literary analogue may reproduce itself on a symbolic level and prove itself ironic by virtue of relationships between events and between linguistic signs. To an extent, the symbolic content of La devoción de la cruz forms part of the pre-history; the pre-text (Christian doctrine) gives value to the symbols, notably the Cross, and to the dramatic action, notably the salvation of the repentant sinner.[1] The plot proper presupposes these values without attempting to fully recreate them in dramatic terms. The symbology thus precedes the literary object, and the movement from the literal to the symbolic--from what is written to the interpretive significance of what is written--is reversed. The dramatic language does not have to supply meaning, but to acknowledge preestablished meanings, since the theological code and the social codes of honor and love prescribe linguistic conventions as well as courses of action. The juxtaposition of an apparent honor plot with the religious plot which encompasses and supersedes it affects dramatic discourse by literalizing a number of linguistic fields, and the innovation of La devoción de la cruz lies in the creation of an ironic language which parallels the central paradoxes of the play.

From the perspective of linear development, La devoción de la cruz may be considered an honor play. Curcio and Lisardo, responsible for Julia, refuse to accept Eusebio as her suitor on the grounds of social inferiority and unconventional courtship procedure. Eusebio uses all means at his disposal to overcome the paternal and filial obstacles to his love. Curcio makes plans to send Julia to a convent, and Lisardo, acting on behalf of his father, challenges Eusebio to a duel. When Eusebio kills Lisardo, Curcio forces his daughter to enter the convent and swears to avenge Lisardo's murder. Eusebio's death in Act III represents a final vindication. Missing from this summary is the circumstantial irony which underlies--and undermines--the honor plot at every stage. Eusebio's unacceptable social status derives from the absence of a known lineage (in effect, from a lack of identity), while the proof of his blood relationship to Julia (the verification of his true identity and social equality) renders him totally ineligible as a pretender. The courtship, the duel, and the vengeance of Curcio become elements of a chain of events erroneously based on Eusebio's position as an outsider. The rectification of this error is nothing less than the destruction, in a conceptual sense, of the honor scheme which serves as the play's chief formal base.

Denied his authentic identity, Eusebio adopts the role of highwayman and, as the archetypal sinner, places himself in line for salvation. Calderón illustrates a doctrinal point by focusing on a single comprehensive and pre-valued symbol. If one is devoted to the Cross (that is, to what the Cross symbolizes, the possibility of redemption through Christ's sacrifice), he may win salvation despite a life of sin. The Cross which accompanies Eusebio from birth functions as a sign of divine forgiveness, Eusebio's respect for the Cross heralds his forthcoming conversion, and the miracles of the Cross prefigure the miraculous confession after death. The culminating moment of the honor plot is the mortal wounding of Eusebio, which leads to the revelation of his identity and moves this plot to the more abstract religious plane. While Curcio's unwillingness to detach himself from the dictates of society binds him to this world, Eusebio and Julia become part of a higher order.[2] The spectacular deliverance in the final scene represents a spiritual climax through the power of the Cross.

The linear scheme of La devoción de la cruz, then, involves the completion of an action: according to the rules of the honor code, Curcio must see Eusebio killed in retaliation for Lisardo's death. A second linear plan ends with the salvation of a sinner, based on his devotion to the Cross. The honor plot provides the sequential foundation of the play, while the religious elements extend and conceptualize the textual message. There is a direct correspondence between certain features of the two systems. In Act I, Eusebio's secular crime (the murder of Lisardo) follows a secular confession (the account of his life). In the second act, his unrighteous acts are complemented by preparations for a spiritual confession. His punishment in Act III, in accordance with the tenets of the honor code, culminates in the confession after death. The discovery of kinship between Curcio and Eusebio (and between Julia and Eusebio) is the final step of a process which exemplifies divine clemency, but this process manifests itself primarily on the pre-textual level, with a Biblical story as model. The circumstances surrounding the birth of Eusebio and Julia, as well as the miraculous escapes from danger throughout Eusebio's life, are treated in narrated passages,

rather than in dramatic events. Even more significantly, Calderón presents the concept of devotion to
the Cross in a predominantly figurative manner.

If the Cross has metonymical value as a symbol of
human salvation through Christ's suffering, the portrayal of devotion as a means of gaining salvation is
synechdochic, with effect indicating cause. Eusebio's
devotion is alluded to, but rarely demonstrated, and
then somewhat ambiguously. Neither compassionate nor
pious, Eusebio responds to the presence, visual or
verbal, of the Cross. He is inspired by an object,
and although he recognizes the divine origin of this
object, his respect is mechanical, or perhaps intui-
tive, rather than reflective.[3] The thematic framework
of La devoción de la cruz depends first on extra-
textual theological principles and examples, to a
lesser degree on situational shifts within the play,
and to a negligible degree on character development.
The final transformation is far less cognitive than
semiotic in nature. The Cross which transports
Eusebio in a heavenly direction (and Julia to the
convent) marks a synthesis of signifier and signified,
as the symbol of deliverance becomes the vehicle of
deliverance. This vision of redemption reifies--and
theatricalizes--the verbal image, transferring its
referential powers to the dramatic medium.

By allowing the honor plot to determine the formal
direction of the play and the religious plot to convey
the symbolic content, Calderón effects a reciprocity
and a tension between the social and spiritual realms.
La devoción de la cruz, as a dramatic form, relies on
the honor plot for movement and for contrast, and as a
source of spiritual meaning, recognizes the universality of Christian symbols. The case of mistaken
identity invalidates the honor plot by converting it
into a contest between man-made laws and divine laws,
while, structurally speaking, the active pursuits of
honor and love counterbalance the passive and extra-
textual qualities of devotion. The linguistic facet
of the dichotomy is embodied in Curcio's refusal to
abstract the significance of transcendent signs, as
opposed to Eusebio's consciousness (through acknowledg-
ment of a "secret cause") of the supremacy of the
signs. Both Curcio's misreading and Eusebio's en-
lightened reading lead to paradoxical conclusions:
Curcio fulfils the requisites of the honor code, but
cannot restore his lost honor; Eusebio commits the
most serious of crimes, yet becomes a candidate for

salvation. Curcio witnesses miracles, but cannot
admit the priority of the divine over the mundane,
for his hierarchical vision extends only to this
world. Eusebio, on the other hand, rebels against
the social hierarchies which have made him a victim,
in favor of a spiritual order which he does not fully
comprehend, but whose symbol he respects. Heeding
the pretextual example (the repentant thief) and the
miraculous foreshadowing of his salvation, he modifies
his behavior according to these signs, while Curcio
remains inflexible.

In Calderón's structural plan, the honor plot has
a sustained formal function and a diminishing thematic
function. As the identity motif achieves its full impact, theological considerations override the precepts
of social performance to control the dramatic events.
The formal analogue mirrors and substantiates the
primacy, on the conceptual level, of the religious
material. The negation of the honor plot not only
reorients the action, but serves as a basis for linguistic artistry; the result is a verbal pattern which
reinforces both the linear development and the thematic
duality of the play. The symbolic value of the dramatic discourse is fundamental to La devoción de la cruz,
with the elaboration of the central image, the Cross,
as the key factor in the transmission of the doctrinal
message. Calderón expands the linguistic scope by
stressing semantic variations: the characters' reaction to language, the interplay between different
modes of speech, and literal language as a source of
irony. While stratified (through analogical relationships) and disjunctive (through disregard for the conceptual categories imposed by the double plot), the
discourse is nonetheless continuous in terms of the
validity of its literal meaning.

The opening scene of La devoción de la cruz, which
precedes the duel between Eusebio and Lisardo, may be
read as a comic analogue of the linear and semiotic
direction of the work as a whole. The rustic character
Gil, whose donkey is stuck in the mud, cries "¿No hay
quien una cola tenga, / pudiendo tenerla mil?,"[4]
alluding to man's bestial nature. He proceeds to
narrate the story of a coach, mired in a stream and
lifted only when the lead horses are tempted by food.
If the Cross is a sign of Eusebio's progression from
criminal to penitent, the tail is a countersymbol,
marking the early stage of the struggle to escape
what Eusebio himself calls "mi fiera condición"

(11. 256-67). The story-within-a-story prefigures the
narratives of Eusebio (11. 199 ff.) and Curcio (11.
1281 ff.), and the elevation of the coach--accomplished
by tempting the horses with an earthly reward--points
to Eusebio's ascension to a divine reward at the end
of the play. In lamenting the fate of the coach, Gil
says, "parecía entre los otros / pobre coche vergon-
zante; / y por maldición muy cierta / de sus padres
(¡hado esquivo!) / iba de estribo en estribo, / ya que
no de puerta en puerta" (11. 27-32). The language of
the description, unusual in its immediate context, is
applicable to the outsider Eusebio, tragically wronged
by his father.

The confrontation between Eusebio and Lisardo
establishes a dichotomy, operative throughout the
play, between types of social consciousness. Lisardo
has inherited from Curcio not only an unyielding sense
of honor, but a resistance to spiritual signs, in this
case the miracles of Eusebio's past, which leave him
unmoved. Eusebio stands in contrast, with no inheri-
tance and with no adherence to society's rules, but
with a consciousness of the abstract nature of the
Cross. Lisardo's challenge to Eusebio (11. 126 ff.)
is a perfect example of the duplicitous literality of
La devoción de la cruz. Without compromising the
contextual usage, Calderón invents a language which
has a more emphatic literal meaning with respect to
Eusebio's true status. Lisardo speaks of himself and
Julia as victims of their father, who has squandered
his fortune and left them only with noble titles. His
first mention of Julia's name is preceded by the phrase
"a los que nacen con ellas" (1. 139), and this ironic
juxtaposition is followed by "Pero al fin, Julia es mi
hermana. / ¡Pluguiera a Dios no lo fuera!" (11. 143-
44), "No os culpo en el todo a vos" (1. 151), and "Si
mi hermana os agradó / para mujer[,] que no era /
posible . . ." (11. 159-61).

The increasingly complex situational irony is
complemented by an increasingly complex use of ironic
language. When Julia bemoans her lost freedom, she
presents her sad state in terms of an analogy. Just
as the once gentle stream may burst forth and destroy
the most beautiful flowers in its path, so grief has
swelled up inside of her and sprung forth as tears:
"Pues mis penas, mis enojos, / la misma experiencia
han hecho; / detuviéronse en el pecho / y salieron
por los ojos" (11. 437-40). Pecho here stands,
metonymically, for heart, but as the site of her

134

Cross, it also stands, metonymically, for salvation. On learning of Lisardo's death, Julia exclaims, "Pues, ¿qué inhumana / fuerza ensangrentó la ira / en su pecho? ¿Qué tirana / mano se bañó en mi sangre, / contra su inocencia airada?" (ll. 756-60). Pecho, mi sangre, and inocencia refer to Eusebio as well as to Lisardo. At the end of the first act, Eusebio reiterates the ironic imagery when he gives Julia the opportunity to avenge Lisardo's death: "Toma esa daga, y con ella / rompe un pecho que te ofende, / saca un alma que te adora, / y tu misma sangre vierte" (ll. 913-16). The figurative language of love is converted into the literal language of identity.

Curcio's discourse reflects his shortsightedness and misdirected sense of values. His reaction to Lisardo's death--"¿Hay más deshonra? / Eusebio me ha quitado vida y honra" (ll. 779-80)--suggests his abandonment of Eusebio, who has had to live in dishonor. Curcio's admonition to Julia, "Queda con él [Lisardo], porque de aquesta suerte, / lecciones al morir te dé su muerte" (ll. 795-96), is ironic, given that it will be Eusebio's death which provides the lesson for Julia. Although Curcio's adherence to the honor code directly inspires the conflict, he remains unaware of his responsibility in the matter, whose source and prime mover is Curcio, self-described as "un padre / a quien el sol no igualó, / en resplandor y belleza, / sangre, honor, lustre y nobleza" (ll. 620-23). Calderón emphasizes this paradoxical situation by including in Curcio's speeches a sustained use of the word tirano, producing an ironic self-referential effect. Curcio simultaneously curses the honor code and rigidly observes its rules. The fact that the initial motivation, his wife Rosmira's suspected guilt, is more than anything the product of Curcio's imagination[5]--that is, it seems in no way to be a public suspicion--reverses the impact of cries such as "¡oh ley tirana / de honor!" (ll. 674-75).

The comic analogue which opens the play is replaced in the first scene of Act II by a description of one of Eusebio's victims. Ricardo says, "Pasó[le] el plomo violento / el pecho," to which Celio adds, "Y hace el golpe más sangriento, / que con su sangre la tragedia imprima / en tierna flor." Eusebio gives the order, "Ponle una cruz encima, / y perdónele Dios," and Ricardo observes, "Las devociones / nunca faltan del todo a los ladrones" (ll. 947-52). The brief scene repeats the imagery of the first act,

with its literal application to Eusebio, and points
forward to the salvation of the "devout" thief.
Eusebio justifies his life as a bandit by condemning
his persecution by the state. As a victim of the
cruel social system, he has no other recourse than
a life of crime. Upon hearing that Julia has entered
the convent, his rage against society broadens to
include the spiritual world: "Que por verme señor
de su hermosura, / tirano amor me fuerza / a acometer
la fuerza, / a romper la clausura, / y a violar el
sagrado; / que ya del todo estoy desesperado" (ll.
1075-80). The recognition of his extreme notoriety
("no puedo ser peor de lo que he sido," l. 1068)
expresses a certain role consciousness. As the
cruelest of the highwaymen and the most unholy of
sinners, Eusebio becomes the least likely--and thus
the most exemplary--aspirant for salvation.6 His
sign of hope in times of despair is, of course, the
Cross.7

Alberto's book, Milagros de la Cruz, serves as
a sign-within-a-sign, rescuing its bearer from a
violent death (as the Cross has rescued Eusebio in
the past) and leading to the priest's offer to become
Eusebio's confessor. With the "Cross" at his heart,
Alberto is literally saved by the book, itself a
literary rendering of miraculous acts, in a scene
which prefigures Eusebio's acceptance of the meaning
of the Cross emblazoned on his heart. The episode
of Alberto stresses past and future, while the peasant
Menga's assertion concerning Eusebio--"con poner tras
la ofensa / una cruz encima, piensa / que os hace
mucha merced" (ll. 1114-16), indicates that at present
the Cross remains an empty sign, intuitively revered
but not understood. Eusebio's mind is on earthly
glory, the seduction of Julia. Unsuspecting of the
consequences of his visit, he states, "la pena de
bajar / no será parte a quitar / la gloria de haber
subido" (ll. 1424-26), echoing the equally ironic
cry of Curcio, "que no hay gloria para mí, / hasta
llegar a vengarme" (ll. 1407-08).8

Eusebio's literal and symbolic fall from the
convent wall is, paradoxically, a decisive incident
in his rise heavenward. Given the opportunity to win
Julia, Eusebio flees from the Cross on her chest,
revering it, almost precognitively, as a sign of his
imminent salvation: "Pues si la hago testigo / de
las culpas que cometo, / ¿con qué vergüenza después /
llamarla en mi ayuda puedo?" (ll. 1617-20). In

viewing the Cross as the means of his own redemption, Eusebio connects signifier with signified; he begins to think symbolically. Calderón underlines this transition by making Julia's reaction a symbolic one. Twice unfaithful to God (as a Christian and as a bride of Christ) and thus the antithesis of the innocent Rosmira, Julia reverses her decision to leave the convent, having convinced herself that God is capable of pardoning all sins. When she discovers that the ladder to her window has been removed (by Eusebio's companions), she takes this as a sign of her destiny and adopts what will be a symbolic role, that of a great sinner and the female counterpart of Eusebio. The answer to her question, "¿Cómo he de subir sin ella [la escalera]?" (l. 1763), is that she will rise by lowering herself to the most profound depths and then be returned to her cell by the Cross.

At the beginning of Act III, Calderón recapitulates the theme of the empty sign. Gil appears, covered with crosses, including a large one over his heart. The motive is self-protection rather than faith, and to avoid Eusebio's wrath, Gil agrees to become a member of the group of bandits. One false identity (the man of devotion) is replaced by another. There follows a comic scene based on mistaken identity, in which Gil's wife and friends fail to recognize him in the new role and almost kill him. From this point, Eusebio, the "real" bandit, will at last comprehend the significance of his devotion and will be saved after death. The change rests upon a recognition of his identity and its relation to the Cross. The mediating factor, and the central portion of this act, is the confrontation between Eusebio and Curcio, ostensibly the climax of the honor plot, but actually the culmination of the ironic structure. In the midst of their struggle, a mysterious bond overtakes them. Curcio alludes to "el que con sangre borra la victoria" (l. 2200), sensing a kinship which nonetheless cannot triumph over his pride. He reenacts the scene of Eusebio's birth, and his son is once again rescued by the Cross.

Eusebio comes to acknowledge his role as sinner, and asks for the rewards of his devotion (and of his role): "luego eres tú Cruz por mí, / que Dios no muriera en ti / si yo pecador no fuera" (ll. 2298-2300). Curcio seems to understand his role in the events ("donde cometí el pecado, / el cielo me castigó," ll. 2369-70), but characteristically--and

definitively--ignores miraculous signs to condemn Julia
for staining his honor. Eusebio's devotion to the
Cross and Julia's public confession of her sins reign
over Curcio's devotion to social dogma, as the brother
and sister ascend the Cross to join their spiritual
father.

In La devoción de la cruz, the sustained linear
plot links this world to a higher realm signified by
the Cross. The honor plot provides a stable form for
the spiritual analogue, as well as a point of contrast
between human and divine laws. The conceptual shift
owes its smoothness to the literal validity of figurative language and to a uniform pattern of irony, both
circumstantial and linguistic. By organizing the
linear movement around the honor code and literalizing
the figurative language, Calderón moves away from the
pure abstractions (the representable ideas) of the
autos sacramentales. He elevates the literary object
by exploring the relationship between worlds--and
words--in opposition. If in La vida es sueño, Calderón produces an all-encompassing metaphorical
structure, in La devoción de la cruz, one must perhaps look to the other side of the metaphor for the
key to dramatic creation.

Arizona State University

Notes

[1]For a discussion of the concept of pretext, see Maureen Quilligan, The Language of Allegory: Defining the Genre (Ithaca and London: Cornell University Press, 1979), pp. 97-155.

[2]Edwin Honig treats the interplay between the honor code and Christian law (with emphasis on the creation of dramatic irony) in "A Strange Mercy Play: Devotion to the Cross," in Calderón and the Seizures of Honor (Cambridge, Massachusetts: Harvard University Press, 1972), pp. 53-80. See esp. pp. 62-70.

[3]Some critics tend to overestimate Eusebio's devotion. Marcelino Menéndez y Pelayo, for example, speaks of "la fe viva que ardía en su pecho y . . . las buenas obras que había hecho durante su pecadora vida." The so-called noble acts, such as saving Alberto and fleeing from Julia, are not really noble acts, and Menéndez y Pelayo does not convincingly refute the objection that Eusebio's faith seems more external than internal. See Calderón y su teatro (Buenos Aires: Emecé Editores, S. A., 1949), pp. 161-62. In a similar vein, Angel Valbuena Briones rationalizes Eusebio's conduct, seeing him as victim of "un desequilibrio entre su concepto del bien y el aceptado por el formalismo de la época. . . . su tragedia consiste en que su marcha hacia el caos es involuntaria y viene forzada por una serie de circunstancias" (Perspectiva crítica de los dramas de Calderón [Madrid: Ediciones Rialp, S.A., 1965], p. 140). The fact remains that Calderón has chosen not to present dramatically the "devotion" of Eusebio. The play contains innumerable inconsistencies and gaps in logic, and its plot simply cannot--and need not--be reasoned out. The devotion consists of Eusebio's awareness of the potentiality of the Cross. For A. A. Parker, ". . . if the Cross is interpreted in the way that both the imagery and the action demand that it should be, it emerges as a dramatic device to symbolize not only Eusebio's salvation (because, though a sinner, he is so through being the victim of another's sin), but also Curcio's punishment, for which Eusebio is the instrument." See The Approach to the Spanish Drama of the Golden Age (London: The Hispanic and Luso-Brazilian Councils, 1957), p. 21, as well as "Santos y bandoleros en el teatro español del Siglo de Oro," Arbor, 13 (1949), 403-10; "Towards a Definition of Calderonian Tragedy," BHS, 39 (1962), esp.

227-28; and "The Father-Son Conflict in the Drama of Calderón," _FMLS_, 2 (1966), esp. 105-06.

[4]Ll. 5-6. All quotations from _La devoción de la cruz_ will refer to Calderón de la Barca, _Comedias religiosas_, ed. Angel Valbuena Prat, 5th ed. (Madrid: Espasa-Calpe, S.A., 1970), pp. 5-117. Line numbers will be indicated in parentheses.

[5]See Bruce W. Wardropper, "La imaginación en el metateatro calderoniano," _Actas del Tercer Congreso Internacional de Hispanistas_, ed. Carlos Magis (Mexico: El Colegio de México, 1968), esp. pp. 926-28, for an analysis of Curcio's overly active imagination.

[6]Robert Sloane deals with the aspect of role-playing in "The 'Strangeness' of _La devoción de la cruz_," _BHS_, 54 (1977), 297-310. He says of Eusebio: "Determined to 'find himself,' to be someone in a society that denies his identity, Eusebio _plays_ at being--rather than _is_--the most terrible bandit of all. He will play his new role with such insistence that he will remove any doubt as to what he is, who he is. Furthermore, in being the wicked man that society will have him be, he will be justifying society's perception: at least his world will finally make sense" (p. 306). Using R. D. Laing's model of the "false self," Sloane contends that the continual interventions of the Cross reveal the inauthenticity of the bandit self. Yet it seems equally true that in the great theater of the world, both Eusebio and Julia genuinely portray only their acquired roles, since their former selves (Eusebio as a man without an identity and Julia as his lover) are based on misconceptions. They never have the opportunity to experience their "real" identities. By stressing their notoriety, one may categorize them as sinners on the road to becoming forgiven sinners. Their violent acts are role requirements; only the death of Lisardo (who has challenged Eusebio) is presented on stage. They are evil in an axiomatic rather than a psychological sense.

[7]For a consideration of human despair as it relates to Eusebio and Julia, see W. J. Entwistle, "Calderón's _La devoción de la cruz_," _BH_, 50 (1948), 472-82. See also the introduction of Francisco Ruiz Ramón to Pedro Calderón de la Barca, _Tragedias_, III (Madrid: Alianza Editorial, 1969), 10-17.

[8]Climbing upward to Julia's cell, Eusebio compares

himself to Icarus and Phaeton in their flights to the
sun (ll. 1411-16). Unknowingly, he alludes to figures
whose stories are much like his own. Icarus' flight
is traceable to his father's crimes (the murder of his
pupil Talos and his offenses against the king of Crete),
and Phaeton's death is the direct result of his initial
ignorance of the identity of his father (Helios).

Calderón's El príncipe constante:

Structure and Ending

W. M. Whitby

It is a question of the play's nature, which translates into a structural problem, that will concern me in this paper. The ending of the play is a structural element, so it is redundant to refer to "structure and ending." But, since the final scenes of El príncipe constante have sometimes been thought to be superfluous or unimportant and have often been imperfectly understood, I would like to single out that aspect of the structure for special treatment.

Edward M. Wilson and William J. Entwistle, with their "Two Appreciations,"[1] are rightly given credit for having initiated, in 1939, what has been and continues to be a period productive of valuable interpretive studies.

Entwistle calls the work "symbolic drama." He sees "behind the human marionettes [my emphasis] . . . eternal and abstract values" (p. 218). "The Constant Prince is Christian Constancy itself, Fortitude, or perhaps most succinctly La Fe" (p. 219). Enrique is El Entendimiento (p. 219), Fénix is beauty (p. 220) and so forth. In the note which Wilson composed after reading Entwistle's article, one finds a statement of what he and later critics see as a fundamental difference of attitudes between the two of them as they look at the play. "Professor Entwistle," he says, "looks at the play in terms of an imaginary auto sacramental. . . . [H]e is preoccupied with the scheme as it probably existed in Calderón's mind, while I have tried to state the way I am moved while I am reading the play. Consequently, I find his approach too schematic; he probably thinks that I do not carry my approach far enough" (p. 217, note).

Albert E. Sloman[2] and, later, R. W. Truman[3] have been the critics who most clearly followed in the path first trod by Entwistle, a path which Wilson in the note to which I have just referred helped mark more distinctly. Truman's article, insisting as it does on the relationship of Constancy to Justice, is an improvement upon Sloman's thesis that Fernando represents Fortitude.[4] It provides explanations for

relationships based on the concept of obligations recognized or rejected between Fernando and Muley, Fernando
and the King of Fez and Fernando and God.

Wolfgang Kayser's study first appeared in Bonn in
1957.[5] Kayser seems unaware of Sloman's book on the
sources of the play, but he does discuss Entwistle's
and Wilson's studies. He finds Entwistle's approach
mistaken: auto sacramental and comedia are two different dramatic forms.[6] He proposes a different way of
viewing and describing the play structurally. In El
príncipe constante, one can trace a series of events
focused on the protagonist Fernando, though this action
moves very slowly at times. This way of looking at the
play corresponds to what Kayser calls the ordo successivorum. But in the final scene, when we see Fernando's
body exchanged for Fénix, we realize that there has
been a correlation Fénix-Fernando throughout the play.
This perception leads us to notice other correlations
as well. The relationship between these characters
and their situations is what Kayser calls the ordo
simultaneorum. The terminology comes from Herder.
Kayser's study is a significant contribution. Alberto
Porqueras Mayo, in his introduction to his edition of
El príncipe constante (1975) calls it an "ensayo tan
citado como poco conocido y leído."[7] It would take
more time and space than I have available here to discuss it as it deserves and requires. The most important point Kayser makes is, I think, that if one looks
only at the ordo successivorum, the structure is loose;
if, on the other hand, one adopts the perspective of
the ordo simultaneorum, the structure becomes tight.[8]

The following year saw the publication of Bruce W.
Wardropper's article, "Christian and Moor in Calderón's
'El Príncipe Constante'."[9] Wardropper's study is well
known and indeed has served as a solid point of departure for most subsequent interpretations of the play,
so I shall not try to summarize it here. It will
suffice for my purpose to describe it (in the author's
words) as an attempt to "[bridge the gulf] between
Wilson's critical particularism and Entwistle-Sloman's
a priori schematic approach" (p. 512). He finds that
the work "falls between" allegory and comedia and that
attempts to interpret it as one or the other must fail.
Besides the opposition or equilibrium between these two
theatrical genres, he refers at the end of his article
to a similar tension between drama and poetry. His
last remark advises us that Calderón is not just a

144

dramatist but a dramatic poet (p. 520).

Wardropper's and Kayser's essays provide mutually complementary means of perceiving the play's ambivalent structure. Broadly, what Kayser refers to as the ordo successivorum corresponds to the work as comedia; the term ordo simultaneorum corresponds very roughly to the work as auto. (Perhaps also to what Wardropper sees as the poetic, as opposed to the dramatic, aspect of the work.) The equivalencies, though they are as I present them an oversimplification, can be helpful to us in defining more sharply what we mean when we say that the play is a comedia which has some of the characteristics of an auto.

In the auto the allegorical personage (already bearing an abstract name) is defined in himself and in relation to other allegorical personages by his actions and words (as well as by theirs). The goal of our understanding is first of all in the character (and ultimately in that of Man), and by character I mean essence. In the comedia (leaving aside questions of symbolism and the like, which would affect its purity--not necessarily its quality) we tend to be interested in character only in a secondary sense; our focus of attention is on the action, as a product of the interplay of character and motivations.

Cause-and-effect relationships prevail in pure comedia (and tragedy). In the auto, the relationships are conceptual, established by convention or authority, by intellectual verisimilitude, or by analogy.

Peter N. Dunn says that regarding the play as Entwistle does "as if it were the sketch for an auto . . . enables us to map out the structure of values."[10] What characterizes the auto in contrast to the comedia in Dunn's definition is space as opposed to time: "The world of values is a space shaped by words and actions." This is the world which the auto captures. The comedia, on the other hand, "has time as one dimension of its feigned reality. Without [this dimension of time] not only the action but also the continuity of the self and its transformations would be unimaginable" (p. 83). It is not without interest to note that Kayser refers to the ordo simultaneorum as spatial, though he prefers to speak of "atmosphere."[11] Perhaps he prefers the word "atmosphere" because what he has in mind is not purely "space" but "space filled with significant essences." Perhaps, too, since space as a concept is

clearly contrasted with time, while atmosphere, on the
other hand, is not as a concept at odds with the idea
of temporal flow, the latter term better suits the
purpose of reconciling the "simultaneous" and "successive" orders.12 Kayser, and before him Max
Kommerell, found time to be a problem in El príncipe
constante. But at least in the case of Fernando
"inner" time is present, and character is transformed.
This fact might seem to make it impossible to maintain
that there is an abstract value associated with Fernando. Actually, as we know, constancy is a quality
which we see in him from the outset of the play and
which can come to characterize him more fully and in
a deeper sense as his situation worsens and he responds
to it with increasing spiritual strength. Secular
constancy becomes spiritual constancy; constancy in
the Christian faith.

Leo Spitzer's article, "Die Figur der Fénix in
Calderón's Standhaftem Prinzen" appeared in 1959.13
The English translation of virtually the entire body
of that article was made available six years later in
Bruce Wardropper's Critical Essays on the Theatre of
Calderón.14 Divested of its twenty-eight footnotes,
which comprise almost a third of its original length,
it is still a rather long article. One must, as
Wardropper recommends, seek out the original for the
"full flavor" of Spitzer's interpretation.

The body of the article is, unfortunately, a
mostly negative contribution to structural studies
and, in my opinion, to our understanding of the play.
Spitzer refers to Kayser's article and in fact gives
the impression that he is taking it as his point of
departure, but he then proceeds to ignore Kayser's
analysis of the structure, putting aside entirely
the concept and strategy of ordo simultaneorum.
Seizing upon Kayser's reference to a "secret partner-
ship" between Fernando and Fénix (perhaps Kayser's
wording was unfortunate), Spitzer explores this
relationship not from the perspective of the ordo
simultaneorum but from that of the ordo successivorum.
In other words, he takes the relationship as literal
rather than as symbolical; he views it dramatically
rather than poetically. He treats Muley as a "comic"
figure and largely ignores the fact that his courtship of Fénix is an impediment to any literal courtship of the Princess by Fernando, forgetting, among
other things, the Prince's important utterance: "si
Fénix su pena es, / no he de competirla yo; / que la

mía es común pena" (vv. 1167-1169; Jorn. II, esc. iv).
Later critics of the play have remarked, either in
general or specifically, on Spitzer's misreadings of
the play.[15] I shall limit myself in this paper to
what I believe is a misreading of a key passage in
the final scene. Before doing so, however, I must
add that Spitzer in his notes--which he seems to have
added after writing his article--does continue the
critical dialogue, commenting favorably or construc-
tively on points made in the earlier studies, including
Kayser's and Wardropper's, or discussing this or that
problematical passage, often in a helpful way. The
article is better with its notes than without them.

Bearing in mind the structural framework sketched
by Kayser, we must ask ourselves repeatedly whether
such and such a phenomenon or situation or set of relationships is to be interpreted within the logic of
physical and psychological cause and effect (ordo
successivorum) or abstractly, metaphorically, analo-
gically (ordo simultaneorum). In other words, do we
allow ourselves to be guided by metonymic or meta-
phoric relationships?

Does the exchange of Fernando's corpse for Fénix
mean that she (as Beauty) is worth no more than a
cadaver? Or that the ransom stipulated (Ceuta) is
being paid symbolically in kind (since Ceuta, like
Fénix, is Beauty)?[16] In this final scene of the third
act, are we to understand "divina imagen" and "muerto
infelice" in accordance with psychological verisimilitude?

These are the words with which Alfonso addresses
the King of Fez, proposing the exchange of Fénix, who
has fallen prisoner to him, for the mortal remains of
Fernando:

> Rey de Fez, porque no pienses
> que muerto Fernando vale
> menos que aquesta hermosura,
> por él, cuando muerto yace,
> te la trueco. Envía, pues,
> la nieve por los cristales,
> el enero por los mayos,
> las rosas por los diamantes,
> y al fin un muerto infelice
> por una divina imagen. (vv. 2732-2741; Jorn.
>   III, esc. xiii)

Spitzer, if he has stirred up some indignation by some elementary misreadings, has done us a service by calling attention to some passages which are not as simple as they may have seemed to earlier critics. "How," he asks, ". . . if the linguistic pomp as well as the 'comparison of values' have taught us to prefer worth to emptiness, can Calderón end with the contrasting of an unfortunate dead man and a <u>divine image</u> of beauty?" Spitzer finds the last two lines surprising because of the "sudden break in style and feeling." He suggests that "perhaps we should read '<u>muerto infelice</u>' and '<u>divina imagen</u>' as if they were enclosed in quotation marks: 'a so-called unfortunate dead man,' 'a so-called divine image.'"[17]

Spitzer, then, reading according to the dramatic sense, finds it strange that Fernando and Fénix should be referred to in such a way and concludes that Alfonso must be enunciating the terms with intentional irony. If, as most of the play's earlier critics have maintained, the exchange of Fernando's remains for Fénix is intended to signify that Beauty is worth no more than a corpse--"a grinning death's head," as Entwistle puts it (p. 220)--some sort of explanation such as Spitzer's was needed.[18]

Jack Sage, after rejecting some of Spitzer's other readings, does find his reading of this passage good, for it seems to him to fit into an ironic pattern: the true phoenix is not the Princess but Fernando (see pp. 566-571; esp. p. 568). Maria Norval, on the other hand, rejects the "suggestion that Calderón's words may be taken to mean the opposite of what they say" (p. 19). These are Alfonso's words, of course, not Calderón's; nevertheless, I believe she is right. Might it not be that what Spitzer sees as intentional or conscious irony in Alfonso's attitude is in reality dramatic irony? The important thing is what the words mean to the spectator or reader. William Empson's definition of dramatic irony is at hand, if we need it: he says that it gives "an intelligible way in which the reader can be reminded of the rest of a play while he is reading a single part of it."[19] "Divina imagen" (within the paradigmatic structure or <u>ordo simultaneorum</u>) is probably intended to remind us that Fénix is, by reason of her beauty, a likeness of Ceuta and that by divine intervention she has become the surrogate of Ceuta in the ransoming of Fernando.

I see no particular difficulty with the epithet
"muerto infelice." What is referred to is Fernando's
mortal remains, the dead body from which the spirit has
departed. It is "infelice" because it has been harshly
treated by time and adversity. "Infelicidad" is defined in the Diccionario de Autoridades as "Desgracia,
desdicha, infortunio," and "Infeliz" as "Desgraciado u
desdichado." "Infelice" is an appropriate adjective to
describe what Fernando's spirit has left in the clutches
of the King of Fez, who has declared,

> Aun muerto no ha de estar libre
> de mis rigores notables;
> y así puesto a la vergüenza
> quiero que esté a cuantos pasen.

> (vv. 2640-2643; Jorn. III, esc. xii)

After the body has been ransomed, Alfonso, promising
to inter it in a temple, refers to it as a "dichoso
cuerpo."

The terms "muerto infelice," then, can be easily
understood both literally and metaphorically. The two
levels coincide, in fact. The problem, such as it is,
concerns the ambiguous meaning of Fénix. I have
already discussed the appropriateness of calling Fénix
"divina imagen" in the ordo simultaneorum. On the
literal level (ordo successivorum) it might seem, at
first glance, that Alfonso would not refer to Fénix in
that way, having just said to the King of Fez, "porque
no pienses / que muerto Fernando vale / menos que
aquesta hermosura; / . . ." (vv. 2732-2734). This
impression appears to be confirmed when the King of
Fez answers, "¿Qué dices, invicto Alfonso?" Why does
he seem not to understand? Sage thinks it is because
"he cannot believe his ears" (p. 168). I think that he
simply does not understand who is meant by any of the
metaphors ("nieve," "cristales," "rosas," "diamantes,"
"enero," "mayos"); all he could be expected to understand is "un muerto infelice," and perhaps, because of
syntax and context, "una divina imagen." Perhaps,
too, he is surprised that the Portuguese should be
more interested in having Fernando's dead body than
in avenging his death.

The varying circumstances of different situations
often determine differences in the way the same matter
is seen or presented. Fernando, in scene vii of Act
III says to Fénix, ". . . más que yo no valéis, / y
yo quizá valgo más" (vv. 2491-2492). When Alfonso

stands before the walls of Fez and addresses the Moorish King, the intent of his words is different. Since the King of Fez believes that with the death of Fernando he no longer has any bargaining power whatsoever, Alfonso must assure him that the Portuguese indeed do value Fernando's remains and are prepared to negotiate for their return. With that in mind, he says,

> Rey de Fez, porque no pienses
> que muerto Fernando vale
> menos que aquesta hermosura,
> por él, cuando muerto yace,
> te la trueco.   (vv. 2732-2736)

But he is, after all, bargaining. When Fernando was alive, a Christian city was his ransom price. Now that he is dead, it is just possible that the King of Fez believes or suspects that he is still worth a great deal to the Portuguese, as in fact he is. With that thought in mind, we may suppose, Alfonso purposely and shrewdly (but not ironically) describes the objects of the exchange in such a way as to make the Moor believe that he is getting the better of the bargain.

All that Alfonso says, then, in his proposal to the King of Fez regarding the exchange of Fénix for Fernando's remains can be understood on a dramatic level; but the significance of the epithets "muerto infelice" and "divina imagen" is not limited to the immediate context. "Divina imagen" in particular is a case of dramatic (not literal) irony, and it should remind us of the ransom price set, the prophecy and the matter of divine intervention in the ransoming.

This analysis would not be complete without some consideration of the two lines uttered by Fénix as the exchange takes place:

> Precio soy de un hombre muerto;
> cumplió el cielo su homenaje.   (vv. 2744-2745)

The first line makes it clear that Fénix sees the exchange as the fulfilment of the mysterious prophecy regarding her. There is, however, no way of explaining on a dramatic level how she could know what the second line means. It is clearly a case of dramatic irony; it refers to the ordo simultaneorum, which has its own poetic logic. The meaning of "cumplió el cielo su homenaje"--which I have never seen explained in any of the many interpretations of the play I have studied--is based on the feudal custom whereby a vassal and a lord made a pact which mutually obligated them.[20] Truman comes close to this idea when he says that

> the burying of Fernando's body with special honour in a church is not simply a favour of heaven unrelated to justice but is, on the contrary, the very fulfilment of justice. God, whose honour has been defended and preserved by Fernando, is bound to bestow honour on him in return. At the end of the play we see that Fernando and God have respected their obligations to each other as justice required. (p. 101)

To make Truman's explanation applicable to the lines under consideration, we need only state the obvious: namely, that Fernando is the vassal, and his lord is God (identified here as "el cielo"). Fernando has defended Ceuta for his lord; and now, in return, his lord redeems him from enemy captivity.

The point to make in this examination of structural problems is that Fénix's two lines, within their dramatic context, are an excellent example of a joint where poetry and drama and Kayser's two _ordines_ converge and are welded together.

There are other aspects of this play which require attention. I would like to have found time to comment on the articles of Robert Sloane,[21] Robert ter Horst and Maria Norval. Peter Dunn in particular raises some interesting points which should be explored further. What I have tried to do is examine what I believe to be the two most accurate ways of describing the structure of El príncipe constante and apply them to an analysis of some key passages in the ending.

Purdue University

[1]"Calderón's 'Príncipe constante': Two Appreciations," MLR, 34 (1939), 207-222.

[2]In The Sources of Calderón's 'El príncipe
constante' (Oxford, 1950) and Chapter VII (pp. 188-
216) of The Dramatic Craftsmanship of Calderón
(Oxford, 1958).

[3]"The Theme of Justice in Calderón's El príncipe
constante," MLR, 59 (1964), 43-52; reprinted in
Critical Studies of Calderón's 'Comedias,' ed. by
John E. Varey (London: Tamesis/Gregg, 1973), pp.
97-109.

[4]Truman's study carries Sloman's (and Entwistle's)
approach forward, of course, building upon what they
achieved. In any event, the most solid and basic
aspect of Sloman's contribution is the comparison
which he makes between Calderón's play and its most
immediate source. Clearly, abstract thought is behind
most of the transformations which turn the earlier play
into El príncipe constante.

[5]"Zur Struktur des 'Standhaften Prinzen' von
Calderón," in Gestaltproblem der Dichtung, pp. 67-82.

[6]He argues (pp. 68-69) by analogy with the case
of La vida es sueño, which is not, of course, entirely
analogous, since there is no auto bearing the title
El príncipe constante. Alonso Zamora says, "El contenido auténtico de la comedia [La vida es sueño] fue
puesto en claro por el mismo Calderón en el auto
sacramental de igual título" (Diccionario de la
literatura española [Madrid, 1953], s.v. "Calderón").
One can agree wholeheartedly with Kayser in rejecting
that statement without necessarily discarding the
possibilities inherent in Entwistle's approach.
Kayser does return to Entwistle's interpretation
briefly at the conclusion of his own analysis (see
note 8, below).

[7](Madrid: Espasa-Calpe), p. xxvii. I shall refer
to this edition when quoting from the play, occasionally altering the punctuation when necessary.

[8]
>So locker die Structur wirkt, solange man
>nur das Hauptgeschehen verfolgt (Nebenhand-
>lungen, haüfiger Szenenwechsel, Zeitspannen

zwischen den Akten, relative Eigenständigkeit
von Szenenteilen, übergreifende Bedeutung von
Daseinsformen), so festigt sie sich, sobald
man die Dichte und Einheitlichkeit der
waltenden Atmosphäre mit einbezieht, in die
Calderón bei der relativen Eigenständigkeit
der Strukturelemente in jedem Augenblick
verstossen Kann. (p. 77)

Returning briefly, in these concluding remarks,
to Entwistle's thesis (see above, note 6), Kayser syas,
"Die Atmosphäre bleibt letzlich unfassbar und lichtet
sich nicht so weit auf, dass dahinter ein geistiges
Bezugssystem, ein begrifflicher Sternenhimmel sichtbar
würde. Eine einseitig allegorische Interpretation wie
in den autos sacramentales würde der Gestaltung nicht
gerecht" (p. 77).

[9]MLR, 53 (1958), 512-520; reprinted in Critical
Studies of Calderón's 'Comedias,' pp. 85-96.

[10]"'El príncipe constante': a Theatre of the
World," in Studies in Spanish Literature of the Golden
Age Presented to Edward M. Wilson, ed. by R. O. Jones
(London: Tamesis, 1973), pp. 83-101; 83.

[11]"Wir bezeichnen diesen Raum bedeutungsvollen
Seins als Atmosphäre" (p. 70).

[12]This atmosphere "übergreift durch ihre Bedeutsam-
keit das Stimmungshafte der einzelnen Szenen, entzieht
sich aber andererseits der begrifflichen Erfassung,
d.h. verflüchtigt sich da, wo das Drama allegorisch
wird" (p. 70). This is a bit vague, but it is still
a rather good description of the effect on the sensitive spectator.

[13]RJ, 10 (1959), 305-335.

[14](New York, 1965), pp. 137-160.

[15]Robert ter Horst, "The Economic Parable of Time
in El príncipe constante," RJ, 23 (1972), 294-306;
note 9 (p. 303); Jack Sage, "The Constant Phoenix,"
Studia Iberica: Festschrift für Hans Flasche (Bern/
München: Francke Verlag, 1973), pp. 561-574; note 23
(pp. 572-573), but, on the other hand, note 37 (p. 573);
Alexander A. Parker, "Christian Values and Drama: 'El
príncipe constant'," Studia Iberica, pp. 441-458;
notes 14 and 15 (p. 457); Maria Norval, "Another Look

at Calderón's _El príncipe constante_," BCom, 25 (1973), 18-28; passim.

When this paper was in what I thought was its final form, Nancy Palmer Wardropper's article, "The Figure of Fénix, Again," came to my attention for the first time. Although its proper bibliographical reference is RHM, Año XXXIX (1976-1977), Num. 4, pp. 167-174, that issue was not published until November of 1980. I am indebted to Bruce Wardropper, to whom I had sent a copy of this paper late in December, for letting me know of its existence, and to Nancy Wardropper for sending me an offprint.

Nancy Wardropper defends Leo Spitzer ably against his critics and defends Fénix even more ably against hers. After reading her article, I am willing to concede that there is a _potentially_ erotic relationship between Fernando and Fénix, but her arguments that Fénix (like Fernando and Muley) is constant (a quality which as she says is associated with the melancholic temperament) would seem to make the "erotic relationship" no more than a mutual attraction which both "partners" must have resisted successfully.

See also Porqueras Mayo's "Hacia una interpretación de la obra" [pp. xxxvi-lxxxi of his ed. cit.], most of which constitutes an effort to accommodate Spitzer's interpretation to a structural description of the work. Porqueras, like myself, attempts to reconcile _ordo simultaneorum_ with _ordo successivorum_. To try to deal here with his essay in the detail which fairness would require would displace the intended focus of this paper.

[16]See my "Calderón's _El príncipe_ constante: Fénix's Role in the Ransom of Fernando's Body," BCom, Vol. VIII, No. 1 (Spring, 1956), pp. 1-4; reprinted in _Critical Studies of Calderón's 'Comedias,'_ pp. 111-116; Kayser, note 24 (p. 82). (See also below, notes 17 and 18.)

[17]P. 159 in Wardropper's _Critical Essays_. In the German version, there is a note (9) on p. 313 in which Spitzer refers approvingly to Kayser's note 24 and to a passage in Wardropper's article, both of which point out the symbolic equivalence of Fénix to Ceuta. Wardropper says (MLR, LIII, 515):

The Moors ask for beauty--Christian beauty--

in exchange for the Prince. It is fitting,
therefore, that they should be paid in
beauty. But the beauty they receive, the
secular ephemeral beauty of Fénix, is ex-
changed--also appropriately--for the
ephemeral body of Don Fernando, the only
thing about the saint which is worldly.

(See also below, note 18.)

[18]See Wilson, p. 216; Entwistle, pp. 220-221;
Sloman, Dramatic Craftsmanship, pp. 207-208. Wardropper, too, after establishing Fénix as the symbolic equivalent of Ceuta via Beauty, which makes
her a fitting substitute for Ceuta as ransom price
for the Prince (I hope I am not reading too much into
Wardropper's words), goes on to refer briefly to the
worth of Fernando's soulless body relative to worldly
beauty (MLR, LIII, 515-516).

Perhaps too much has been made of the exchange
of Fernando's body for the living beauty of Fénix as
a way of comparing values. I am inclined to agree
with Peter N. Dunn's suggestion that "we should think
of the moral aspect of the play as something which
belongs to the general verisimilitude of the action,
rather than the justification of the action" (p. 86).

[19]Seven Types of Ambiguity (New York: Meridian,
1955), p. 53.

[20]The term "homenaje" is defined as follows in
the Siete Partidas:

> et homenage tanto quiere decir como tornarse
> home de otri et facerse como suyo para darle
> seguranza, sobre la cosa que promete de dar
> o de facer, que la cumpla; et este homenage
> non tan solamente ha logar en pleyto de
> vasallage, mas en todos los otros pleytos
> et posturas que los homes ponen entre si
> con entencion de complirlas.

(Part. IV, 25, 4)

[21]"Action and Role in El príncipe constante,"
MLN, 85 (1970), 167-183.

Función y significado de Muley en

El príncipe constante

Alberto Porqueras-Mayo

La crítica ha estudiado ya muchos aspectos de esta obra juvenil para coincidir en que se trata de una de las más bellas que han salido de la pluma de Calderón. Basta recordar, por su importancia, los testimonios de Goethe y M. Menéndez Pelayo.[1] En general los investigadores observaron el fondo histórico (la verdadera prisión del príncipe portugués por el rey de Fez) para resaltar la desviación y concentración artística de Calderón al especializarse en la tensión heroica del príncipe Fernando. Para ello el dramaturgo tuvo que alterar la verdad histórica en aras de una más universal verdad poética ya que en la obra literaria el príncipe portugués no acepta el canje de Ceuta, exagerando todavía más la forma de santidad del protagonista. La verdad histórica es que sí estaba dispuesto a este canje, que, por diversos motivos, no pudo realizarse.

Otra zona de la crítica más reciente se ha ocupado del tema secundario, teñido de colores de amor mundano, al establecer, por debajo del triángulo oficial amoroso que representan Fénix, Tarudante y Muley otra latente relación entre Fénix y Fernando. Se ha visto entonces que, literariamente, esta proyección es más intensa y sutil que el tema principal heroico, aunque surge fundido a él y, rebasándolo, lo subraya y unifica gloriosamente al final de la obra.[2] Y es precisamente Muley el personaje-puente encargado de conectar el tema principal y secundario de la obra. Pero la manipulación calderoniana de este personaje adquiere complejidades insospechadas que conviene estudiar con cierto rigor y detalle, aunque con las limitaciones de espacio de la presente ocasión. De esta manera, espero, se ampliará la comprensión artística de la obra y de las técnicas calderonianas. Se trata de un acercamiento inicial a tan atractivo personaje para el público de la época.

Muley[3] es arrancado del fondo tradicional español; procede de la vida que se refleja en los romances fronterizos. La sola presencia de Muley (y por supuesto la melancólica belleza de Fénix también)

asegura un tratamiento poético de la materia histórica
y una ampliación exótica del mundo cristiano. No
olvidemos que Calderón dará, a menudo, mucha importancia a los personajes-puente capaces de intercomunicar las zigzagueantes acciones principal y secundaria.
Pensemos, para citar un solo ejemplo, en Clotaldo de
La vida es sueño. Allí, por tratarse de una obra
filosófica, el enlace axial que representa Clotaldo
será enormemente calculante y razonador, característica
bastante generalizada, por cierto, de los personajes-
puente. El príncipe constante, con su fondo épico-
lírico, demandará un engarce a través de un personaje
bien versado en poesía y cortesanía capaz de "funcion-
ar," al menos argumentalmente, en el mundo refinado
de Fénix y Fernando, las almas más delicadas y sensi-
bles de la obra.[4] Su profesionalidad guerrera,
especialmente en la vertiente oficial del argumento,
le hace también apto para intercomunicar los intereses
históricos de dos potencias políticas, antagonistas
en la obra, es decir, el reino portugués y el de Fez.

La aparición de Muley se produce en la escena V.[5]
Pero la primera mención ocurre en la escena anterior,
la IV, aquella, en que el rey de Fez anuncia a su
hija Fénix que debe casarse con Tarudante, el infante
de Marruecos. Y le entrega un retrato de su futuro
esposo. Fénix, princesa melancólica y desamorada,
exclama en un aparte:

> ¡Ay Muley
> grande ocasión has perdido! (p. 9)

Es curioso que la primera mención a Muley ocurre en
el aparte citado en función "triangular" respecto a
la futura relación oficial de Fénix-Tarudante. La
existencia de Muley aparece como un fondo mental
(podríamos pensar en un background en el sentido de
Wölfflin) sin realidad física todavía en la escena.
Este "fondo mental," en cuanto al triángulo amoroso,
se siente a lo largo de toda la obra, hasta el final
en que pasa aparatosamente a ocupar un primer plano.
Pero hasta entonces la relación amorosa oficial
sancionada por el rey de Fez, padre de Fénix, es solamente la de Fénix y Tarudante.

La escena V, a pesar de su función de relleno
en muchos aspectos, me parece muy importante para
comprender el desarrollo de la obra y el papel importante de Muley. A ella voy a dedicarme con especial
atención. Leemos en la acotación: "Sale Muley con

bastón de general" y en el manuscrito C^6 se describe
incluso el primer gesto de este personaje "y arrodí-
llase." El espectador sabe ahora, por primera vez,
que Muley es militar al servicio del rey de Fez. A
su función de galán, con su profesionalidad militar
se le inyectan atributos de posible heroísmo, como
después se verá, y de posición social privilegiada al
ser general. Más tarde, cuando le cuenta al fin del
primer acto a Fernando su vida, nos enteramos de que
es sobrino del rey de Fez. Este "nepotismo" podría
salvar la ley del decoro al aparecer un tan joven
general. He aquí como un exordio muy literario, en
redondillas, que prepara el largo discurso en romances
que viene después:

> Quien penetra el arrebol   (alusión al
> de tan soberana esfera,   monarca)
> y a quien en el puerto espera (alusión a su
> tal aurora, hija del sol   hija, Fénix)
>
>   (p. 10)

Se trata, pues, de un rendido homenaje al rey al que
antes ha dicho "dame gran señor, los pies" para en
seguida pasar al otro plano de galán y cortejar a
Fénix, a quien además le dice "dame, señora, la mano."
Es decir, ya se señalan los dos niveles de todo el
parlamento. El mismo Muley resalta en su servicio
político cualidades que perduran a lo largo de toda
la obra: "con amor, lealtad y fe." Por los apartes
nos enteramos que Fénix, sorprendida por la aparición
de Muley, muestra turbación por tener el retrato de
Tarudante en las manos, retrato que también ha notado,
y disimulado, Muley. He aquí ya una característica
típica de los personajes-puente: el ser grandes
disimuladores.

Hay que notar que el rey de Fez nunca ha tenido
en cuenta la voluntad amorosa de su hija Fénix, ni los
sentimientos amorosos expresados ahora, aunque veladamente, por Muley, a quien corta por lo sano: "En fin,
Muley, ¿qué hay del mar?" (p. 11) Es interesante
observar que Calderón crea dentro de la escena un
pequeño teatro, o al menos, una audiencia para el
parlamento de Muley. Léese en la acotación escénica
"siéntase el rey y las damas." Hay que pensar que
Muley seguiría de pie para declamar, en alto estilo
literario, una relación en romances (como aconsejaba
para las relaciones Lope de Vega en su Arte Nuevo)
ante tan elegante audiencia: el rey de Fez, su hija

Fénix y las damas de honor que acompañaban a Fénix.
Estos varios niveles receptivos explican que junto a
la información política y militar Muley no olvida a
su dama para adornar poéticamente el lenguaje con
imágenes pictóricas, a las que se ha mostrado tan
aficionada Fénix en las primeras escenas. Calderón
es muy dado a poner en labios de sus importantes
personajes-puente, además de en el protagonista de
la obra, largos parlamentos. Piénsese una vez más
en Clotaldo de La vida es sueño. Calderón en esta
obra primeriza que constituye el Príncipe Constante
todavía no usa los monólogos a que será tan aficionado
después, y que pueden matizar con interpretación objetiva por parte del espectador, la acción de las tablas.
De aquí, pues, la importancia estructural de Muley,
que empieza a traslucirse ya. Me refiero al hecho
de que a través de la conexión de acontecimientos
exteriores con el argumento interno de la obra, puede
producir en la inmediatez de las tablas tensiones
íntimas en los personajes que le rodean, y que, a
veces, los efectos de los datos externos, asumen la
función interiorizante de los monólogos.

Empieza Muley su declamación romancística con
esta paradójica afirmación: "Ni hablar, ni callar,
podré" que señala ya su caracterización dilemática,
llena de contradicciones, como muchos personajes
calderonianos, especialmente los "personajes-puente."
Con ello se anuncia ya los grandes dilemas de Muley
que aparecerán después claros en la obra, especialmente su amistad con Fernando y su lealtad política
al rey de Fez.

Calderón, repito, ha arrancado a Muley de la
tradición galante de los romances fronterizos, gusto
que pudo recibir directamente, sobre todo, de su
admirado Góngora, a quien pronto plagiará para mostrar
su homenaje de admiración con el romance morisco
"entre los sueltos caballos." La descripción de
Muley de ahora tiene también mucho del ritmo mental
de un romance fronterizo. Se trata de una especie
de escaramuza arrancada de la tradición de las
guerras granadinas aquí transformada en expedición
naval. Repárese en el comienzo: "Salí como me
mandaste." Aquí la escaramuza galante ha sido ir a
observar la situación de la cautiva Ceuta. Nótese
los paralelos de Ceuta-Fénix y precisamente, la falsa
etimología de "hermosura" que se ofrece para Ceuta,
ciudad que aparece, pues, como una ciudad-novia (en
la tradición árabe) y ahora en posesión de los enemigos

cristiano-portugueses. Muley al hablar de Ceuta afirma:

> aquella, pues, que los cielos
> quitaron a tu corona
> quizá por justos enojos
> del gran profeta Mahoma . . . (p. 13)

Esto nos interesa por el papel que tiene también Muley,
aquí, de coro de tragedia griega, para aludir al pasado
y proyectar el futuro, a lo que aludiré después.

Notemos que, en esta obra de ambiente marino,
Calderón se vale de Muley para abrir una ventana
decorativa y describirnos el mar. Los autores
teatrales abren a menudo, a través de relaciones,
estas ventanas decorativas. Piénsese, por ejemplo,
en la "loa a Lisboa" inserta en El burlador de
Sevilla de Tirso. Ya los románticos alemanes, además
de su profundidad filosófica, admiraban en Calderón
la sensibilidad marítima meridional. A Calderón, su
afición literaria al mar, le venía sobre todo, pienso,
del mundo gongorino del Polifemo y de las Soledades.
También, podría pensarse, acaso, que el mar representa
el elemento impetuoso y natural que ya se opone a la
corte de Fez. Algo así como el monte en Segismundo
de La vida es sueño que se opone al mundo palaciego
de Basilio, y acaba por triunfar.[7] Voy a citar la
primera descripción manierista del mar en esta obra,
con difíciles imágenes, insertas en una sintaxis
gongorina,[8] difíciles de intelegir por un auditorio
normal:

> Yo lo sé porque en el mar
> una mañana, a la hora
> que, medio dormido el sol,
> atropellando las sombras
> del ocaso, desmaraña
> sobre jazmines y rosas
> rubios cabellos, que enjuga
> con paños de oro a la aurora
> lágrimas de fuego y nieve
> que el sol convirtió en aljófar,
> que a largo trecho del agua
> venía una gruesa tropa,
> de naves [. . .] (p. 14)

Estas descripciones temporales (aurora o crepúsculo)
venían de la tradición grecolatina (Homero y Virgilio,
especialmente) se incorporan a la literatura pastoril
y de aquí, ocasionalmente, pasan al teatro. Sabido

de sobras es la abundancia de términos pictóricos en
una zona específica de este parlamento de Muley, versos
232 a 268 (p. 14 y 15 de mi edición): "pinceles,"
"unos visos, unos lejos," "perspectiva dudosa," "dis-
tancia," "mil engaños a la vista," etc. Muley, con
ello, establece un contacto directo con la princesa
Fénix, tan aficionada al arte pictórico, como ya he
señalado. Literariamente, Muley le sirve a Calderón,
además, en esta ventana poética para incrustar estas
técnicas pictóricas (a las que tan aficionado era el
dramaturgo) más propias de la poesía elevada (lírica
o épica) en el estilo dramático. También, en cuanto
al contenido, es muy importante aquí la función de
Muley: se trata de una bisagra comunicativa a través
de la cual los elementos externos, fuera de la escena,
van afectando y decidiendo la misma acción dramática
que tiene lugar en el teatro. En esta zona preliminar
de la obra podríamos considerar también a Muley en una
doble función de prólogofaraute, es decir, mensajero,
como ya en el teatro griego, y de coro de antigua
tragedia al matizar, interpretándolo, el pasado y
aludir a un posible castigo en la pérdida de Ceuta
(ya lo hemos visto) o también al presagiar el futuro
en tono profético. He aquí un pasaje importante:

> que quizá se cumple hoy
> una profecía heroica
> de Morabitos, que dice
> que en la margen arenosa
> del Africa ha de tener
> la portuguesa corona
> sepulcro infeliz [. . .]   (p. 20)

Dentro del arte manierista el detalle, la anécdota,
cobra mucha importancia artística. De aquí la nave
cristiana, individualizada, que se hunde en la tormenta, observada por Muley que se acerca en actitud
de romance fronterizo: "llegué a ella, y aunque moro."
La anécdota se individualiza todavía más. Y un cristiano cautivo sirve de informante. Piénsese en el
soldado traidor de La vida es sueño, recientemente
tan estudiado por varios investigadores. Pues bien,
la información transmitida ahora va envuelta en la
atmósfera de los romances fronterizos:

> Catorce mil portugueses
> -----------------------
> Mil son los fuertes caballos
> -----------------------------   (p. 19)

He aquí otra función para la que Calderón echa
mano de Muley a través de este parlamento: anticipar
los grandes temas de la obra a través de sentencias.
Veamos las tres más importantes:

>   que también saber huir
>   es linaje de vitoria   (p. 16)
>
>   que el tener en las desdichas
>   compañía, de tal forma
>   consuela, que el enemigo
>   suele servir de lisonja   (p. 17)
>
>   [. . .] que el vivir
>   eterno es vivir con honra   (p. 18)

Muley ha terminado este largo parlamento, del que
sólo he observado algunas características, y el rey le
contesta en redondillas, al mismo tiempo que se levanta,
él y sus damas. Gracias a la acotación del manuscrito
C, donde leemos "levántense" nos enteramos de este
importante detalle escénico. Tenemos, pues, que con
el cambio de métrica y con el movimiento del pequeño
auditorio que se levanta, queda enmarcado el espectáculo
declamatorio de Muley, constituido, todo él, como una
ventana decorativa que ahora se cierra.[9]

El rey de Fez, al mismo tiempo que decide dirigir
sus ejércitos al encuentro de los portugueses, subraya
una vez más las habilidades de este personaje fronterizo que es Muley al encargarle que entretenga al
enemigo "en escaramuzas diestras." Y termina el
propio rey contagiado del tono galante-guerrero que
late en el romance anterior:

>   porque Ceuta ha de ser mía
>   y Tánger no ha de ser suya   (p. 21)

Después viene la escena VI en que quedan solos
Fénix y Muley. Ahora Calderón reafirma el tema de
los celos, como característica de Muley, a través
sobre todo de dos sentencias:

>   si celos mis penas son
>   ninguno es cortés con celos   (p. 21)
>
>   . . . que, en habiendo celos
>   se pierde el respeto a todo   (p. 22)

163

Una vez más vemos las sentencias que se encargan de
"colocar" los temas que la misma acción dramática está
desarrollando o desarrollará después. Los celos se
encrespan en seguida en una dińamica esticomitia,10
para, hacia el final de la escena, en un tono galante
y cortesano que engarza muy bien con la atmósfera
fronteriza del parlamento de Muley en la escena
anterior, exclamar Fénix:

> A Tánger, que en Fez te espero
> donde acabes de quejarte (p. 24)

Encontramos de nuevo a Muley, en la escena XI, cuando
cae prisionero de Fernando. Toda la escena está
redactada en romances, de nuevo, y se intercalan, sin
citar la procedencia (y hay que considerarlo como un
homenaje a la popularidad de Góngora) versos enteros
del romance de tema fronterizo "entre los sueltos
caballos." No insisto en el obvio carácter fronterizo
de esta escena, en su función puramente literaria
(para lo que sirve muy bien Muley, como hemos visto),
con acontecimientos anacrónicos--que subrayan el
carácter literario--con la misma obra que está pre-
sentando Calderón y otros detalles de sobra subrayados
por la crítica anterior. Lo que sí me interesa es
recalcar el paralelismo métrico y de tono, con el
parlamento de la escena V de Muley, que ya venía
preparando esta "materia fronteriza" de ahora. En
cuanto al contenido destacaría tres aspectos del
curriculum vitae de Muley:

> 1) Sobrino del rey de Fez
>   soy, mi nombre es Muley Jeque (p. 35)
>
> 2) nací en brazos de la muerte (p. 35)
>
> 3) gozando en auras süaves
>   mil amorosos deleites. (p. 37)

Vemos, pues, que 1) nos explica el generalato de Muley,
como ya he señalado más arriba 2) alude a su nacimiento
desgraciado, como tantos personajes calderonianos,
hecho que posibilita, después, además de su gratitud
por los acontecimientos posteriores, la compasión ante
la desgracia de Fernando y 3) su íntima relación
amorosa con Fénix, que despierta la curiosidad e
interés humano de Fernando ante Fénix, todavía desconocida para él.

Ahora, en esta escena, se inyecta una nueva

característica en Muley, la amistad agradecida hacia
Fernando, que, en los actos segundo y tercero, llegará
a ser en su caracterizacíon más importante que los
mismos celos. Estas afinidades entre Fernando y Muley,
que nacerán a raíz de este encuentro y del consiguiente
perdón por parte de Fernando, posibilitarán argumentalmente la función de puente que ejercerá Muley entre los
intereses musulmanes y la posible liberación de
Fernando.

En las tablas se reproducen aspectos de la batalla
entre las huestes de Tarudante y el rey de Fez, por una
parte, y los ejércitos portugueses. Y en la penúltima
escena de este primer acto, Fernando cae prisionero.
Y allí Muley se entera de la verdadera identidad de
su generoso perdonador de antes. Ahora, definitivamente, Muley queda unido a los vaivenes de Fernando,
por su intención intermediaria ante el rey de Fez.
Calderón, a través de los celos de Muley, apunta una
falsa pista ante un nuevo posible rival amoroso. He
aquí el pasaje:

> Fernando. Iré a la <u>esfera</u> cuyos rayos sigo.
>
> Muley. (¡Porque yo tenga, cielos (Aparte)
> más que sentir entre amistad
> y celos!) (p. 45)

Me he detenido en el primer acto, y sobre todo en
la larguísima escena V, porque allí se ofrecen ya los
aspectos más importantes del personaje Muley. Ahora
será posible ir más de prisa. Ya hacia el principio
de la segunda jornada, después de la aparición de
Fénix, se le une Muley que interpreta la profecía de
la caduca africana, según la cual Fénix será el precio
de un hombre muerto. Muley le da un viraje a esta
profecía aplicándola, celoso, a sí mismo: se trata,
según Muley, de su propia muerte producida por la
entrega de Fénix a Tarudante.

En la próxima escena Muley saluda a Fernando, en
el jardín, y se queja, todavía impresionado por la
profecía que acaba de escuchar, de su mala estrella.
Ya sabemos que Fernando desde el fin de la primera
jornada, conoce ciertos amoríos de Muley, y que
precisamente por ellos le perdona. Ahora, curioso,
le pregunta por ellos. De nuevo Muley insinúa más
relaciones sexuales, que Calderón puede veladamente
indicar porque, al fin y al cabo, se trata de la
vertiente musulmana de la obra:

                    Fueron en mí
        recatados los favores.
              El dueño juré encubrir . . .   (p. 54)

De todas maneras le comunica en forma de enigma, el
nombre de su amada, usando de nuevo la paradoja "decir-
callar" que ya le había caracterizado desde el primer
momento como personaje desconfiado, casuista, calcula-
dor y, ahora, además, por supuesto, celoso, para con
ello Calderón dejar abierta todavía la falsa pista de
un encuentro amoroso Fénix-Fernando:

              Fénix mi amor y cuidado;
        y pues que es Fénix te digo,
        como amante y como amigo
        ya lo he dicho y lo he callado.   (p. 54)

Es ahora, precisamente, cuando Fernando nota el in-
esperado zarpazo de los celos en Muley, y Calderón
aprovecha el momento para calmar, hasta cierto punto,
a los espectadores, a través de un aparte de Fernando:

              si Fénix su pena es,
        no he de competirla yo . . .   (p. 55)

    Hay que tener en cuenta este lazo de honda amistad
entre los dos seres desgraciados que son Fernando y
Muley, porque evidentemente contribuirá, más tarde, en
Fernando, además de su ascendente santidad, a rechazar
la intensa atracción física que la presencia de Fénix
producirá en el príncipe portugués.

    Fernando, en la obra literaria de Calderón,
rechaza el canje de Ceuta, propuesto en la embajada
diplomática de su hermano Enrique. A partir de ahora,
esta negativa del príncipe provoca las más feroces
represalias del rey de Fez. Muley, personaje-puente
y por tanto a menudo presenciador, silencioso, de lo
que ocurre en la escena, exclama en un aparte:

              Ya ha llegado la ocasión
        de que mi lealtad se vea.
        La vida debo a Fernando,
        yo le pagaré la deuda.   (p. 68)

A partir de ahora Calderón hace que Muley simbolice la
amistad, y ya los celos ocupan un segundo plano, nunca
más ya aparentes ante Fernando como rival. La amistad
a Fernando, en un momento, vacilante, predominará
sobre la lealtad al rey de Fez, en este Muley

conflictivo, y por tanto capaz de intercomunicar dos
mundos distintos de la obra. Me refiero a la entrevista
Fernando-Muley de la escena XV en la que éste la propone un plan de huida. Hay una serie de acontecimientos y finas dialécticas entre los dos personajes,
de los que emerge un Muley confuso, indeciso, salvado
por la santa renuncia de Fernando, que Calderón como
contraste a los vaivenes psíquicos de Muley, puede
definitivamente, al final de la segunda jornada, pre-
sentar como el príncipe constante que justifica el
título de la tragedia:

> Sí aconsejas, porque yo,
> por mi Dios y por mi ley,
> seré un Príncipe Constante
> en la esclavitud de Fez. (p. 85)

Una vez situada en el primer acto la importancia
de Muley, y complicada en el segundo su actuación de
conducto que va uniendo y matizando con su presencia
los diversos intereses de los otros personajes, no
puede sorprendernos que el primer personaje que hable
en el tercer acto sea Muley. Si en esta obra muchos
de los personajes representan ideas abstractas, en
técnica reminiscente de los autos sacramentales, como
quería, un tanto exageradamente, Entwistle,[11] Muley
simboliza, ya lo hemos dicho, la amistad. Veamos sus
primeras palabras expresadas, curiosamente, en un
aparte:

> Ya que socorrer no espero,
> por tantas guardas del Rey,
> a Don Fernando, hacer quiero
> sus ausencias, que esta es ley
> de un amigo verdadero. (p. 86)

Muley intercede directamente ante el rey, justificando
su intercesión, que desde un principio rechaza el rey,
en su cualidad de guarda personal de Fernando, que le
autoriza a informar a su superior sobre el estado del
preso. Calderón echa mano aquí de Muley para contarle
al rey de Fez, y por tanto a los espectadores, un
lapso de tiempo transcurrido entre la terrible prisión
a que se ha visto sometido Fernando y el momento presente. Para estos flashbacks Muley es el personaje
más utilizado por Calderón. La otra característica
de Muley, los celos, aparecen en la escena siguiente
provocados por la presencia física de Tarudante.
Muley, personaje conflictivo, queda obligado a servir
a Fénix. He aquí las palabras del rey dirigidas a

Muley:

> Prevente,
> que con la gente de guerra
> has de ir sirviendo a Fénix,
> hasta que quede segura
> y con su esposo la dejes. (p. 98)

Lo curioso es que ahora, más que los celos, nos enteramos por el aparte que es el sentido de la amistad el que predomina en Muley:

> Esto sólo me faltaba,
> para que, estando yo ausente,
> aun le falte mi socorro
> a Fernando, y no le quede
> esta pequeña esperanza. (p. 98)

La presencia de Muley es ya, cuantitavamente, poco destacada en este tercer acto. Una vez establecida su gran amistad con Fernando, queda subrayado al final que es esta amistad lo que salvará a Muley y posibilitará el que parecía imposible matrimonio con Fénix. Dice hacia el final, en efecto, el vencedor Alfonso al rey de Fez:

> A Fénix y a Tarudante
> te entrego, Rey, y te pido
> que aquí con Muley la cases,
> por la amistad que yo sé
> que tuvo con el infante. (p. 121)

Ante los espectadores de la época la presencia de Muley en la trama se sentía como algo importante y deseado. Ello explica las amplificaciones que en lo relativo a este personaje, ocurren ante una audiencia de carácter más popular, como la que escuchó la versión que nos ha conservado el manuscrito de la Biblioteca Nacional.

En un futuro próximo me referiré con detalle a este manuscrito. Voy a citar solo dos ejemplos de las líneas finales ya que la versión del manuscrito prepara a los espectadores mucho mejor para el protagonismo de Muley respecto a Fénix. En efecto, leemos en el manuscrito (donde modernizo la ortografía):

> Si se habrá olvidado Alfonso
> con estos nuevos pesares
> que era amante de Fénix
> llegaré otra vez a hablalle

aunque no es tiempo, señor
en esta ocasión hablarte
por amigo de Fernando
vuelvo otra vez a rogarte
que Fénix no va contenta
a Marruecos, Tarudante
no le ha tocado una mano.[12]

También pintoresca es la competición generosa entre
Tarudante y Muley, antes de efectuarse, por el rey de
Fez, el rescate de la princesa Fénix y de los dos
rivales amorosos, que encontramos en la última página
del manuscrito.

Tarudante.   Líbrese Fénix Señor
             que yo ofrezco mi rescate
             entrega luego a Fernando
             y dale la vida a un ángel.

Muley.   Entrégale y yo le ofrezco
             por Ceuta los alijares
             que tengo orillas del mar
             y es poco por el infante.

Con estos ejemplos (podría citar muchas otras amplificaciones del manuscrito respecto a Muley) queda
subrayado que ya en el siglo XVII Muley era visto
por las audiencias españolas como un personaje importante en la trama de la obra.

En esta paper me he acercado a este exótico
personaje que Calderón se encargó de adornar con un
gran relieve poético. Pero además, como hemos visto,
su posición axial en la estructura de la obra le
permite importantes soldaduras argumentales, especialmente entre la acción principal y secundaria, al
mismo tiempo que sirve, en la acción secundaria,
especialmente con sus expresados celos no solo ante
Tarudante sino también ante Fernando, de reforzar la
falsa pista calderoniana de una posible seducción de
Fernando por parte de la melancólica princesa mora.

University of Illinois, Urbana

[1]Pueden encontrarse en la introducción a mi
edición de Clásicos Castellanos (Madrid, 1975), págs.
xiii y xiv. En esta misma introducción se encontrará
la bibliografía relevante sobre la obra. Todas las
citas en este trabajo se refieren a esta citada
edición, y se añade la página correspondiente. Los
subrayados siempre son míos. Para los trabajos más
recientes puede consultarse ahora Kurt und Roswitha
Reichenberger, Bibliographisches Handbuch der Calderón-
Forshung. Manual Bibliográfico Calderoniano. Kassel:
Verlag Thiele & Schwarz, 1979, Teil I.

[2]Véase Leo Spitzer, "Die Figur der Fénix in Calderón's Standhaften Prinzen," RJ X (1959): 305-55 y en
mi "En torno al Príncipe Constante. La relación
Fénix-Fernando," Actas del Quinto Congreso Internacional de Hispanistas (Bordeaux: Instituto de
Estudios Ibéricos e Hispanoamericanos, 1977) I, 687-
97. Prácticamente en este artículo reagrupo, unifi-
cándolas, las ideas ya expuestas en la citada edición
de Clásicos Castellanos. En realidad el primero, en
rigor, en notar la correlación Fernando-Fénix fue
Wolfgang Kayser, "Zur Struktur des Standhaften Prinzen
Von Calderón" incluido en su libro Gestaltproblem der
Dichtung (Bonn, Bouvier, 1957), 232-56. Véase especialmente las páginas 246-52. Es obvio que Spitzer re-
cibió el primer estímulo de este trabajo. Sobre la
relación Fénix-Fernando (en la que, por supuesto,
Muley sirve de vehículo) quisiera subrayar ahora que
Calderón contaba con una larga tradición de musul-
manas, a veces princesas, enamoradas de cristianos,
cautivos o no, tradición que flotaba en la atmósfera,
sin que Calderón tuviera que ser más explícito. He
aquí un ejemplo importante que bien pudo conocer
Calderón. Se trata de Tirant Lo Blanc de Joanot
Martorell donde leemos que una reina mora requiere
en amores a Tirant, pero éste la rechaza: "E la tua
mercè no em tinga a mal lo que et diré, encara que
jo no en sia mereixedora, car sobre tots los hòmens
del món te volria per marit e per senyor. E si jo
fos estada en llibertat e no temés infàmia, ab tu
me'n fóra anada. E si la tua noblea me desempara,
¿on trobaré jo refugi ni esperança de persona tal
qui a mes dolors remei puixa donar sinó tú, o la
mort, qui és la fi de tots los mals?" (edición de
Martín de Riquer, Barcelona, Seix Barral, 1969, 2ª
edición, II, p. 323).

[3]A fines del acto primero nos enteramos de su nombre completo, Muley Jeque. Sobre el nombre Muley, nos informa Covarrubias: "Cerca de los árabes es lo mesmo que "don" en Castilla," Tesoro, p. 819a. Ya Norman Maccoll en la introducción a su Select Plays of Calderón (Londres: Macmillan, 1888) afirmaba en pág. 15: "Muley is an Andalusian warrior such as he is described in the pages of Hita and in the ballads." Pero no llegó a comprender su importancia y le parecía que no tenía nada que ver con el tema principal. En realidad Maccoll no estaba, como lógicamente, todavía preparado para comprender las complejidades del arte barroco y manierista. Su sensibilidad literaria era también bastante reducida. Convendría añadir también que, ante los espectadores, el sólo nombre de Muley ya lo reviste de exotismo, cosa que no ocurría con el nombre de Fénix. Véase en la nota número cuatro que Immermann la hace aparecer blanca en la escena.

[4]Es sintomático que en el experimento dramático que realizó Immermann para el teatro de Düsseldorf entre 1833 y 1838 a Fénix se la presentó sin embedurnarla de negro. Se trató de la única excepción en el círculo moro de los personajes de la obra. Así se destacaba su igualdad con Fernando. Para más detalles sobre estas representaciones dirigidas por Immermann, véase Karl R. Pietshmann, "Calderón auf der Deutsche Bühue von Goethe bis Immermann," Maske und Koturn, III (1957), 317-39. Para un resumen de este trabajo véase mi citada introducción, xii-xv. También tenemos muchos detalles de la representación dirigida por Goethe en Weimar en 1811. Precisamente en un curioso y raro libro, Johann Schulze, Uber der Standhaften Prinzen de Don Pedro Calderón (Weimar: im Verlage des Landes, 1811) encontramos interesantes detalles sobre esta representación y en la página 26 se reproduce un pintoresco grabado en el que aparece el actor Oels, representando el moro Muley.

[5]Aunque es verdad que, seguramente, en futuras ediciones, convendría eliminar esta división de escenas que no figuran en el texto original (y a veces son caprichosas en las ediciones posteriores) de momento nos sirven para entendernos y a ellas se ha referido la crítica tradicional. Sigo la división de escenas establecida en mi edición que suele coincidir con la división propuesta en ediciones anteriores por otros investigadores, especialmente a partir de Hartzenbusch.

[6]Así, con esta denominación, me refiero al manuscrito letra del siglo XVII que se conserva en la Biblioteca Nacional de Madrid, número 15.159. La mayoría de estas acotaciones del manuscrito se han incorporado en notas en mi citada edición.

[7]Expongo estas ideas en mi ensayo de presentación de La vida es sueño para una edición de divulgación de Selecciones Austral (Madrid, 1979), 3ª edición, véase especialmente pág. 20.

[8]Se trata de una técnica parecida a la gongorina el intercalar aposiciones y atributos en una frase tan simple como "en el mar, una mañana, venía una gruesa tropa de naves." Esta técnica respecto sobre todo a una estrofa famosa de la dedicatoria a las Soledades mereció ya un detallado análisis de Leo Spitzer, "Zu Góngora Soledades" en Volkstum und Kultur der Romanen, 2 (1930), 249-58 y de Walter Pabst en La creación gongorina en los poemas Polifemo y Soledades (Madrid: Consejo Superior de Investigaciones Científicas, 1966), 28-38. Por supuesto que estas aposiciones, y las mismas observaciones pictóricas que vendrán después ("perspectiva dudosa," etc.) subrayan ya el carácter analizante y razonador, respecto a la realidad que surge en la obra, de este importante personaje que es Muley. Nótese también, después, cuando alude a dos profecías usa en ambas ocasiones el adverbio quizá que tiñe así las mismas profecías de misteriosa incertidumbre.

[9]La mayoría de críticos alemanes del romanticismo, empezando por Goethe, atacaron el gongorismo y "amaneramiento" (que hoy entendemos, positivamente, gracias a las investigaciones recientes sobre el manierismo) de Calderón, especialmente en fragmentos como el parlamento de Muley. Sabemos, incluso, que este parlamento sufría drásticos cortes en las tablas germanas. Este era el caso, por ejemplo, del experimento de Immermann, en el que suprimía la explicación de Ceuta y todo lo relativo a la flota. Es interesante notar que su auditorio normal, poco sofisticado, según Edward M. Wilson en "An Early Rehash of Calderón's El Príncipe Constante," MLN 76, 8 (1961), 785-991, como el de una provincia española de la época, donde tendría lugar la representación que nos ha conservado el manuscrito C, gozaba de este delicado parlamento que nos ha mantenido íntegro, sin cortes de ninguna clase.

[10]Véase David Wise, "Stichomytia. A Rhetorical Device in Four Plays by Calderón" en Segismundo XII, 1-2 (1978), 133-42.

[11]Me refiero a la zona de William J. Entwistle en "Calderón's Príncipe Constante: Two Appreciations" en MLR 34 (1939), 218-22. Para Entwistle Muley representa bizarría. Me parece mucho más acertada la aplicación a esta obra, como hace Spitzer, de técnicas emblemáticas. En este uso me parece que Muley sería un buen emblema para el concepto amistad.

[12]Se trata de la pág. 66 del manuscrito, donde se indica que se trata de un aparte, pero no señala que a partir de "aunque no es tiempo" se trata evidentemente de un diálogo con D. Alfonso.

Conflict in Calderón's

Autos Sacramentales

Donald T. Dietz

In his book The Enjoyment of Drama, Milton Marx
writes: "The essence of drama is conflict. Every
dramatic situation arises from conflict between two
opposing forces."[1] In this same chapter devoted to
theatrical conflict, Marx posits the following: "In
order to make the struggle or conflict exciting, which
is one of the synonyms of dramatic, the playwright
must make the odds fairly even."[2] The first portion
of this paper will analyse the nature of the dramatic
conflict in the Calderonian autos sacramentales. The
second part will illustrate how Calderón conscientious-
ly tried to "make the odds even" in constructing the
plots of his allegorical dramas.

Marx, in the book just cited, distinguishes three
types of conflict: that between two individuals, that
between the individual and an outside force--society,
the supernatural, destiny or fate--and that between
the individual and himself. I believe it helpful to
conceive of conflict from a structural point of view
in the treatment of Calderón's autos sacramentales
and their artistic development. I prefer to categorize conflict in terms of "horizontal" and "vertical." Horizontal conflict is a struggle of allegorical personages from two opposing camps: side A is
pitted against side B, the "good" forces against the
"bad." Vertical conflict is a dramatic situation in
which allegorical figures in the same camp fight each
other thus creating dramatic tensions among themselves.

Basically the conflict found in the early autos
and farsas of the Rouanet collection and the pre-
Calderonian autos of Sánchez Badajoz, Valdivielso,
Lope de Vega, Tirso de Molina, and others is of the
horizontal type.[3] Louise Fothergill-Payne in her book
which deals with the autos sacramentales prior to
Calderón corroborates this principle:

> Cualquiera que sea el argumento, siempre habrá
> dos bandos contendientes que abierta o velada-
> mente se hallan en conflicto: el eterno con-
> flicto entre El Bien y El Mal.[4]

Fundamental to the development of this pattern
of horizontal conflict is the alignment of the
personae dramatis. All of the allegorical figures
in the evil camp act in unison as a single dedicated
team to oppose all of the figures in the good camp
who also function harmoniously as a unit. Generally
the pattern goes something like this. On the side of
evil, the Devil (Demonio, Lucifer, Luzbel, Luz de
Tinieblas) captains his forces and he is ably assisted
by either the World (El Mundo) or the Flesh (La Carne)
or both. On the evil team may be found Vice (El
Vicio) or any number of vices, more often than not,
Pride (El Orgullo, La Soberbia), because pride effec-
ted Satan's downfall from the camp of the good angels
and this same vice, according to tradition, accounted
for man's fall from paradise. Lucifer's antithesis
is Christ (Cristo, Cordero, Príncipe de Luz) who
marshals his forces of the good, Grace (La Gracia),
the virtues, the saints, etc. The battle between the
two contesting sides is waged over man (El Hombre, El
Peregrino, Género Humano) who initially gives in to
the evil spirits but who eventually sees the light
and receives salvation through repentance (Penitencia,
Contrición) and Mercy (Misericordia).

Sometimes man's nature or inner-self becomes the
battleground. In this case, war is waged between
man's two natures, his rational and sensual (Razón
vs. Apetito) or his physical and spiritual (Cuerpo
vs. Alma). The literary tradition of allegorizing
the struggle which takes place in man's inner-self
comes from Prudentius' Psychomachia and is deeply
rooted in the Spanish medieval poetry of the debates.[5]
The point is that even when man is dissected and this
inner struggle is allegorized by the dramatist, the
battle between the figures aligned in the two camps
of man's dual nature provides the main source of
dramatic conflict.

To be sure, the "good" versus "bad" approach may
also be found in the Calderonian autos sacramentales.
It is impossible to conceive of theater without the
presence of a protagonist-antagonist situation.[6] I
do not intend in this paper to dwell on the obvious,
but rather my goal is to focus upon Calderón's advance-
ment in theatrical technique and upon his enhancement
of conflict so essential to the dramatic. More specifically, I wish to establish Calderón's employment of
vertical conflict to augment his theater, where allegorical figures of the same side create dramatic

tensions among themselves. We will observe that Calderón gradually advanced as an auto writer to employ
vertical conflict in his more mature works where he
recast allegorical figures of earlier pieces.

Angel Valbuena Prat categorizes Calderón's La
cura y la enfermedad under that group of autos sacramentales which depict mankind's salvation-history
story of the creation, fall, and redemption.[7] Another
allegorical play belonging to this same classification
is Calderón's La vida es sueño. La cura y la enfermedad was penned sometime between 1652 and 1659 while
La vida es sueño appeared some fifteen years later in
1673.[8] The latter play is therefore representative
of Calderón's later years as an auto writer. Actually
the 1673 version of La vida es sueño is a reworking
of an earlier manuscript version with identical title
whose date is still uncertain.[9] La cura and both versions of La vida are the only ones written by Calderón
in which the four elements, El Aire, El Agua, El
Fuego, and La Tierra make appearances and assume significant dramatic roles.[10] Edward Wilson, some years
ago, studied the imagery of the four elements in Calderón's comedia and I have contrasted in another
study the dramatic function of these four allegorical personages in the two auto versions of La vida.[11]
My purpose here is to briefly contrast Calderón's
dramatization of the four elements in his early La
cura by the development of horizontal conflict and his
adaptation of these same allegorical figures by the
vertical mode in La vida. In La cura, El Aire, El
Agua, El Fuego, and La Tierra are rather extensively
involved in the play's action. Furthermore, their
dramatic roles are determined principally by their
relationship to one of the central protagonists. La
Naturaleza (Human Nature). In the garden of Eden, the
elements are friendly towards man until he sins; after
the fall, to allegorize the disruption of the natural
order of things, they are hostile to him. Man fully
recognizes that, as part of creation, his human nature
is intrinsically bound to that of all other created
things and that to upset one is to upset the other.
The destruction of this delicate balance between man
and nature is evidenced in these words of La Naturaleza
after she has willfully accepted Sombra:

> Y pues corresponder veo
> cuatro Elementos a cuatro
> humores, que descompuestos
> de natural equilibrio,

177

han enfermado en mi pecho. (p. 760)

At the end of the play, after Redemption, the four
figures relate amiably to man once again. The point
I wish to stress is that no matter what position the
elements take vis-a-vis man in the plot, they do so
as a block, in unison; when there is antagonism
between them and man, they are all hostile toward
him with never a trace of dispute among themselves.
We have here a good example of horizontal conflict.

There is another interesting aspect with regard
to the four elements in the play which foreshadows
Calderón's later treatment of them in La vida. In
La cura, the allegorical figure of El Mundo is seen
where in La vida there is no such figure. Actually,
in La cura, the presence of El Mundo and each of the
four elements is structurally unnecessary since the
four elements are really a conceptual extension of the
one, El Mundo. The four elements often refer to themselves in the play as "moradores del Mundo," and
there is a cumbersome structural relationship that
is evident in which El Mundo always precedes their
appearance on stage and calls them onto the scene. It
is interesting to note that in most of his autos
sacramentales where the world appears as a dramatic
figure, Calderón conceives of it differently than did
most of his predecessors who, it will be remembered,
saw the world as a member of the potent evil trium-
virate with the flesh and the Devil. Calderón's El
Mundo assumes a neutral attitude toward man and it is
man who uses the world for good or evil. We will recall El gran teatro del mundo where Mundo serves the
Creator (Autor) and offers itself as the stage upon
which man can play out his role in his passage from
cradle to grave.

As I have stated, in La cura, the four elements
are conceptually and structurally wedded to El Mundo;
always acting in unison, they never oppose one another.
However, there are some poetic lines by El Mundo in
the play which clearly indicate Calderón's subtle
awareness that the elements taken compositely comprise
one world, but taken individually they are opposed to
one another, as for example, fire to water, earth to
air, etc. In one of the instances in which El Mundo
summons the elements onto the stage, he addresses them:

Elementos que la hermosa
máquina del Universo

178

unís unos de otros, siempre
amigos y siempre opuestos. (p. 757)

This baroque conceptualization of the harmonious
and at the same time discordant nature of the four elements which is only verbalized in La cura receives full
dramatization in La vida. Although what I have to say
regarding the four elements and conflict is applicable
to both versions of the auto, for the sake of simplicity
at this point in my study, I wish to refer only to the
more refined refundición of 1673.

The drama begins with an excellent example of
vertical conflict and dissension in the same camp.
Listen as the curtain rises:

> Agua. Mía ha de ser la corona.
> Aire. El laurel ha de ser mío.
> Tierra. No hará mientras yo no muero.
> Fuego. No será mientras yo vivo. (p. 1387)

These explosive opening verses are followed by several
more in which each of the elements argues its case as
to why each alone should have dominion over the world.
The altercation gets so heated that, on stage, in full
view of the audience, "luchan los cuatro":

> Tierra. Con Aire y Agua compito.
> Aire. Yo con el Agua y el Fuego
> que son los dos con quien lidio.
> Agua. Yo con el Aire y la Tierra.
> Fuego. Yo con la Tierra y contigo. (p. 1380)

At this point, while the elements are physically fight-
ing, to add to the confusion that already reigns in
the theater, the stage is inundated with the cacophony
of thunderous voices emanating from behind the scenes.
These are the voices of the three God figures and the
music of the chorus:

> Músic. ¡Agua, Tierra, Fuego, Aire!
> Los Tres. ¡Qué contrariamente unidos!
> Músic. ¡Qué contrariamente unidos!
> Los Tres. ¡Y unidamente contrarios!
> Músic. ¡Y unidamente contrarios!
> Los Tres. En lucha estáis, divididos.

> (p. 1388)

God, allegorized in three figures, enters and

immediately imposes order on the chaos. From then on,
the four elements function in unison and are at the
disposal of both man and the Creator in the manner we
have already witnessed in La cura.

For my second example of vertical conflict in
the Calderonian autos sacramentales, I again turn to
the refundición of La vida es sueño, especially to the
three God figures of the Trinity. Poder, Sabiduría,
and Amor represent respectively the Father, Son, and
Holy Spirit. Returning once again to the first portion of the play, after harmony has been restored to
nature, Poder gets the "Soberana Idea" to create
another creature, this time to his own image and
likeness. In a lengthy discussion among the three
God figures, Poder shares his ideas and the other two
react. Sabiduría, reflecting upon his Father's intentions, forewarns him of certain dangers, predicts
that man will succumb to the Devil, and foresees that
he will have to assume human form to remedy the
situation. Poder, as though he had enough of his
Son's "wetblanket," cuts him off and turns the floor
over to the third member of the family: "Cesa / que
el Amor se ha enternecido" (p. 1391). Amor advises
Poder to go ahead with his plans but to endow man
with reason and the other intellectual faculties, as
well as with the senses. Amor, above all, urges Poder
to let man exercise his own choice in all his actions.
Poder listens attentively to his two Divine counterparts and for a brief moment, hesitates. He appears
undecided. His mind briefly toys with the tragic
possibility that man will end up as his first creature,
another Satan:

> Aquello (vuelvo al discurso)
> la Sabiduría me dijo;
> y esto me dijo el Amor,
> cuando me tenía indeciso
> si en la segunda criatura
> me sucediera lo mismo
> que en la primera. (p. 1391)

But Poder's mind is set; his love is overflowing and
demands regeneration. His hesitation turns into
determination:

> A sacar me determino
> de la prisión de no ser
> a ser este oculto Hijo,

que ya de mi Mente ideado
y de la Tierra nacido,
ha de ser Príncipe vuestro.   (p. 1391)

Later in the play, man, of course, falls and we
see the three God figures coming together for consul-
tation once again. This time the dramatic tension is
extreme. Poder has "to eat crow," for he sees that
man was weak as Sabiduría had forewarned and that he
abused the gifts which he had so generously endowed
man on Amor's recommendation:

¡Oh, Eterna Sabiduría,
bien sus peligros anuncias!
¡Oh, Eterno Amor, mal el Hombre
de tus beneficios usa!   (p. 1400)

Poder burns with a sense of just anger and he is prepared to even the score with man. He condemns man to
a valley of tears and suffering: "Sufra, llore, gima
y sienta" (p. 1400). But God's just attribute must
be balanced with his all-merciful nature. Amor reminds him of this fact:

¿Quién duda
que el Amor siempre es Amor?
y aunque tu sentencia es justa,
también lo es su apelación.   (p. 1401)

At this precise moment, Sabiduría does his part in the
salvation scheme by offering to accept the incarna-
tion, which to him, was inevitable.

In the Spanish allegorical tradition, Calderón
was one of the first to tackle the visualization on
stage of the intricacies of the mysteries associated
with the Roman Catholic dogma of the Trinity.[12]
Prior to Calderón, God the Father, Creator, the first
Person of the Trinity, had been portrayed alone or
together with the Second Person of the Trinity, God
the Son, Redeemer. The ability to undertake such
profound theological mysteries and dare to manipulate
them on stage while, at the same time, to extract the
full dramatic potential of vertical conflict that
these Trinity figures afforded was a gradual process
for Calderón. For example, one other auto, El nuevo
hospicio de los Pobres, written in 1668, contains
the three Trinity figures but never portrays any
dramatic tension among them such as we have seen in
La vida.[13] Even Calderón's first rendition of La vida

181

does not contain the dramatic dialogue and interaction that we have just witnessed in the 1673 version. In fact, the Trinity is not even complete in the manuscript version, for only the traditional Father (Verbo) and the Son (Sabiduría) are present in the play.[14]

Calderón could increase the dramatic intensity of his autos sacramentales over the years only when he became more adept at theology and more secure in his dramatic principles. In previous studies, I have shown that Calderón developed aesthetics for writing his autos.[15] A very high regard for balance symmetry anchored his aesthetic principles.[16] If early he was structuring his plays around only one, two, or three of the religious figures, in later years the complement was completed as he centered his plays around four religious figures, Idolatría, Paganismo, Judaísmo, and Gentilidad; characteristically these four religious figures were accompanied, respectively, by the four continents America, Africa, Asia, and Europe. And so it was with regard to the law figures, Natural (Ley Natural), Written (Ley Escrita) and Divine (Ley Divina); if one or the other was missing in his early attempts at dramatization, the full complement appeared in later works.

With regard to conflict, the same aesthetic principle of balance and symmetry holds true. Long before Milton Marx wrote his The Enjoyment of Drama, Calderón sensed that sides should be even in a play in order to make the action fair and plausible and thus to hold the public's attention. In one of his autos on the Gospel parable of the Sower and the Weeds, La semilla y la cizaña, believed to have been written toward the end of his life in 1678, Calderón created a tightly structured and perfectly symmetrical allegory characteristic of his later years.[17] In this auto, in a manner I have just described, the allegorical figures of the four continents act in relation to their respective religions. The continents are attacked by the four plagues, Weeds (Cizaña), Locust (Ira), North Wind (Cierzo), and Rot (Niebla). The four continents and the four plagues correspond neatly to the four seeds of the Gospel story, each of which falls upon different soils with corresponding results. The point is that the four plagues are pitted against the four poles of the earth, a fair duel of four against four. In one verse of La semilla y la cizaña, Calderón actually gives evidence of his awareness of the need to keep the odds even. In a lengthy

182

passage, Cizaña asks his three evil companions to
unite against the earth's four continents:

> Y así, pues, en cuatro partes
> de la tierra nos avisa
> la letra que ha de caer
> esta Semilla, que, mixta,
> es Semilla y es Palabra,
> y la tierra dividida
> en cuatro partes está
> y somos cuatro las Iras,
> en buen duelo cuatro a cuatro [mine]
> trataremos de destruirla. (p. 590)

In conclusion, Calderón went far beyond the
traditional concept of the "good" versus the "bad"
in the development of his plots. As he became
familiar with the theological nuances embodied in
the mysteries of his Faith, he gradually discovered
possibilities of enhancing his dramatic art. He
began to incorporate into his theater vertical conflict where previously he had not realized its possibility. Occasionally, especially in his later years,
his formulas for dramatic art were directly expressed
in the text of his theater.

Texas Tech University

Notes

[1] *The Enjoyment of Drama* (New York: Appleton-Century Crofts, 1961), p. 21.

[2] *Ibid.*, p. 23.

[3] Leo Rouanet, ed., *Colección de autos, farsas, y coloquios del siglo XVI*, 4 vols. (Madrid: Biblioteca Hispánica, 1901). The classical work on the pre-Calderonian *auto* has been Bruce W. Wardropper's *Introducción al teatro religioso del siglo de oro: Evolución del auto sacramental, 1500-1648* (Madrid: Revista de Occidente, 1958).

[4] *La alegoría en los autos y farsas anteriores a Calderón* (London: Tamesis Books Limited, 1977), p. 46.

[5] For a study of Prudentius' influence on the pre-Calderonian *auto* see "La *Psychomachia* de Prudencio y el teatro alegórico pre-calderoniano," *Neophilologus*, 59 (1975), 48-62.

[6] For an analysis of the development of the protagonist-antagonist relationship in the pre-Calderonian *auto* see Fothergill-Payne's *La alegoría*, chapters 2 and 3, pp. 78-131.

[7] For a thematic classification of Calderón's *autos* see Angel Valbuena Prat, "Los autos sacramentales de Calderón: Clasificación y análisis," *RHi*, 61 (1924), 1-302. See also his edition of the *autos*, *Calderón de la Barca: Obras completas* (Madrid, 1952), III, 32-35. Quotations from the *autos* appearing in this study are made from this edition.

[8] Angel Valbuena Prat (*Obras*, III, 749) sets the date of *La cura* at 1657-58. Harry W. Hilborn in his *A Chronology of Calderón's Plays* (Toronto, 1938), p. 114, dates the *auto* c. 1655-59. Alexander A. Parker in his "Chronology of Calderón's *Autos Sacramentales* from 1647," *HR*, 37 (1969), p. 187, places the *auto* roughly within the same years, 1652-57. All agree as to the date of this version of *La vida*.

[9] The manuscript version of *La vida* appears in Angel Valbuena Prat's edition (*Obras*, III, 1861-75). There is a lot of confusion as to the date of this early version. Valbuena maintains simply that it was

written between Calderón's well known comedia of this same title and the 1673 version (Obras, III, 1859). The comedia appeared in the first edition of the Primera Parte of 1636. Alexander Parker feels that this early version together with El veneno y la triaca and the first version of El divino Orfeo "must all have been written before 1638." See his "The Devil in the Drama of Calderón," in Critical Essays on the Theater of Calderón, ed. by Bruce W. Wardropper (New York University Press, 1965), p. 9, n. 9.

[10] In one other auto, La inmunidad del sagrado, the four elements appear as dramatic personae, but their dramatic roles are very limited. They appear only once at the very end of the play. Angel Valbuena Prat (Obras, III, 1109) and Hilborn (p. 114) give 1664 as the auto's date. Given the minor role of the four elements in this play, I am surprised at the late date attributable to the auto and especially in light of the extensive roles of these same figures in La cura and the first version of La vida, both of which supposedly have earlier dates. Characteristically, Calderón took great care to integrate his dramatic personages into every phase of his plot; this is especially true of those plays of his later period after 1660. See my book, The Auto Sacramental and the Parable in the Spanish Golden Age Literature (Chapel Hill: The University of North Carolina Press, 1973), especially pp. 186-193.

[11] Edward M. Wilson, "The Four Elements in the Imagery of Calderón," MLR, 31 (1936), 34-47; Donald T. Dietz, "Toward Understanding Calderón's Evolution As an Auto Dramatist: A Study in Dramatic Structure" in Studies in Honor of Ruth Lee Kennedy (Chapel Hill: Estudios Hispanófila, 1977), pp. 51-55 especially.

[12] Sister M. Francis de Sales McGarry discusses Calderón's treatment of Divine Persons, God the Father, and God the Son, in her The Allegorical and Metaphorical Language in the "Autos Sacramentales" of Calderón (Washington, D.C.: The Catholic University of America, 1937), p. 38. McGarry does not even recognize the fact that Calderón attempted to visualize the Trinity by presenting all three persons on the stage. One of the more profound mysteries of the Trinity is described in theological terms as "intelligible immanation." For a discussion of how Calderón dramatized this doctrine see my The "Auto Sacramental" and the Parable, p. 154.

[13] For a structural study of El nuevo hospicio see my The "Auto Sacramental" and the Parable, pp. 153-158.

[14] For a structural study of the two versions of La vida see my article, "Calderón's Evolution," especially pp. 51-54.

[15] See my The "Auto Sacramental" and the Parable, pp. 186-193; also see my article, "Calderón's Evolution," pp. 54-55.

[16] Two landmark studies on symmetry and balance in Calderonian theater are Lucien-Paul Thomas, "Les jeux de scène et l'architecture des idées dans le théâtre allegorique de Calderón," in Homenaje a Menéndez Pelayo, II, 501-520; Dámaso Alonso, "La correlación en la estructura del teatro calderoniano" in Seis calas en la expressión literaria española (Madrid: Gredos, 1963), pp. 111-175.

[17] For a detailed structural analysis of this play see my The "Auto Sacramental" and the Parable, pp. 98-107.

Theme and Metaphor in the <u>Auto</u> <u>Historial:</u>

Calderón's <u>Los</u> <u>encantos</u> <u>de</u> <u>la</u> <u>Culpa</u>

J. Richards LeVan

Despite the general appreciation we have today for the literary theory behind Calderón's <u>autos</u>, readers of the <u>autos</u> have been remiss in putting that theory to use as an instrument of analysis. As a result, the allegories are sometimes misunderstood or simply dismissed. For two reasons, this is especially true, I think, of the <u>autos</u> based on well-known stories. One, because the reader is familiar with the story from a different context, he is likely to have preconceived notions about the theme, and two, because he is often not familiar enough with the allegorical method by which the play was constructed, he is likely to seek the meaning of the <u>auto</u> in its external plot. Calderón developed a special technique to enable himself to use familiar old stories to express new themes. Apparently, he experimented first with "historical" subjects taken from the Bible and Church or Spanish history--hence the term <u>auto</u> <u>historial</u>.[1] For purposes of critical analysis, however, this category of <u>autos</u> may be broadened to include mythological fables as well, because in allegorizing well-known plots, whether "historical" or fictitious, Calderón utilized the same technique. The reader of an <u>auto</u> <u>historial</u> who overlooks the nature of this technique and fails to use the allegorical form to discipline his analysis, will arrive at only a partial understanding of the play.

<u>Los</u> <u>encantos</u> <u>de</u> <u>la</u> <u>Culpa</u>, an <u>auto</u> which dramatizes the Homeric fable of Circe and Ulysses, offers a fine example of the technique of the <u>auto</u> <u>historial</u>.[2] Calderón's two earlier <u>comedias</u> on the Circe story are both disappointing because Circe and Ulysses' morally stigmatized romance did not make for convincing drama when treated as a love theme.[3] But on the allegorical stage of the Corpus Christi festival, the Circe fable became the vehicle for a moral investigation of much greater import. <u>Los</u> <u>encantos</u> <u>de</u> <u>la</u> <u>Culpa</u> illustrates the role played by the Eucharist in reversing the damaging effects of anxiety on mental and spiritual health. The originality of this theme, so distinct from the conflict of sensuality and moral duty traditionally associated with the fable, is achieved by

means of a system of analogies in which the key elements of the fable, including its thematic conflict, function as metaphors pointing beyond themselves to express an abstract scheme of a wholly different order. The sensuality motif of the fable becomes a metaphor for the seductive charms of sin, and the action depicts not a torrid love story but a psychological conflict in which the human will is ironically enticed into sin by appeals to its natural desire for good. Lust is not singled out here for moral condemnation as a vice per se, for it too functions in a metaphorical sense: sin seduces the will by twisting its love of good into a perverted "lust for life."

As the title suggests, this system of analogies is built upon a single, basic metaphor which links the theological concept of sin with the story's principal narrative element, enchantment. The correspondence between "culpa" and "encanto" is precise, yet manifold in its implications. First of all, in this fable "enchantment" means "transformation"; sin is the corruption or "transformation" of man's inner nature. Secondly, enchantment is a magical enslavement from which the victim can be freed only through an equally supernatural antidote, just as man is liberated from slavery to sin by divine grace. Thirdly, the word "encanto," in its plural form, is used in Spanish to denote the seductive charms of a beautiful woman: in other words, sin is somehow inherently attractive to man. And furthermore, encanto in Calderón's time was an equivalent for apariencia or engaño, a falsification of reality by supernatural means.[4] Especially in the seventeenth century, sin and moral disorder were held to be results of the inability to distinguish appearance from reality. The fundamental analogy between the story as a metaphor and Calderón's theme extends therefore to the allegory's portrayal of Christian salvation. Man's dis-enchantment from sin must begin with des-engaño. Viewed as metaphor, Ulysses' release from Circe's spell corresponds perfectly to neo-Stoic moral philosophy, although desengaño can only initiate man's liberation from sin. The magical counter-charm to sin's power is the grace, imparted through the Eucharist, which brings about a "retransformation" of man's inner being, known in theological terms as justification, "the sanctification and renewal of the inward man."[5] As the allegory's fundamental analogy, the enchantment metaphor establishes a natural and convincing correspondence between the overall scope of the theme and its figurative vehicle, the Circe fable.[6]

In constructing an allegory, as A. A. Parker has
shown, Calderón first conceived his theme in terms of
imaginative thought pictures--conceptos imaginados--
which form the core of an auto's argumento.7 In the
auto historial, the conceptos imaginados function as
leitmotifs, permeating the poetic language of the dialogue and adapting the plot, characters and setting
of a known story to the new theme. Constant in meaning, though shifting in form, these images relate every
event back to the overriding conceptual framework. The
dramatic conflict is thus redefined and the action becomes metaphor. The spectator must look through the
figurative action to perceive the logic of the theme
unravelling within.

The theme of Los encantos derives from one of St.
Augustine's sermons based on a passage from the Gospel
of Matthew (14:24-33).8 In the Gospel narrative, Peter
steps from a boat in which the disciples are crossing
a lake during rough weather, and attempts to join
Jesus, who walked out from shore. Peter takes a few
steps but is seized by fear; he begins to sink and
finally cries out to Jesus for help. Interpreting
the episode, St. Augustine remarks that men naturally
call out to God in fear when confronting the storms of
"this life's adversity," and he continues by warning
his listeners that in times of peace and security,
when the "smile of temporal happiness" blinds men to
their need of God, they must seek to remain aware of
that need by discovering a storm within: "See if there
be no inner wind which overturns thee." Augustine's
straightforward insights into the relationships between fear, faith, false security and sin served Calderón as a basis for illustrating the psychological
functions of the Eucharist.

Calderón's conceptos imaginados echo the familiar
Christian motifs of Augustine's sermon: the opening
scene of the play introduces el Hombre tossed about on
the stormy sea of life, seeking a safe harbor for his
fragile, defenseless ship. El Hombre is a voyager
accompanied by a crew of five Senses and by Entendimiento, the pilot of "aquesta humana nave." Acknow-
ledging the metaphorical nature of the storm, el Hombre
alludes to biblical commentators like Augustine to
clarify this concepto imaginado for the audience:

> En el texto sagrado
> cuantas veces las aguas se han nombrado,
> tantos doctos varones

        las suelen traducir tribulaciones,
        con que la humana vida
        navega zozobrada y sumergida.   (25-30)

Tribulation has two meanings. It can refer both to
external adversities and to the internal suffering
which accompanies them. Thus when man seeks a harbor
he has two options: to find a seguro puerto where
there are, ostensibly, no external adversities, or to
find a feliz puerto of inner peace and serenity which
can ensure safe passage through any storm which may
arise. Entendimiento, advocating the latter, encourages
the sailors to continue their appeals to heaven:

        Todos.   ¡Piedad, Cielos!

        Entend.   Si los llamáis, serenidades crea
                    vuestro temor cobarde, y que no sea
                    este bajel, que en piélagos se mueve,
                    sepulcro de cristal, tumba de nieve,
                    que el Cielo a humildes voces
                        siempre abierto
                    al náufrago piloto es feliz puerto.

                                        56-62)

The sea then calms, and as the threatening storm passes,
the crisis of el Hombre's spirit is resolved in peace
and renewed hope. Moments later, however, a mountain
island appears on the horizon and el Hombre's spirit
soars as he directs his ship to the deceptive safety
of this port of tangible, worldly security.

    This opening scene introduces the conceptos
imaginados--the voyager, the ship, the storm, the
harbor--and these establish the auto's dramatic conflict: man must choose his puerto. The nautical
imagery fixes the thematic vocabulary and serves as a
backdrop against which the action is to be interpreted. Thus, when the sailors are transformed into
beasts, el Hombre suffers a nightmarish "tormenta"
(481), which ends, after his repentance, with the
entrance of Penitencia under a rainbow, bringing peace
of mind and restoring his hope and courage. La Culpa,
as though competing with Penitencia, welcomes el Hombre
to her "seguro puerto" (566) and urges him to escape
future storms by seeking protection in her "noble
asilo . . . blando albergue y feliz puerto" (579-80).
The use of recurrent images like these has the effect
of taking the audience's vision off the stage action,

as a story, and refocusing it on the interplay of
concepts set forth in the introductory scene.

Calderón conceived the theme of Los encantos
wholly in psychological terms. This is not one of
the autos which dramatize theological dogma. The
action, characters and conceptual imagery together
constitute, as a metaphor, the sphere of a single
mind.9 In watching the play, the audience observes
the mental processes which occur as an individual falls
into sin and subsequently finds release from it. The
storm images depict fear and inner tribulation; the
harbor, hope and peace; and the ship, which moves in
water while driven by air, the hybrid nature of the
human psyche, part spirit, part body (i.e., the
senses). The metaphorical sense of el Hombre's role
as the play's protagonist can best be understood in
terms of a single psychic faculty. Cast as Ulysses,
a voyager, lover, and master of craftiness, el Hombre
feels and does as a character on stage what the will
feels and does as a faculty in the soul. The will
desires good and well-being and, like the shrewd
Ulysses, uses clever deceptions to avoid harm or
evil.10 But el Hombre uses his cautelas and astucias
primarily to outwit his own Entendimiento, and this
pinpoints the will as the culprit behind man's engaño,
his inner self-deception. Furthermore, the will's
desire is love and it should therefore seek union with
God, the absolute good. Since the relationship between
man and God is often expressed as a covenant of marriage,
the will is like Ulysses in that its duty is to remain
faithful to a distant spouse. To do otherwise is to
engage in harlotry, an image used by Old Testament
prophets to condemn the Hebrews for the worship of
false idols.11 In this allegory, Circe's promiscuity
is therefore not primarily sexual: it is a metaphor
for the will's degenerate love of a false god. And
thus, in a song celebrating her queen's triumph,
Lascivia identifies the idol of el Hombre's sinful
devotion:

> Si quieres gozar florida
> edad entre dulce suerte
> olvídate de la Muerte
> y acuérdate de la Vida.   (1073-1076)

The "passion" in conflict with man's duty to love God
is not the body's sexual lust but the will's "lust for
life." Man sins when he turns his love toward life as

an end in itself, when his will seeks life, not God, as the highest good.

In conjunction with its Eucharistic theme, Los encantos demonstrates the manner in which the fear of death can be "transformed" by moral desengaño and divine grace into a positive spiritual force within man's psyche.[12] Beneath the tribulations of everyday life lies a pervasive anxiety, an awareness of the threat of death, which can be only partially allayed by the hopes men mistakenly place in worldly forms of security. The psychological pressures which influence man to choose worldly life as a harbor for his deeply-rooted fears and sense of vulnerability are the "charms of sin" which the Circe allegory exposes. But the allegory also manifests the psychological process through which the irrational effects of man's fear can be reversed, and a disenchantment effectuated. First, echoing Augustine's advice ("See if there be no inner wind which overturns thee"), desengaño works through the memory, frightening the will with the spectre of death and shattering the hopes inspired by the "smile of temporal happiness"; and second, divine grace works through the Eucharist, infusing in man the theological virtue of hope and the Real Presence of God, thus transforming the fragile "humana nave" into "la nave de la Iglesia" (1257-8), the Body of Christ. Anchored to hope in "el puerto de Hostia" (1303), man is invulnerable to the threat of death and its anxiety.

Recent studies of Los encantos de la Culpa have overlooked this psychological theme because of an imperfect recognition of the auto's technique, the manner in which certain conceptual images combine to set forth a theme and then govern the adaptation of a metaphorical historia to it.[13] Hans Flasche, whose study is by far the most perceptive, rightly emphasizes the importance of the nautical metaphors--the mariner, ship, storm, and port--and explains that their recurrence throughout the play determines the thematic substructure of the action.[14] Nevertheless, rather than interpret these fundamental images as they relate to each other on a conceptual level, he reads them as separate allusions to traditional Christian symbolism. This method leads him, for instance, to interpret the "feliz puerto" metaphor as Rome. Calderón may indeed have intended a witty reference to this symbolic city (whose ocean port is in fact named Ostia). But more significantly, "el puerto de Hostia" here depicts a state of the soul in which man is transformed through the

Eucharist from a threatened, fear-ridden individual into an invulnerable member of Christ's Body, the collective Church. In his analysis of the "love" scene in Circe's garden, Flasche correctly analyzes a conceptista image comparing Circe to dawn, the common factors being the seductive power of natural beauty, the beauty of woman and the charm of sin. But again, because he does not relate these images to the thematic conceptos, his analysis does not point out that what dawn suggests to el Hombre--and what sin offers man--is the promise of life. The hope-inspiring countenance of dawn is the "smile of temporal happiness" about which Augustine warned his listeners centuries before. Two conceits describing the human ship, "sin escamas delfín, cisne sin plumas" (82), prove enigmatic to Flasche. Alluding to traditional Christian iconography, he suggests that the dolphin may symbolize Christ, but in fact the conceits signal man's helplessness in the face of the tormentas of his existence. Though man is partly a spiritual being, he cannot return directly to his celestial home; like a swan without feathers, he cannot fly but must voyage across the seas of the physical world. Dolphins, superb swimmers famous in legend for rescuing drowning sailors, were taken by mariners to be a sign of approaching storms; yet man is a dolphin that cannot swim ("sin escamas") and save even himself. Fully at home in neither of the two worlds he inhabits, out of his element both as a spiritual and physical being, man lives an existence in which mortal threat is an inescapable fact. And like a swan, therefore, he senses the approach of death and, defenseless, can only "sing," crying out like el Hombre's crew, "¡Piedad, Cielos!" Man, "sin escamas delfín, cisne sin plumas," is a creature of anxiety. Because Flasche stops just short of fitting all the images together, Calderón's most penetrating insights go largely undetected. The tormenta, as Flasche recognizes, is an inner struggle and man's deceptions are indeed signs of moral weakness; viewed together, however, the metaphors help explain why men sin: both tormenta and cautela point to vulnerability and fear as primary causes of sin.

James Maraniss, in his book On Calderón, speaks of the "chesslike ease" with which Calderón manipulates his conceptos imaginados, but in studying Los encantos he does not identify them or question their significance.[15] For him Calderón's "playing with fixed fancies . . . conveys, above all, an unwillingness or inability to deal successfully with the problems of living in time."[16] And yet, in Los encantos, Calderón does precisely what Maraniss holds he is unable or unwilling to do. Calderón's concern was that man's mental stability, his rationality and faith are gravely undermined by anxieties and fears provoked by the setbacks of everyday life: the threats of illness, financial disaster, personal loss, social disgrace, death (189-198). Addressing the crisis of faith in the individual who succumbs to fear during his "walk" over the stormy waters of life, St. Augustine reminded his congregation to call on the Lord, as Peter did: "[I]f thou totter, if some things there are which thou canst not overcome, if thou begin to sink, say, Lord, I perish, save me." Calderón's allegory of the Circe fable celebrates Corpus Christi by studying that psychic crisis and by dramatizing the power of the Eucharist, as an instrument of grace, to sustain man's hope as he wrestles with the conflicts of his existence.

University of Texas, Austin

[1]See A. A. Parker, The Allegorical Drama of Calderón: An Introduction to the "Autos Sacramentales"
(Oxford and London: Dolphin Book Co., 1943), pp.
160-164.

[2]Los encantos de la Culpa, Obras completas: Autos
Sacramentales, III, ed. Angel Valbuena Prat (Madrid:
Aguilar, 1952), pp. 405-421. References to the text
will be given in parentheses by line number following
Valbuena's Clásicos Castellanos edition, Calderón de
la Barca: Autos Sacramentales (1972; 5th rpt.,
Madrid: Espasa-Calpe, 1967), II, pp. 69-114. Valbuena's interpretation of Los encantos (see the prologue to the Clásicos Castellanos text, II, pp. lix-
lx) is incorrect because he bases his reading on the
Circe comedia, El mayor encanto, Amor; the plots being
so similar, he assumes the themes are also and perceives in the auto no abstract level of meaning.
Valbuena, following Cotarelo, suggests 1649 as the
auto's probable date, but its style and technique
indicate that 1636-40 is a far more likely conjecture.

[3]Polifemo y Circe (1629), a collaboration with
Mira de Amescua and Pérez de Montalbán, Biblioteca
de Autores Espanoles, XIV, 413-428. And El mayor
encanto, Amor (1635), BAE, VII, 390-410.

[4]See "encantador" and "encantamento" in the Diccionario de Autoridades (Madrid: Editorial Gredos,
1963).

[5]Canons and Decrees of the Council of Trent,
trans. H. J. Schoeder (St. Louis: Herder, 1941), p. 33.

[6]Cf. Parker, pp. 81-82.

[7]Parker, pp. 72-82.

[8]Sermo LXXVI, Patrologiae Latinae, ed. J.-P.
Migne, XXXVIII (Paris: Migne, 1865), columns 479-483.
English quotations taken from Sermon XXVI, Sermons on
Selected Lessons of the New Testament by S. Augustine,
Bishop of Hippo, a Library of Fathers of the Holy
Catholic Church, Anterior to the Division of East and
West, trans. Members of the English Church, I (Oxford:
Parker and Rivington, 1844), p. 220.

[9]Cf. Parker, p. 164, concerning the prototype of the auto historial, La cena de Baltasar. In Los encantos, Penitencia and Culpa represent states of the soul, and their influence on the action illustrates the mental processes and attitudes which correspond to penitence and sin, respectively. Likewise, the Vices (Circe's handmaidens) are "habits" of mind (in the Aristotelian sense).

[10]In a brilliant flash of agudeza, Calderón found in Ulysses' resourceful cunning two parallels to the nature of the will. First, like Ulysses, the will is "cauteloso" (34), that is, ever-watchful for signs of danger and always prepared to outmaneuver it with some stratagem. Second, to save itself, the will may resort, if necessary, to "astucias" (31), that is, engaños. In other words, the will's aversion to evil--its fear of death--foments its resistance to the voice of reason (which would remind it of death) and incites its acceptance of false, misplaced hopes. See "astucia" and "cautela" in the Diccionario de Autoridades.

[11]See Jeremiah ch. 3; Ezekiel chs. 16, 23.

[12]Cf. Otis Green, Spain and the Western Tradition: The Castilian Mind in Literature from "El Cid" to Calderón (Madison: Univ. of Wisconsin Press, 1966), IV, p. 77, n. 1: "Both Quevedo and Terrones del Cano are arguing in favor of a culture of death which is a conception of man and his earthly existence wherein the awareness of death functions as a positive sign; it is a stimulus, not a hindrance, to living and acting, and it makes possible an understanding of the full and total meaning of life." And Parker, p. 106, n. 18: "Calderón accepts the Augustinian but non-Thomistic conception of memory as a power of the soul, and makes it appear as a dramatic character alongside of the understanding and the will. But he cannot dramatize the Augustinian definition of it, and therefore gives it a new (and dramatically most important) significance for which the scholastic systems offer no philosophical justification. It appears as the character that directs man's thoughts to God by means of 'acuerdos mortales' (the thought of death) and thus makes of the memory a spiritual power by means of which God enlightens the mind in a special way." In Los encantos the memory operates more as an emotional stimulus than as an intellectual "sign." Here Calderón reveals that the memory's spiritual power derives

196

from its ability to marshall the passion of fear in
the service of reason and bring it to bear on the will:
memory stimulates desengaño by literally frightening
the will.

[13]Studying "La correlación en el teatro calderoniano," Dámaso Alonso, in Seis calas en la expresión
literaria española, 3rd ed. (Madrid: Gredos, 1963),
does not look beyond the sensuality theme, and over-
emphasizing the role of the five senses, he seriously
distorts the dualistic structure of the play: "La
pluralidad pentamembre es el verdadero fundamento y
punto de arranque de toda la obra. . ." (p. 140).
Delfín Garasa, in "Circe en la literature española
del Siglo de Oro," Boletín de la Academia Argentina
de Letras, Buenos Aires, 19 (1964), 228-271, calls
the allegory transparent and reads it as a comedia a
lo divino, finding only the conventional theme.

[14]Die Struktur des Auto Sacramental "Los encantos
de la Culpa" (Köln: Westdeutscher Verlag, 1968).

[15]On Calderón (Columbia, Missouri: University of
Missouri Press, 1978), pp. 18-28.

[16]Maraniss, p. 28. With respect to its theme
Maraniss sees little more in Los encantos than the
illustration of certain articles of faith and dogma
(reflecting the fable's traditional moralization),
and thus he says," [T]he play presents no really
difficult conflict. . ." (p. 22). Actually, however,
the play dramatizes the divisive contention in man's
psyche between his passionate affirmation of life and
his fearful awareness of death. El Hombre cries:

> En dos mitades estoy,
> partido (¡pasión tirana!)
> entre el horror de mañana,
> y la ventura de hoy. (1123-6)

The conflict is so difficult, in fact, that it cannot
be completely resolved; even in his triumphant exit,
el Hombre looks back with yearning to Culpa's en-
chanted island (1317-20). Cf. Parker, pp. 192-3.

Adjetivación y dramatización en un

auto sacramental calderoniano

Hans Flasche

No se ha analizado todavía la relación entre
adjetivación y dramatización en la obra de Calderón.
Esperamos que la disquisición siguiente sirva al
conocimiento de la correspondencia en cuestión en
el auto "La Vida es Sueño." El Diccionario de la
Real Academia Española define el concepto de la adjetivación con las palabras "Acción de adjetivar o
adjetivarse" y dice que el verbo "adjetivar" significa
"aplicar adjetivos." En cuanto al término "dramatización" hay que pensar, según el diccionario citado,
en la "acción y efecto de dramatizar." El verbo
"dramatizar" se refiere al acto de "dar forma y condiciones dramáticas." Después de haber dado estas
explicaciones es necesario poner en claro la palabra
"drama." La acción dramática presupone tensión y
lucha, especialmente en el hombre que constituye el
centro de lo que pasa. El drama calderoniano, famoso
por su concentración, presenta a un hombre que deja
ver, durante un espacio de tiempo de corta o larga
duración la oposición entre vida terrenal y vida
futura.

Resulta enormemente difícil formarse un juicio
sobre las ideas de Calderón relativas a la importancia
de la adjetivación el el drama. Creemos, sin embargo,
que es posible apreciar la intención del artista de
hacer patente su tema gracias al análisis de ciertas
formas de adjetivación.

Las opiniones referentes a la importancia del
adjetivo en el texto de una obra literaria son dis-
crepantes. El lingüista inglés Weekly escribió en
1931: "Tal vez el adjetivo sea la parte menos
esencial de la oración." En su "Arte Poética"
Vicente Huidobro acentuó el papel del adjetivo
diciendo: "El adjetivo, cuando no da vida, mata."
El dictamen sobre el alcance del adjetivo depende
naturalmente de las perspectivas del crítico. El
crítico literario que no se orienta únicamente sobre
los valores lingüísticos, considerando sin embargo la
lengua como uno de los ingredientes más relevantes del
texto, tandrá sin duda alguna el adjetivo por un
elemento constitutivo del drama.

Para poder examinar el adjetivo en "La Vida es Sueño" es imprescindible caracterizarlo brevemente como parte de la oración. Distinguimos entre adjetivos calificativos y determinativos. Considerando los adjetivos determinativos, la lingüística moderna prefiere el término "no calificativo." "Azul" es un adjetivo calificativo, "este" un adjetivo no-calificativo. En el dominio de los adjetivos calificativos distinguimos entre adjetivos derivados de un substantivo que determina el uso, y los adjetivos no derivados. Pensemos en la palabra "azul" por una parte, en la palabra "prodigioso" (tan frecuente en la obra calderoniana) por otra. Según el Diccionario de Autoridades, "prodigioso" significa una cosa "que incluye en sí prodigio" y también "excelente, primoroso y exquisito."

Examinaremos en esta conferencia tan sólo los adjetivos añadidos a substantivos, a saber, los adjetivos caracterizadores que podemos llamar, como lo hace el Diccionario de Autoridades, también "epitetos." (Este término deriva del substantivo "ἡ ἐπίθεσις ") No tenemos la intención de incluir el participio, que ocupa una posición entre el verbo y el adjetivo.

En cuanto al significado, los lingüistas conocen muchas posibilidades de diferenciación. Es imposible enumerarlas en esta comunicación. Tocante al lenguaje calderoniano, nos parece muy útil separar adjetivos que designan cualidades evidentes de otros que se refieren a cualidades que no se sobreentienden. Encontramos en la obra de Calderón, que queremos analizar, la yuxtaposición "vejez caduca" y la secuencia "letal sueño." Sería objeto de un estudio especial verificar la frecuencia de las dos maneras de proceder.

Tan sólo una única lectura de nuestro auto sacramental deja ver que Calderón se sirve del adjetivo en grandes proporciones. Hacemos constar en su texto lo que podríamos llamar densidad, concentración, frondosidad o proximidad de adjetivos. Todavía no podemos afirmar que "La Vida es Sueño," obra tardía de Calderón, tiene un rango particular. En la obra literaria de Racine el número de adjetivos aumenta a partir de "Andromaque" hasta "Esther" (exceptuando "Iphigénie").

El juicio sobre la anteposición o posposición del adjetivo es una de las tareas más difíciles, y apenas realizable satisfactoriamente sin previos y extensos estudios con que se enfrenta el investigador. Según la opinión de Hayward Keniston ("The Syntax of Castilian Prose"), la posposición significa insistencia en una cualidad característica del substantivo; la anteposición, reacción de la sensibilidad del hablante o del autor. En cuanto a Calderón esta distinción no vale en todos los casos. Además hay que añadir que muchas veces es muy difícil tomar una resolución respecto al efecto de querer acentuar mediante la anteposición o la posposición.

Como en estudios anteriores, rechazamos en esta conferencia toda hipótesis que explique la posición del adjetivo por la necesidad de tomar en consideración cualquier analogía métrica. La maestría de Calderón está por encima de tales reflexiones y cálculos.

Para llegar a unas conclusiones definitivas en el sector de la adjetivación, especialmente respecto al valor de cada adjetivo en una acumulación de epítetos, sería imprescindible tener en cuenta la puntuación. Pero el estado actual de la investigación no nos permite manifestar una opinión satisfactoria, porque precisamente la puntuación de los manuscritos y de las ediciones encierra todavía muchos misterios.

Examinando ahora el texto del auto sacramental queremos aclarar los pasajes que llaman la atención del oyente y del lector actual. Durante la lucha relativa a la primacía de los elementos, el Agua dice a sus tres compañeros: ". . . si sobre las aguas / el Espíritu divino / de Dios es llevado, al Agua / debéis los demás rendiros. /" En conformidad con la fórmula muy frecuente "Espíritu Santo," el adjetivo caracterizador "divino" se encuentra, en el reparo del elemento acalorado, después del substantivo. En virtud del empleo de dos palabras relativas a Dios ("el Espíritu divino / de Dios es llevado . . .") el Agua intenta crear el fundamento que sirva a su reivindicación.

La repetición del adjetivo constituye una de las maneras de proceder más importantes de nuestro autor. La Sabiduría, segunda persona de la Santísima Trinidad, pone de relieve la cordura de la primera persona diciendo: ". . . el Sumo Poder / a los cuatro (sc. elementos) ha dividido, / mantenidos en igual / balanza, igual equilibrio;/" El encabalgamiento fortifica la repetición, contribuyendo así a aumentar la atención del oyente. Se ilustra la igualdad en cuestión por la posición del adjetivo al final del verso, por el encabalgamiento, por la repetición y por la anteposición doble del adjetivo. Prescindiendo de todo esto, el término "equilibrio" ya contiene el elemento "igualdad."

Muchas veces las personas hablantes en el drama manifiestan lo que quieren acentuar por medio de la acumulación de adjetivos diferentes. En virtud de este procedimiento el artista Calderón produce una intensificación del contenido del substantivo. Encontramos uno de los ejemplos más característicos en el discurso de la Sabiduría. Dice refiriéndose a la Tierra: "los hombres descubra, en quien / descanse el grave, el prolijo / peso de tanto eminente / universal edificio./" Las palabras antepuestas "grave" y "prolijo" constituyen una apreciación expresamente subjetiva de los atributos peculiares del peso. Debido al enlazamiento inmediato de un substantivo acompañado por dos adjetivos el poeta-filósofo enseña lo imponente del mundo corpóreo.

Delante de uno de los cuatro adjetivos intencionadamente antepuestos, Calderón coloca el adverbio "tanto." Se le puede caracterizar en muchos versos como elemento que da impulso a la adjetivación. Las párticulas "tan(to)," "más," "muy" y "no" no tienen influencia en la posición del adjetivo. Por lo tanto se comprende fácilmente que en nuestro texto el número de los adjetivos antepuestos e introducidos por "tan" es más o menos igual al de los adjetivos introducidos por "tan" y pospuestos.

Oyendo o leyendo las palabras pronunciadas por la tercera persona de la Santísima Trinidad (llamada "El Amor") relativas a la Tierra ". . . en quien, / ya familiares, ya esquivos, / diversos brutos habiten, /" echamos de ver una manera de expresión calderoniana todavía no descubierta. La combinación del empleo predicativo y atributivo, la intercalación reiterada del adverbio "ya," la reasunción de dos adjetivos predicativos por un adjetivo atributivo ("diversos") confieren a la descripción una extraordinaria viveza.

A pesar de la elección de epítetos sencillos y muchas veces usados, la anteposición, por una parte, y el paralelismo de los versos por otra, dan brillo dramático al comienzo de un discurso de la persona alegórica El Poder: "Gran corte del universo, /

leales vasallos míos,/.

Es absolutamente natural que el autor dramático
inserte en los razonamientos de carácter teológico--y
en nuestro texto se trata de razonamientos de este
género--palabras llenas de significación transcendental.
El Príncipe de las Tinieblas recibe el "eterno castigo"
merecido. El Poder anuncia el proyecto de la creación
del hombre diciendo: ". . . mi eterna / Sabiduría me
dijo . . . /." Esta declaración inmediatamente ex-
tendida y desplegada por la Sabiduría ("Yo, que sé
todas las ciencias") es enormemente dramática en tanto
que la unidad de las tres personas divinas queda
determinada como unidad que dura por el espacio de
la eternidad. Esta unidad caracterizada por la palabra "eterno" se pone en evidencia, de un lado, gracias
a la referencia doble a la persona hablante ("mi eterna
/ Sabiduría me dijo"), y de otro, debido a la continuación inmediata del discurso realizado por la Sabiduría. Queremos mencionar aquí que los adjetivos calderonianos se ofrecen en el pasaje citado y en muchos
otros, no sólo como adjetivos plásticos, inherentes,
ornamentales, objetivos, sino también como adjetivos
temáticamente importantes que acentúan al mismo tiempo
una apreciación subjetiva. Por lo demás estos adjetivos se refieren muchas veces a la esfera de la
religión. Dios, que es ya eterno por definición
implícita, aparece según la voluntad del hablante
como Dios eterno. Creemos que es lícito decir en
sentido inverso que el dominio de la religión se
traduce lingüísticamente a menudo y en gran escala
en expresiones adjetivas.

El lenguaje de las personas divinas en el teatro
calderoniano se caracteriza también por su majestuosi-
dad. La notamos en el discurso de la Sabiduría que
invita a admirar "todo ese azul zafiro." En esta
advertencia lo majestuoso se produce en virtud de la
yuxtaposición de la palabra adjetival "todo," gracias
al demostrativo "ese," debido al epíteto que designa
un color y, finalmente, a consecuencia de la mención
de una piedra preciosa que ya en los libros bíblicos
es símbolo del cielo.

La terminología calderoniana relativa a los
colores y en la cual hasta ahora nadie ha reparado es
muy abundante. En "La Vida es Sueño" se nos deparan
diecinueve nombres de colores (diecisiete adjetivos
y dos participios). Aun cuando se trata de cualidades
inherentes, Calderón prefiere la anteposición,

probablemente motivado por la acción y el deseo de
acentuar. Tomando como base de un verso la incor-
poración adjetival, el dramaturgo desea subrayar la
relación entre el color y el hablante. El adjetivo
comprende la sensación, la presencia personal y
afectiva del contemplador.

Calderón llega a una dramatización especial en
virtud de su uso variable del adjetivo y la concate-
nación simultánea con técnicas lingüístico-estilísti-
cas. Citemos como ejemplo algunas palabras de la
Sabiduría que ponen la mira en la eternidad divina:
"yo, para quien el presente / tiempo solamente es
fijo, / pues si miro hacia el pasado, / y si hacia
el futuro miro, / es tiempo presente todo, / futuro
o pasado siglo;/." Esta aclaración deja ver, y en
varios respectos, que el tiempo se ofrece a Dios
únicamente como tiempo presente. El adjetivo "presente," que se encuentra al final de la primera línea,
reunido por el encabalgamiento con la palabra "tiempo"
en el verso siguiente, recibe un acento tan intenso
que no es posible desconsiderarlo. El quiasmo formado
por la tercera y la cuarta línea prepara el quinto
verso. En el la secuencia "presente tiempo" se convierte en "tiempo presente." Esta transformación
llama la atención sobre el adjetivo "presente" que,
según la intención del autor dramático, debe ser caracterizado como cualidad constitutiva en el razonamiento de la persona divina. En "La Vida es Sueño"
Calderón se sirve veinte y una veces del encabalgamiento que acabamos de mencionar, a saber del encabalgamiento que, dramatizando, pone de relieve una
palabra o un pensamiento.

Evidentemente el actor dramático hace mucho
efecto si se vale de varios procedimientos retóricos.
Ocurre esto cuando Calderón reúne el encabalgamiento,
la triplicación de la construcción sintáctica y la
acumulación de adjetivos antepuestos que siguen el
mismo rumbo. Respecto a la creación del hombre por
la omnipotencia divina leemos: ". . . si del lóbrego
seno / de la tierra, el duro silo / de sus entrañas,
el ciego / vientre de su oscuro limbo / ... / ... /
... / ... / la sacan a luz . . . /." Es un hecho
incontestable que la idea de la salida del hombre de
la oscuridad (idea frecuente en la obra calderoniana)
se introduce muy claramente por las palabras "lóbrego,"
"duro," "ciego" y "oscuro" y, naturalmente, los substantivos respectivos.

Le importa al dramaturgo que una cualidad salga tan distintamente que el espectador pueda aquilatarla en su alcance referente a los sentidos. Compruébalo la substitución de la combinación adjetivo-substantivo (o substantivo-adjetivo) por "lo" y adjetivo. El Fuego es caracterizado por la expresión "lo brillante," el Aire por "lo lucido," el Agua por "lo prodigioso" y la Tierra por "lo rico." En esta ponencia nos limitamos a analizar la yuxtaposición substantivo-adjetivo. Por lo tanto no podemos entrar en los pormenores de la composición "lo y adjetivo."

Sin tener en cuenta las maneras ya mencionadas de emplear el adjetivo (especialmente en armonía con los diálogos dramáticos llenos de convicción) tenemos el deber de examinar muchas otras. El Poder exterioriza su intención de crear al hombre y llevarle al paraíso de la forma siguiente: "hoy del damasceno campo / a un hermoso alcázar rico / ... / ... / le trasladaré . . ./." Por medio de un adjetivo antepuesto y otro pospuesto, el esplendor del alcázar confrontado con el campo damasceno se manifiesta como un regalo de la gracia divina. Calderón presta viva atención a la práctica de los adjetivos circundantes. No se trata de un encarecimiento repetitivo, sino de un encarecimiento intensificativo. La intensificación se reconoce con toda claridad gracias al hecho de que el artista continúa describiendo el lugar ya determinado por dos adjetivos circundantes. Dice el Poder: ". . . a oposición de azul cielo / será verde paraíso,/." Establece por lo tanto un paralelo entre la hermosura del paraíso y el cielo. La anteposición de los adjetivos "azul" y "verde" deja ver que los colores no son considerados únicamente como cualidades inherentes sino también como cualidades particularmente caracterizadoras y opuestas. A lo que parece la descripción realizada por el Poder manifiesta el empeño de corresponder a los ruegos de la tercera persona de la Santísima Trinidad.

Huelga decir que las maneras de proceder calderonianas hasta aquí recordadas ocurren en nuestro texto con mucha frecuencia. Así es que descubrimos la intención de circundar el substantivo de dos adjetivos en versos que incluyen un adjetivo determinativo antepuesto (precisamente con el efecto de acentuar) y un adjetivo pospuesto caracterizador. "Y yo, aquel fuego nativo," dice el Fuego que quiere ayudar a formar el hombre.

Acabamos de mostrar que, conforme a una de las
tendencias calderonianas, un adjetivo conteniendo una
cualidad inseparable del substantivo puede ocupar el
plano correspondiente, en el lenguaje de todos los
días, al adjetivo marcador pospuesto. Pensemos en la
expresión "ese azul zafiro"! Haciendo constar esto,
no queremos decir que nuestro dramaturgo proceda
esquemáticamente. La Sombra encolerizada por la
alegría reinante en su ambiente, a consecuencia de
la creación inminente del hombre, oye la música que
solemniza el acontecimiento que se aproxima. Exclama
entonces: "¿Cuándo el acento fué rayo veloz, / trueno
el eco, relámpago la voz, / ... / ... / sino hoy
...?/." No obstante la perturbación de la persona
hablante, el poeta puede decir en este caso "rayo
veloz" (en vez de "veloz rayo") porque los términos
"rayo," "trueno," "relámpago" confieren al habla de
la actriz irritada energía realmente suficiente.
Cuando la figura alegórica alarmada se refiere, en
el mismo razonamiento, a la esfera lejana de Dios,
el autor dramático le pone en la boca las palabras
"Patria horrible cruel / ... /." Insertando esta
definición no expresa la señal característica por
medio de la anteposición, sino de la duplicación.
Tan sólo después de una investigación sistemática de
la adjetivación en toda la obra calderoniana podre-
mos decir si, respecto a la sucesión de adjetivos,
piensa en determinados principios.

Dejando aparte la duplicación ahora mismo citada,
la persona que se dirige contra la creación del hombre
dispone de la posibilidad de repetir el mismo enlace
de adjetivo y substantivo, unido con la figura retórica
del quiasmo. El hombre puede considerarse como "última
obra del Poder, / última obra de la Ciencia, / ... /
del Amor última obra / .../."

A la irritación del Príncipe de las Tinieblas
respecto a la existencia del hombre se añade en
seguida el asombro del ser que perdió la gracia.
Corrobora su admiración relativa a la naturaleza
humana sirviéndose de una exclamación con interjección
introductoria: "¡Oh humana naturaleza!" Esta exclamación equivalente a la construcción "¡Oh tú que eres
humana naturaleza!" nos enseña que existe una relación
estrecha entre la anteposición del adjetivo por una
parte a una exclamación que lo contiene por otra.

A través de las disquisiciones hechas hasta aquí

se puede comprobar que las maneras de proceder calderonianas y las diversas consecuencias en el dominio
de las cualidades son en realidad muy numerosas. Pero
desde el punto de vista cuantitativo tenemos que mencionar todavía otras modificaciones. La importancia
de una localidad caracterizada por dos adjetivos circundantes es intensificada por un pronombre demostrativo. Exclama la Gracia: "Hombre imagen de tu Autor, /
de esa enorme cárcel dura / rompe la prisión oscura, /
a la voz de tu Criador./"

Cada lector del auto sacramental sabe que después
de esta invitación de la Gracia el texto calderoniano
presenta las estrofas extraordinariamente admirables y
muy conocidas en las que el hombre se compadece de su
libertad reducida. ¿Por qué admiramos estas estrofas?
Las admiramos, entre otras cosas, porque el dramaturgo
del Siglo de Oro opta por una substitución que la gusta.
Reemplaza la palabra "cielo" por "campo" añadiéndole
un adjetivo que recuerda el substantivo substituido.
El hombre, inventado por Calderón, dice, refiriéndose
al sol: ". . . con la majestad / de su hermosa claridad / azules campos corrió, / ... /." Mediante el substantivo pluralizado, raras veces usado en este contexto, e igualmente en consideración al adjetivo antepuesto pluralizado también, la expresión "azules campos"
surte mayor efecto en la imaginación del espectador,
del oyente y del lector que la yuxtaposición "azul
cielo." Mencionemos algunas substituciones parecidas:
"campaña cerúlea" en vez de "cielo," "claro espejo" en
vez de "agua," "escamado navío" en vez de "pez,"
"intacta luna" en vez de "virginidad."

Las estrofas en cuestión, que impresionan a fuer
de una belleza muy sencilla, lograda con adjetivos
corrientes, recuerdan la lírica renacentista. En las
décimas que son completamente diferentes, en comparación con las discusiones posteriores llenas de problemas relativos a la caída del hombre y a su redención, el hombre dice respecto al ave con que se parangona: "va con ligereza suma / por esa compaña bella, /
.../."

El papel considerable de la adjetivación en el
drama calderoniano se desprende del uso de adjetivos
muy corrientes pero todavía no palidecidos, es decir
sin disminución o atenuación de su importancia original.
¿Sería por eso posible descubrir una dramatización insensata en la definición del mar que reza: ". . . la
vaga humedad / de tan grande inmensidad"? Hay que

observar, sin embargo, que la palabra "grande" intensificada por "tan" significa en el verso citado: "Todo lo que excede y se aventaja a lo ordinario y regular." (Diccionario de Autoridades.) Por lo tanto es lícito creer que el poeta Calderón conoce diversas inmensidades. "Grande," por asociación semántica, significa también "amplio," "ancho," "dilatado," "espacioso." Calderón podría haber dicho también: "de tan vasta inmensidad." Pero a pesar de la aliteración en "v," la expresión resulta más opaca, más compacta y Calderón preferiría la vibración de las nasales sonoras ("de tan grande inmensidad"). El adjetivo "ancho" tiene también la nasal sonora, pero, claro está, le falta la connotación de grandeza que Calderón instintiva o intencionadamente quiere conservar: grandiosidad y espaciosidad. Es decir, el poeta tiene razón, y el adjetivo "grande" es insustituible.

Al cabo de la queja extensa del hombre, pronunciada antes de recibir la luz de la gracia, leemos después de la investidura con esta luz, el razonamiento del Príncipe de las Tinieblas. A pesar de estar enfadado e irritado ensalza la dignidad del hombre. Denomina el traje de la inocencia otorgado por Dios "rico aparente vestido." Destaca por lo tanto la justa proporción y el esplendor del vestido por dos adjetivos antepuestos. El dramaturgo que se sirve muchas veces de la polisémia de los términos alcanza un resultado considerable dando a la palabra "aparente" otro significado que por ejemplo en la combinación "sofi(s)tería aparente."

Calderón continúa la acción dramática según una sentencia del Antiguo Testamento. Leemos en el Libro de los Proverbios: "Contritionem praecedit superbia, / et ante ruinam exaltatur spiritus." Por cierto, de momento esta exaltación es detenida por una duda. Pero toma incremento. Bajo una perspectiva lingüística este incremento llega a expresarse por la intensificación del contenido del significado del adjetivo. Además de la intensificación por medio de "tan" ya observada se nos ofrece la intensificación por medio de "más." Durante su admiración de la propia hermosura, refrenada por un asombro lleno de vacilación, el hombre exclama: "¿Pues quién me trajo a una esfera, / tan rica, tan suntuosa / y tan florida, que en ella / la más reluciente estrella / aun no se atreve a ser rosa?" Poco después se llama a sí mismo "la criatura /

más perfecta del orbe." Se echa de ver muy claramente
que la adjetivación ("más reluciente"--"más perfecta")
no indica tan sólo la plenitud de la gracia antes de la
caída sino también la tragedia siguiente con todo su
espanto. Contribuyen a esta representación del antag-
onismo entre elevación y degradación las exclamaciones
del hombre caracterizadas por epítetos cultos--por
ejemplo "¡Qué fábrica tan augusta!"--y también las
exposiciones de los elementos que favorecen la caída.
El Aire habla de la subida del hombre a "más eminente
solio."

En los diálogos que aumentan la tensión antes de
la catástrofe, antes del goce de la dorada poma, Calderón introduce la alternación entre anteposición y
posposición del adjetivo. La Sombra que en virtud de
una visión de la Madre de Dios tarda en realizar la
seducción, pide disculpa por su demora diciendo que ve
"una cándida azucena / junto a una rosa purpúrea, /
.../." Debemos mencionar no sólo la manera de expresarse tan llena de irresolución de la Sombra sino
también su dicción hímnica y seductora en la cual Calderón hace valer nuevamente un epíteto culto: ". . .
las estrellas / en su campaña cerulea, / mis oráculos
de fuego / son.../." A este autoelogio el hombre
contesta: "¡Qué raro bello prodigio!" Calderón
transforma la exclamación "¡Qué prodigio!" por via
de la expresión "¡Qué raro prodigio!" en la construcción "¡Qué raro bello prodigio!" es decir en el sin-
tagma con dos adjetivos antepuestos. El significado
de las palabras "bello"--"raro"--"prodigio" llama la
atención del oyente y del lector. La Sombra es una
figura que causa desgracias. Nos atrevemos a preguntar si el dramaturgo se acordó del término latino
"prodigium." "Prodigium" marca en la mayoría de los
casos un signo milagroso que pronostica desdicha.
Entre otras cosas el Diccionario de Autoridades explica
"prodigio" por medio de las palabras "suceso extraño."
De todas formas es lícito creer que el poeta que se
sirve de los términos "raro" (a saber "extraordi-
nario") y "prodigio" tiene la intención de dar a
entender lo inquietante del interlocutor.

Llamando la atención del hombre sobre el ser que
trae mala suerte el Entendimiento habla de "... una /
serpiente ... / ... incautamente astuta, / .../." En
"La Vida es Sueño" encontramos una sola vez un adjetivo acompañado de un adverbio con la desinencia--
"mente," mientras que en otros textos calderonianos
hay muchos ejemplos que demuestran a predilección del

autor dramático por la yuxtaposición en cuestión. El
Diccionario de Autoridades interpreta "incautamente"
mediante las palabras "Sin cautela ni prudencia." Es
posible que Calderón, incluyendo en su auto la expresión "incautamente astuta," piense en el hecho de
que la serpiente, a pesar de su astucia, sigue siendo
imprudente porque avanza con demasiada temeridad.

El Entendimiento caracteriza la serpiente como
"negra noche oscura." Se sirve de una manera de decir
que se encuentra varias veces en el texto, a saber, de
la anteposición y posposición simultáneas del adjetivo
(por ejemplo "hermoso alcázar rico"). En cuanto al
verso que acabamos de citar es de suponer que Calderón,
pensando en la declamación, haya querido tomar en
cuenta una pequeña pausa entre "negra noche" y "oscura." La palabra "oscura" hace resaltar la negrura
de la noche, pero también implica torcida, aviesa
intención.

La Sombra, persona seductora, glorifica al hombre
que ya flaquea, llamándole "eterno edades futuras."
Salta a la vista la diferencia entre el singular
("eterno") y el plural ("edades futuras"). Además
llama la atención la ausencia de una preposición pre-
cedente a la forma plural. Es concebible que el
autor dramático, escogiendo la yuxtaposición "eterno
edades futuras" haya querido destacar particularmente
la idea de la eternidad. Hubiera sido imposible
hacerla tan patente por medio de otra construcción
sintáctica. La eternidad no contiene edades, pero,
según parece, Calderón no se fija en esta verdad.
Dicho sea de paso que la identificación de la eternidad con edades eternas la encontramos en otros textos
de la literatura universal. (El español conoce
también esa aglutinación--eterno edades futuras--
para concretar, sustantivar, para formar entidades,
"sustantivaciones" o ideaciones, frente al procedimiento de la caracterización por medio de preposi-
ciones. En el contexto la expresión "eterno edades
futuras" podría significar también "ser proyectado
eternamente al futuro" que eso sería igualmente la
eternidad en cuanto inacabable expectación.)

Después del pecado del hombre, la luz de la
Gracia dice que la caída será herencia del orbe,
"miserable herencia suya." El oyente se de cuenta
que estas palabras constituyen, hasta cierto punto,
una inversión de la secuencia "aquel fuego nativo,"
es decir, de la secuencia "demostrativo--substantivo--

adjetivo." Calderón es un inventor admirable de variaciones. El pronombre demostrativo "aquel" parece revelarse como elemento acentuado gracias a la expectativa que incluye. El adjetivo "miserable" manifiesta la insistencia que el autor le confiere, tanto en virtud de la enteposición como por el contenido semántico.

Calderón sabe aprovecharse no sólo de las posibilidades proporcionadas por la posición del adjetivo, sino también--acabamos de insinuarlo--del contenido semántico del adjetivo. Prescindiendo de la combinación "incautamente astuta," ya interpretada, es indispensable mancionar las palabras con que el hombre, quejándose de lo que hizo, caracteriza a la serpiente. "El áspid era sin duda / el que, con humano rostro, / bien que inhumana hermosura, / me dío la hechizada poma; / ...(./." Salta a la vista la antítesis "humano-inhumano." Pero es mucho mas importante llamar la atención sobre el hecho de que el adjetivo "inhumano" (es uno de los quince adjetivos formados en nuestro auto por medio del prefijo "in-") equivale tanto a cruel" como a "sobrehumano." Sabemos que en vocabulario de Apuleyo "inhumanus" quiere decir "divinus."

Gracias a una fuerza que es caracterizada como inhumana en dos sentidos, el hombre llega a ser una "bronca informe estatua bruta." Para determinar el estado del hombre después de su desdicha, Calderón utiliza tres adjetivos peyorativos, anteponiendo dos de ellos. Se trata, si dejamos aparte expresiones parecidas a "esa enorme cárcel dura," de otra forma nueva e intensa de dramatización. Poco después el mismo Dios, arrepentido de haber creado al hombre, llama a la fuerza seductora "... fiera / poderosa Sombra injusta, / ...(./." Respecto al título del auto es digno de atención que el hombre caído de su altura cree encontrarse en un "letal sueño." La vida se presenta como un sueño calificado de muerte. La ecuación "La Vida es Sueño" queda reducida a "La Vida es letal Sueño." Calderón conoce la diferencia que hay de unos sueños a otros. Cada sueño constituye una especie de vida de diferente valor.

Después de haber incluido una antítesis en su descripción de la serpiente seductora ("humano rostro"--"inhumana hermosura") se sirve de este recurso retórico añadiendo, de modo especial, los adjetivos antitéticos a un solo substantivo para multiplicar así lo dramático de la situación. La

primera persona de la Santísima Trinidad, simulando
ser ignorante, se entromete en el curso de la conversación relativa a la situación del hombre haciendo una
pregunta. Los cuatro elementos contestan, adjeti-
vando cada vez de manera muy diferente: "Dígalo la
mía (esto es luz) eclipsada. / Díganlo mis flores
mustias. / Destemplados mis alientos. / Mis claras
corrientes turbias./" Estas últimas palabras pronunciadas por el Agua manifiestan en términos especialmente categóricos la metamorfosis fatal causada por
la caída: "Mis claras corrientes (están ya) turbias."

El hombre llega a conocer toda su desgracia
cuando se da cuenta de su culpa. La acción de darse
cuenta trae consigo "heroicos anhelos." Es imaginable
que el hombre hable de "heroicos anhelos," a saber
ambiciones, porque el amor divino ha tomado ya antes
la resolución de rescatarlo. Pueden ser llamadoa
"heroicos," es decir "ilustres o pertenecientes a los
héroes" (Diccionario de Autoridades), porque dejan
presentir una decisión en favor de Dios.

Oyendo las palabras ";Gloria a Dios en las al-
turas, / .../," el hombre exclama: ";Qué lejanas
voces / tan misteriosas son éstas, / ...!/." Aparece
una triplicidad ("lejanas"--"misteriosas"--"éstas")
que expresa gran sorpresa gracias a la posición
diferente de los adjetivos, al uso del adverbio
"tan" y, por añadidura, de una palabra determinativa.

La adjetivación calderoniana realizada con mucha
y madura reflexión se destaca todavía más claramente
donde se menciona la salvación próxima por medio de
la Sabiduría, es decir, por medio del amor de la
segunda persona de la Santísima Trinidad. En este
contexto la humillación a causa del pecado se hace
patente por los epítetos usados: "tosca piel y basta
jerga / vistió la Sabiduría / de humana naturaleza./"
En "La Vida es Sueño" Calderón suele preferir la
anteposición de la palabra "humano." En el pasaje
citado parece tratarse de una acentuación muy particular, porque el autor tiene presente la encarna-
ción. El adjetivo "humano" debe simbolizar lo que
Dios hizo en provecho del hombre.

La emoción que Calderón desea hacer patente
también lingüísticamente en su auto se manifiesta
hacia el final, cuando el hombre se refiere al
resultado de la acción teatral, caracterizándolo
como "viva muerte" y "muerta vida." La anteposición

y la posposición de palabras semánticamente antitéticas reunen la vida de Cristo que sufrió la muerte ("viva muerte") y la muerte del Príncipe de las Tinieblas todavía vivo poco antes ("muerta vida").

Para dar a conocer su disposición de ánimo especial relativa a la situación teatral en cuestión y para intensificar la reacción del espectador, Calderón antepone hasta cuatro adjetivos. El sacramento del bautismo, o sea la "...clara, pura, tersa, / natural Agua..." lava la ofensa del hombre.

Una vez más Calderón traduce el carácter dramático del auto sacramental por medio de la adjetivación y en este caso precisamente por el empleo de una de las palabras de gran trascendencia, seguido del cambio de posición. Cuando la Tierra ofrece "vides y espigas" como "viandas eternas" para el acto del sacramento, el Príncipe de las Tinieblas pregunta: "¿Qué es ser eterna vianda?"

Según Keniston la anteposición del adjetivo se encuentra sobre todo en la poesía dramática. Podemos decir que la práctica de Calderón confirma esta hipótesis. En comparación con los adjetivos pospuestos, Calderón aumenta al doble los adjetivos antepuestos. Hay que añadir todavía que más de cincuenta adjetivos se hallan tan sólo delante del substantivo correspondiente. Nuestro análisis, tal como queda expuesto, es una tentativa por descubrir el papel realmente importante de la anteposición del adjetivo en el acontecer dramático. Pero paralelamente creemos haber puesto de relieve la destreza de Calderón en lo que atañe a la anteposición, ya sea en virtud del empleo de dos adjetivos, ya sea mediante las múltiples alteraciones de la construcción sintáctica.

University of Hamburg

213

El stile rappresentative en la comedia

de teatro de Calderón

Alicia Amadei-Pulice

Cuando Dámaso Alonso expone la fórmula general de las correlaciones en el teatro calderoniano, él mismo reconoce las limitaciones del método estilístico en su aplicación al estudio del teatro. No podemos acercarnos al teatro--nos dice--leyéndolo al nivel de la expresión meramente lingüística porque "el signo idiomático del teatro, el lenguaje del teatro, es fónico y visual, es decir, temporal y espacial a la vez."[1] Recientes estudios semióticos han enmendado las fallas de los acercamientos "literarios" al teatro, haciéndonos ver que este género es en realidad un arte politécnico en el cual se conjugan varios sistemas de significación extralingüísticos, siendo los principales, como acertadamente lo viera Dámaso Alonso, el fónico y el visual.[2]

Pero la semiótica es una ciencia moderna, el teatro es un arte antiguo. Lo que se ha venido elucidando en esta última década acerca de los niveles de significado de la acción teatral no es más que un redescubrimiento de las convenciones teatrales que habían sido creadas y codificadas con el nacimiento mismo del teatro moderno, es decir, el teatro que nace en Italia a fines del siglo XVI.

Con la aparición del edificio teatral, y me refiero específicamente a teatros como el Olímpico de Vicenza, el teatro Farnese de Parma, prototipo del teatro de Buen Retiro de Madrid, y otros pequeños teatros palaciegos, nace un nuevo arte de representar: el stile rappresentativo.

En Italia, con la aparición de la escena, profunda, tridimensional y en perspectiva, vemos que el antiguo poeta dramático se ve en la necesidad de cambiar la estructura del drama. La puesta en escena hace claramente visible a los espectadores discrepancias entre lo que se dice en el texto poético y lo que se ve. El antiguo poeta dramático, que escribía sus obras para ser simplemente recitadas o leídas, se va a encontrar con problemas insospechados; de hecho va a tener que reestructurar el drama. Este pasaje

crítico que va de la recitación del texto dramático a
su representación lo registra Angelo Ingegneri en el
tratado Della Poesia Rappresentativa (Ferrara, 1598).[3]
Ingegneri advierte que el autor dramático debe ahora
tratar de figurarse, antes de escribir la obra, la
topografía escénica, como si la viera, con los edi-
ficios, las perspectivas, las calles, el proscenio,
debe preveer las salidas y entradas de personajes,
los gestos, las miradas y hasta detalles como la
proyección de la voz o la imitación del eco, a fin
de evitar errores en lo que se percibe desde la sala.
Este texto de suma importancia en la historia y evolución de las convenciones teatrales nos revela que,
hasta el momento de la aparición de la escena, el
texto dramático se escribía para ser leído o recitado
y, después de la aparición de la escena, el texto
cambia y adquiere características representativas, es
decir, se le añaden dos lenguajes, el fónico y el
visual. En el tratado de Ingegneri, y también en el
de Francesco Buonamici, Discorsi Poetici (Florencia,
1597)--y ambos autores merecen una exposición más
amplia que la que nos permite el tiempo--se establecen
todas las convenciones que le dan al teatro moderno
su lenguaje particular.[4] Se define en el nivel visual
la función "representativa," icónica, del aparato
escénico, la función ilusionista de trompe l'oeil de
las perspectivas pintadas que establecen el lugar
artificialmente recreado de la acción, donde el ser
histriónico asume también características representativas, es decir sígnicas, pasa por lo que no es,
y representa por medio de gestos, posturas y miradas.
En el nivel fónico, se especifican todos los valores
expresivos de la voz, la función de la música instrumental en la escena y otros "efectos" sonoros como el
eco, que pasan a tener un papel preponderante en la
representación.

     Esta nueva manera de representar, el stile
rappresentativo, opera un cambio fundamental en todos
los niveles de captación del espectáculo y afecta
también a la exposición de la acción, la cual se
exhibe dualmente:

     L'Azione contiene due parti cioè la Voce, e il
     Gesto; nelle quai due parti è riposta la totale
     espressione e efficacia della favola . . . l'una
     riguarda l'udire, e l'altra riguarda il vedere.
     E ciascuno prova le cose in se, e si commove
     per esse, secondo ch'egli le ascolta, e le
     rimira.[5]

En la poesía _rappresentativa_ toda la inteligencia
de la trama o _favola_ reposa en lo que se percibe por
los ojos y los oídos. Es más, los representantes se
escuchan y se miran entre ellos, mostrando conmoverse
o admirarse por lo que ven o escuchan. En lo que
concierne a la Voz, Ingegneri recomienda el uso de
la voz modulada y expresiva en correspondencia con
la acción, ya sea sumisa, ronca, clara, iracunda,
suave, feble o feroz. En la parte que se refiere al
Gesto, aclara que éste consiste en los movimientos
del cuerpo, de las manos, del rostro y, sobre todo,
del movimiento de los ojos.

Aquí están concisamente delineados los dos aspectos de la acción teatral en cuanto ésta se hace representativa: el fónico y el visual. Estas características son exclusivas del género teatral y son las que
lo diferencian de otros géneros _literales_, como la
novela o la poesía, o el drama para ser recitado o
leído--pensemos en el _lesedrama La Dorotea_, de Lope,
"teatro de papel"--cuya captación no está supeditada
a la puesta en escena. La poesía _rappresentativa_,
por otro lado, se independiza del _nivel literal_, se
expresa sensorialmente, y se percibe también por los
ojos y los oídos. Contemporáneamente al tratado de
Ingegneri el Pinciano hace una clasificación de
géneros dramáticos o "especies" basándose también en
la manera de captación:

> . . . en toda especie de fábula es la verosimili-
> tud necesaria pero mucho más en las dramáticas y
> representativas, las cuales mueven mucho más al
> ánimo _porque entra_ su _imitación por el ojo; y
> por ser acción sujeta a la vista, la falta es
> mucho más manifiesta, más que en aquellas especies
> de fábulas que entran por el oydo_ o lectura, _como
> son las comunes_.[6] (Subrayado mío.)

Como vemos, el Pinciano clasifica dos especies
dramáticas: una, cuya acción (fábula)[7] entra por el
oído o la lectura, y la otra, la manera representativa,
que entra por la vista. Ingegneri y el Pinciano coin-
ciden en este punto: la separación de los géneros
dramáticos se basa en la manera de _percibirlos_. Esta
observación nos remite a considerar dos escuelas, dos
especies si se quiere, de la comedia española en tanto
que se perciben de manera distinta, ya sea por el oído
o lectura solamente, o por el oído y la vista.

De hecho, constatamos que la comedia de corral,

la comedia lopesca por ejemplo, era un género dramático poético que establecía la comunicación por medio del oído. Lope es muy explícito sobre esta manera de captación en el Arte Nuevo:

> Oye atento, y del arte no disputes;
> que en la comedia se hallará de modo,
> que, oyéndola, se pueda saber todo.[8]

El énfasis en el aspecto auditivo de la comedia que colegimos de estas líneas se confirma en la misma configuración del corral. La plataforma de los recitantes no estaba montada para la visualización de la acción; el tablado estaba emplazado a más de 2,50 mts. de altura.[9] No hay duda que el sentido que más predominaba en la captación de la trama era el oído. Los lugares escénicos, a falta de mutaciones, estaban suplidos por los recitantes quienes llevaban a los oyentes por lugares simplemente imaginados, nunca vistos. El lugar en que ocurre la acción no se hace presente a los ojos de nadie, surge, como por arte de magia, de lo que indican verbalmente los recitantes. Por ejemplo, en Los embustes de Fabia se dice:

> Este es palacio: acá sale
> Nerón, nuestro emperador,
> que lo permite el autor,
> que de esta industria se vale;
> porque si acá no saliera,
> fuera aquí la relación
> tan mala, y tan sin razón,
> que ninguno la entendiera.[10]

La verosimilitud con el lugar que se imita se consigue a través de palabras recitadas. En el teatro, por otro lado, la escena imita el lugar de la acción, representándolo visualmente. El espectador teatral no se guía por su imaginación, ve el lugar, lo interpreta con los ojos y reconoce la substitución sígnica: i.e., que los bastidores no son tela, sino paisaje. El lenguaje teatral no es estrictamente poético, es visual; la metáfora no es operante en este sistema representativo, el aparato escénico asume su función y se transforma en una "metáfora visible." Para Lope, contrariamente, la comedia permanece dentro del ciclo de la palabra poética, es "un género de poëma o poësis," afirma, y "la imitación se hace de tres cosas, que son plática, verso dulce y armonía, o sea la música."[11] Todos éstos son sistemas auditivos y temporales. La intelección de una obra como

Fuenteovejuna o Los embustes de Fabia, no pierde nada
si se escucha a ojos cerrados. En la "especie"
comedia de Lope la dimensión visual está ausente. La
comedia de corral, es un género "imaginativo," o si
se quiere--como lo califica John Weiger--un "género
auditivo."[12]

Con la aparición de la escenografía italiana en
la corte madrileña notamos, como era de esperar, un
fenómeno similar al que registra Ingegneri en Italia:
el énfasis de la representación se pone en el aspecto
visual de la obra, el aspecto textual se eclipsa.
Ante las escenas mutables y las maravillosas transformaciones que montó Giuglio Fontana para La gloria
de Niquea del conde de Villamediana, el relator dice
sucintamente: "Fue de lo más excelente y (si pudo
ser) lo representado pasó de lo escrito."[13] Lo cual
nos indica que el texto lingüístico cede paso a la
representación sensorial en la escena. Hurtado de
Mendoza indica en la relación del espectáculo que,
efectivamente, se trata de la introdución de un género
distinto al de la comedia:

> . . . Ya advertí al principio que esto que
> extrañará el pueblo por comedia, y se llama en
> Palacio "inuención," no se mide a los precetos
> comunes de las farsas que es una fábula unida,
> ésta se fabrica de variedad desatada, en la que
> la vista lleva la mejor parte que el oído, y la
> ostentación consiste más en lo que se ve, que
> en lo que se oye.[14] (Subrayado mío)

La "invención," cuyos antecedentes encontramos en
las representaciones florentinas del mismo nombre, es
una pieza corta, con unas pocas escenas, no tiene "una
fábula unida," es decir, no tiene una acción compleja;
sin embargo la diferenciación con la comedia, el
género auditivo que acostrumbraba a oir el pueblo,
es notoria. Aquí están frente a frente los dos
géneros; en el género representativo, claramente,
"la vista lleva la mejor parte que el oído."

Con las fiestas de Aranjuez comienza la época de
la escenografía italiana; la época "imaginativa" va
a ceder el lugar a la época de la visión perspectivista.
En el siglo XVII la perspectiva es el patrón dominante
en todas las artes, más ún en el teatro, arte espacial.
El barroco es la edad de la visión plena, del dominio
de lo visual sobre lo auditivo, de las "apariencias"
escénicas, y sobre todo, de la visión ilusionista del

trompe l'oeil, base perceptual y filosófica de la comedia de teatro de Calderón. Calderón será el genio de la visión escénica y dramática, concebida ya al stile rappresentativo. Cosimo Lotti, y luego Vaggio del Bianco y Francesco Rizzi, pondrán en sus manos la más avanzada escenografía perspectivista con bastidores laterales fácilmente mutables que le permitirá producir maravillosos "efectos" visuales.

Sobre estos dos pilares sensoriales, el oído y la vista, en tanto que ellos son los recipientes de los fenómenos acústicos y visuales que juegan en la acción dramática, Calderón construye la estructura primordial de su teatro: un teatro que oscila entre miradas y voces, silencios y lamentos, ciegos y videntes, cantos y perspectivas, sordos y murmuradores, pintores y cantantes, en fin, todas las combinaciones posibles entre los dos efectos. La particularidad de su obra descansa en una sensibilidad extremada de los dos sentidos principales, la vista y el oído, los "efetti" que proviene del melodramma toscano. Los principios estéticos del melodramma y del recitativo, acompañados por la escenografía perspectivista, se acusan en las tablas españolas desde por lo menos 1622, con el estreno de la primera "invención."[15] Las conexiones de la comedia de teatro con el melodramma florentino, y con la teoría y práctica del recitativo es un tema demasiado vasto para tratar aquí; dejo pendiente por esta razón este aspecto de la obra calderoniana, advirtiendo, sin embargo, que los efectos fónicos corren paralelos a los aspectos visuales de la acción.

Calderón preserva el texto de la comedia lopesca, la estructura en tres jornadas, los personajes claves y el tema favorito del público español, el honor. Le superpone al texto poético los dos niveles de captación sensorial, los efectos vocales y musicales escénicos, los ayes, los suspiros, los lloros y lamentos desgarradores, los ecos, el canto en estilo recitativo, y toda otra derivación fónica afín. El lenguaje visual, por otro lado, y en simultaneidad, se expresa sobre el fondo espacial, tridimensional, cóncavo y perspectivista de la escena, en el intercambio de las miradas de los representantes, los gestos histriónicos, en el aparecer y desaparecer visual, en cómo es visto o desea ser visto el personaje, en lo que él ve, su ángulo particular de visión, lo que se descubre o eclipsa a su mirada, en los desdoblamientos de los seres histriónicos en retratos o espejos, y en toda otra dirección que toma el haz visual, ya sea en la

220

escena o desde el punto de vista del espectador.[17]

En cualquier obra de Calderón que abramos al azar
encontramos indefectiblemente esta dualidad: ojos y
oídos; voces y miradas. Estas son las dos coordenadas
básicas de la acción representativa--ya establecidas
por Ingegneri--que aparecen en todas sus obras, desde
las primeras de su inicio en el teatro cortesano en
1623, hasta las obras escritas en el último año de su
vida en 1681. En La gran Cenobia representada, según
nos informa Valbuena Briones, el 23 de junio de 1625,
aparecen paralelamente los dos sentidos. Aureliano,
es un personaje que, como tantos otros que habitan el
mundo calderoniano, se encuentra en la encrucijada del
"engaño de los sentidos":

> En efectos tan dudosos,
> ¿pueden mentir los oídos?
> ¿pueden engañar los ojos?
> No, pues es cierto lo que veo;
> no, pues es verdad que oigo.
>
>   (La gran Cenobia, I, pág. 73, vol. I)[18]

El personaje calderoniano siempre se debate en la
incertidumbre de lo que se le presenta a los ojos.
Recordemos la entrada de Rosaura en La vida es sueño:

> ¡Quién ha visto sucesos tan extraños!
> Mas si la vista no padece engaños
> que hace la fantasía,
> a la medrosa luz del día,
> me parece que veo
> un edificio.

Es la edad de los "ojos hidrópicos," de la
estética de la admiración, de la mirada que no se
sacia de mirar:

> Segismundo ....
> Con cada vez que te veo
> nueva admiración me das,
> y cuando te miro más,
> aún más mirarte deseo.
> Ojos hidrópicos creo
> que mis ojos deben ser;
> pues cuando es muerte el beber,
> beben más, y de esta suerte,
> viendo que el ver me da muerte,
> estoy muriendo por ver.

221

Esta primera escena de La vida es sueño encierra, con una densidad inigualada en otras obras, uno de los mejores ejemplos de la "óptica barroca," la exaltación del ojo y la mirada intensa del personaje. La dialéctica de las miradas siempre nos alerta al significado último de la acción que reposa en este mirarse y admirarse con apasionamiento al que se refería Ingegneri, típico de este estilo de representar. La dirección que toma el haz visual de los protagonistas es de suma importancia en la elucidación de la trama, especialmente en casos en que el honor toma proyecciones visuales. Véamos este pasaje de Amor, honor y poder donde la vista le revela al protagonista un latente agravio a su honor. Enrico ve al rey forcejeando con su hermana:

> Enrico. [Aparte.]
> ....
> ¿Qué es lo que miro? ¡Cielos!
> Sin los celos de amor, ¿da el honor celos?
> Pero erraron los labios;
> que éstos ya no son cielos, sino agravios.
>
> Estela. Suelta, suelta la mano,
> que viene (¡ay de mí triste!) allí mi hermano.
>
> Rey. Mal mi pena resisto.
> ....
>
> Enr. ¡Oh quién no hubiera visto
> su agravio! Mas si es grave
> infamia en el honor que no la sabe,
> pues tan injustamente
> culpa también al inocente,
> (¡Tirana ley!) doblada infamia hallara,
> si, mirando mi agravio, me tornara.
>
> (Amor, honor y poder, II, pág. 79, vol. II)

En el mundo visual de la escena calderoniana el agravio al honor se descubre visualmente: de allí los innumerables ¡Qué miro! que encontramos en obra tras obra.[19] Por otro lado, el ocultamiento, el escondite, indica una posible admisión de culpabilidad. Los valores sígnicos de esta escena se hacen más claros al verla, al ver los ojos sorprendidos del hermano que espía al rey desde los bastidores. La escena está concebida visualmente, stile rappresentativo.

Ese asombro de verse y de oírse que los representantes muestran siempre en seguimiento de este estilo, lo encontramos en este intercambio entre

Rosaura y Segismundo en La vida es sueño:

> Segis. ....
>   tú sólo, tú has suspendido
>   la pasión a mis enojos
>   la suspensión a mis ojos
>   la admiración al oído.

Captación sensorial superlativa a la que Rosaura
contesta en reciprocidad:

> Con sombro de mirarte,
> con admiración de oirte,
> no sé qué pueda decirte,
> ni qué pueda preguntarte.
>
>   (I, pág. 503, vol. I)

Esta visión que va del uno al otro, donde cada
uno se siente a la vez observado por el otro, crea una
visión interpersonal, una metaperspectiva, que se puede
reducir a esta fórmula: mi visión de la visión que el
otro tiene de mí.[20] En otras palabras, el personaje
mira y se siente visto. Esta visión que el otro tiene
de él le afecta enormemente, ya sea en su honor o en su
ser. Segismundo, al verse visto por Rosaura exclama
furioso:

> Pues la muerte te daré,
> porque no sepas que sé
> que sabes flaquezas mías.
>
>   (I, pág. 503, vol. I)

En otras palabras, traduciendo esta frase a la
dialéctica de las miradas en la escena, tenemos esta
visión de Segismundo:

> Yo sé [porque te vi],
> que tú sabes [porque te vi, viéndome],
> que yo sé [porque tú me vistes viéndote
>   verme].

La manera en que Rosaura lo percibe, la metaperspectiva que él recibe de la visión de ella, en
su condición miserable, le enfurece hasta querer
matarla. Este grado de hipersensibilidad visual es
típico de tantos personajes, como lo es la fórmula
metaperspectivista, que se repite, con variaciones,
en cada uno y todos los dramas calderonianos. La
función de la metaperspectiva está siempre en relación

con la acción dramática y es crucial para su significado final. Lamentablemente, la exposición textual
que requiere mostrar su función en una obra no cabe
en los límites de esta presentación.

La acción en las obras calderonianas cobra otro
significado si seguimos los efectos visuales y sonoros,
las miradas y las voces, en sus perspectivas y tonali-
dades tal como se representara. Es en vano tratar de
imaginar la acción como poesía dramática; Calderón
supera la época imaginativa de la comedia. Su comedia
de teatro crea una realidad visual--aunque esta sea la
ficticia de la escena--donde los personajes se ven y
se escuchan como en el mundo paralelo de la vida real.
La comedia de teatro de Calderón tiene la fuerza
expresiva de lo que se ve que es mayor a lo que se
pueda imaginar.

Así nos lo dice Calderón:

> Quien ve una beldad divina
> a sus mismos ojos cree,
> y, realidad en quien ve,
> es sombra en quien imagina.

(Los tres efectos de amor,
II, pág. 1202, vol. I)

University of California, Los Angeles

Notas

[1]Dámaso Alonso y Carlos Bousoño, Seis calas en la
expresión literaria española (Madrid: Gredos, 1970),
pág. 163.

[2]Véase Umberto Eco, "Elementos preteatrales de
una semiótica del teatro," Semiología del teatro
(Barcelona: Editorial Planeta, 1975), ed. José M.
Diéz Borque y Luciano García Lorenzo. Eco diferencia
tres campos de investigación semiótica: la kinésica,
que estudia los gestos; la paralingüística, que
estudia las entonaciones; y la prosémica, que estudia
las distancias espaciales. Págs. 100-101. Patrice
Pavis, en Problèmes de Sémiologie Théatrale (Montreal:
Université du Québec, 1976) distingue en el teatro dos
realidades, una visual y una lingüística, el referente
lingüístico, comprende el mundo de la palabra que puede o no ser visto en la escena; el referente visual,
se remite al decorado y la aparición de los personajes,
pág. 40. Roman Jakobson, por otro lado, distingue
entre una oposicion fundamental entre los signos
auditivos y signos visuales que coincide con la premisa
nuestra. Véase, "Visual and Auditory Signs," Selected
Writings, II (La Haya: Mouton, 1959).

[3]Della Poesia Rappresentativa et del modo di
rappresentare le favole sceniche. Discorso di Angelo
Ingegneri (Ferrara, 1598). ". . . ed avvenendo poi il
piu delle volte, che le cose loro sono solamente lette,
e non mai rappresentate, esse [los poetas dramáticos]
non possono accorgersi degli inconvenienti che di
necesità accaderebbono nella loro rappresentazione.
Converrebbe adunque, che il Poeta, il quale si da a
fare alcuna opera Dramatica, primieramente si
figurasse dinanzi agli occhj la Scena, divisandone
fra di se gli edificj, le prospettive, le strade, il
proscenio, e ogni altra cosa opportuna per l'adveni-
mento di quel caso, ch'ei si prende ad imitare; e ne
facesse nella sua mente propia una cotal pratica, che
non uscisse personaggio, che non gli sembrasse vedere
onde essi si venisse, ne si facesse sul detto proscenio
gesto, ne vi si dicesse parola, ch' egli in certo modo
nol vedesse, e non la udisse, mutando, e migliorando,
a guisa di buon Corago, e di perfetto Maestro, quegli
atti, e quelle voci, che a lui non paressero bene a
proposito" (pág. 509). El subrayado mío indica la
parte visual y auditiva que el poeta debe tener en
cuenta al representar la obra escénica.

[4] Discorsi Poetici nella Accademia Fiorentina in difesa di Aristotile dell' Eccellentissimo Filosofo Messere Francesco Bounamici (Fiorenza, 1597). Bounamici señala el valor sígnico, representativo, que tiene el aparato escénico. Para él la verosimilitud no se obtiene mediante la imaginación, sino se crea a base de una suposición. El espectador debe aprender el valor sígnico que tienen los bastidores: el decorado no es Roma, sino que simplemente indica el lugar. En este tratado de Bounamici se encuentra la definición del "signo" así como lo entiende modernamente la semiótica: "le similitudini sono naturali, i segni pendono dalla volontà nostra, le similitudini essendo naturali non si mutano ne può fare l'uomo, che ne lo specchio non apparisca l'imagine mia con le medesime delineationi, & colori che sono in me; ma che io significhi una cosa ò con altra è posto nel arbitrio dell'uomo" (pág. 105). En este tratado distinguimos el paso sutil de una época, el Renacimiento a otra, el Barroco, marcado este último por una revolución sígnica en la escena: se supera la similitud natural y se pasa a la representación sígnica, de lenguaje más expresivo, rico y creador, y a la vez, más ficticio, características del lenguaje teatral desde entonces.

[5] Ingegneri, pág. 535.

[6] Alonso López Pinciano, Philosophía Antiqua Poética (Madrid, 1596), ed. Alfredo Carballo Picazo (Madrid: Consejo Superior de Investigaciones Científicas, 1953), II, pág. 200. Acerca de la teoría de la representación en el Pinciano véase Sanford Shepard, El Pinciano y las teorías literarias del Siglo de Oro (Madrid: Gredos, 1970), págs. 105-12.

[7] La palabra "fabula" tenía en ese momento este significado: "A la Fabula llama el Maestro Alma de la Tragedia: assi la parte principal de ella. Esta es la Acción imitada o representada, i la Constitución de su parte. A la que Aristoteles llama Acción, nosotros llamaríamos en la Tragedia, como en la Comedia, el Argumento, la Materia, la Traça." Jusepe Antonio Gonzales de Salas, Nueva Idea de la Tragedia Antigua (Madrid, 1633), pág. 20.

[8] Lope de Vega y Carpio. Rimas . . . con el Nuevo Arte de hazer Comedias deste tiempo. Año 1609. En Madrid. Por Alonso Martín. Reproducido por Alfred Morel-Fatio, "'L'Arte Nuevo de Hazer Comedias en este tiempo' de Lope de Vega," Bulletin Hispanique, 3

(1901), pág. 383.

[9]Véase Othón Arróniz, Teatros y escenarios del Siglo de Oro (Madrid: Gredos, 1977), pág. 67.

[10]Cito a Lope por Américo Castro y Hugo Rennert, Vida de Lope de Vega (Madrid: Anaya, 1968), pág. 118.

[11]Lope, Arte Nuevo, pág. 375.

[12]John G. Weiger en Hacia la comedia: De los valencianos a Lope (Madrid: Cupsa, 1978) expresa la misma idea sobre la "audibilidad" del texto: "Para Lope la comedia consiste ante todo en los elementos que escuchará el público," pág. 46. En mi tesis doctoral, "Hacia Calderón: Las bases teórico-estéticas del teatro barroco español," UCLA, 1981, he llegado a las mismas conclusiones que Weiger, aunque partiendo de premisas diferentes. Mi razonamiento se basa en la comparación genérica entre la comedia de corral y la comedia de teatro, caracterizándose esta última por su representación en el recinto teatral con la preceptiva escénica y musical de origen italiano que la acompaña y que es radicalmente distinta a la práctica española anterior.

[13]Antonio Hurtado de Mendoza, Obras poéticas, ed. de Rafael Benitez Claros (Madrid: Ultra, 1947), pág. 22.

[14]Mendoza, págs. 21-22.

[15]Para las conexiones entre la "invención" y el melodramma florentino remito al lector al capítulo I de mi tesis.

[16]Revivo este término difenciador que fue viable y útil en su momento histórico. Comedias de teatro se llamaban a aquellas producciones en las cuales no se dejaba nada a la imaginación del espectador y se empleaba el aparato escénico en contraste con las comedias de capa y espada que usaban una simple cortina como fondo. Véase Hugo A. Rennert, The Spanish Stage in the Time of Lope de Vega (1909; reimp. New York: Dover, 1963), pág. 86. Calderón escribe comedias de teatro, es decir, teniendo en cuenta el rico aparato escenográfico. Siguiendo la distinción que hace Rennert notamos que Calderón realmente no escribe comedias del tipo de capa y espada.

[17]Las proyecciones visuales son siempre perspectivistas y obedecen a la nueva reestructuración espacial del teatro y de la escena después del tratado de Guidobaldo del Monte, Perspectivae, libri VI (Pesaro, 1600). El punto de vista en el teatro, es decir el punto de vista del espectador, está geométrica y ópticamente definido. Para más detalles sobre la función de la perspectiva en el teatro calderoniano véase el capitulo III de mi tesis.

[18]Don Pedro Calderón de la Barca, Obras completas (1966; reimp. Madrid: Aguilar, 1969). Prólogo y notas de A. Valbuena Briones. Las notas siguientes que se refieren a textos de Calderón corresponden a esta edición.

[19]Este aspecto visual de las obras calderonianas ha sido recientemente explorado con brillantes resultados por William R. Blue en "'¿Qué es esto que miro?': Converging Sign Systems in El médico de su honra," Bulletin of the Comediantes, 30 (1978), págs. 83-96. Su acercamiento semiótico se centra en los niveles de captación visuales y verbales de esta obra en particular. En mi tesis doctoral, fundándome en textos históricos, señalo que la obra calderoniana, como género de comedia de teatro, se estructura obligadamente en estos dos niveles de captación, el visual perspectivista y el tonal-vocal proveniente del dramma per musica italiano, que exhiben la acción en la representación de una manera sensorial. La frase clave "¿Qué es esto que miro?" que ha llamado la atención de Blue, como así también otras frases similares, se encuentran en todos los dramas calderonianos y es parte del sistema perspectivista que es inherente a la conformación de este género.

[20]Utilizo para el estudio de las relaciones visuales en la escena el término metaperspectiva acuñado por Ronald D. Laing para el estudio de las relaciones interpersonales en la vida real. Laing nota que en la vida, y contrariamente a la visión (ego)ísta que propuso Freud, la percepción que los otros tienen de nuestro ser, la visión que presentamos a los ojos de los demás altera y define nuestra identidad, incluso nos hace actuar de cierta manera. "My field of experience is, however, filled not only by my direct view of myself (ego) and of the other (alter), but of what we shall call metaperspectives-- my view of the other's (your, his, her, their) view

of me. I may not actually be able to see myself as others see me, but I am constantly supposing them to be seeing me in particular ways, and I am constantly acting in the light of the actual or supposed attitudes, opinions, needs, and so on the other has in respect of me" (R. D. Laing, H. Phillipson and A. R. Lee, Inter-personal Perception (New York: Harper & Row, 1966), pág. 5. Calderón emplea consistentemente esta fórmula metaperspectivista, y su hallazgo posiblemente esté en relación con el descubrimiento de la perspectiva escénica que afecta no sólo cómo se ve el personaje desde la sala, sino cómo éste es visto por los otros personajes que, a su vez, lo contemplan siendo con-templados.

Cavemen in Calderón (and Some Cavewomen)

J. E. Varey

Ignacio de Luzán, writing in 1737, before the reconstruction of the Madrid corrales de comedias, proclaims the superiority of visible-change stage machinery over the décor of the Spanish commercial theatres, which had changed little if at all from the days of Lope de Vega and Calderón: "Siempre tengo por mejor la [disposición] de mutaciones y bastidores que no la que comúnmente se usa en España, donde cuatro paños o cortinas inmobles representan todo género de lugares, cosa sumamente violenta para la imaginación del auditorio."[1] The two ground plans of the Corral del Príncipe and the Corral de la Cruz, drawn by an architect in 1735, both show a large platform stage, and pillars supporting a balcony which runs across the rear of the stage. No indication is given of a wall cutting off the back-stage area from the playing-space, and it is therefore to be presumed that curtains, hanging from below the balcony, served as a back-drop to the action.[2] N. D. Shergold's analysis of the stage directions of early comedias also supports this theory.[3]

Many plays make use of parallel entrances and exits through two "doors" at the rear of the stage. Calderón, a dramatist with a well-developed taste for symmetry in staging, uses the motif constantly. It is very probable that these entrances were not actual doors, but gaps in the curtain. The stage directions of some plays indicate the need for three such entrances. In Cubillo de Aragón's La perfecta casada are to be found the following stage directions: Sale al paño, por la puerta derecha, Rosimunda, con manto; Sale Don Cesar al paño, por la puerta siniestra; Sale Estefanía por la puerta de enmedio.[4] A stage direction of Act I of La prudente Abigail by Antonio Enríquez Gómez demonstrates that the third entrance was centre stage and suggests that it formed part of the back-stage area: Toquen caxas, y salgan por los dos lados del tablado a un tiempo, soldados de Saul i Dauid, y descubrase en medio del tablado, al vistuario, vna cueba; y de ella salgan Saul y Dauid, y venga Dauid cubierto el rostro y diga Saul.[5] This area, then, corresponds to the discovery-space of the Elizabethan theatre, often referred to as the "inner stage."

The discovery-space was revealed by the drawing

back of curtains, as can be seen from the following quotation from Act II of Tirso de Molina's La celosa de sí misma:

> Sé sumiller de cortina,
> descubre aquesa apariencia,
> tocarán las chirimías;
> que en las tramoyas pareces
> poeta de Andalucía.[6]

The lines mention the music which often accompanied such a discovery, and also suggest that stage-hands were employed to draw back the curtains. A less flattering description is to be found in a traveller's account which describes the theatre of Cadiz in 1694: "As for their Scenes and Ornaments, a Mountebanks Scaffold is an illustrious contrivance to 'em: Two or three dirty Blankets pin'd across the Stage, serves for the Curtain, that is, The flat Scene before which they Act and when they have anything to show behind that, they draw the Wollen Scene, and then the Audience may suppose what they will."[7] At times play-texts refer to the opening of a door or doors to disclose the discovery-space, as in Act I of Calderón's Los cabellos de Absalón, where the protagonist says: "Este es de Amón el cuarto; ya has llegado / más del efecto, que del pie, guiado," and David commands: "Abrid aquesa puerta." However, the stage direction reveals that in reality a curtain was used: Corren una cortina, y está Amon sentado en una silla, arrimada a un bufete, y de la otra parte Jonadab (STAGE DIRECTION 128). Joab's following speech suggests that a light could be seen in the discovery-space:

> Ya, señor, está abierta
> y al resplandor escaso que por ella
> nos comunica la mayor estrella,
> al príncipe le mira,
> sentado en una silla.[8]   (128-32)

One might well ask how it could be possible for the spectator to see a light, particularly the feeble light of a candle, when, as we know, plays were always performed in the commercial theatres in broad daylight.[9] The geographical orientation of the theatres is of relevance: the main axis of the Príncipe was East/West, and that of the Cruz South-East/North-West. The afternoon sun would therefore fall from the right-hand side of the spectators who stood or were seated facing the stage. The patios of the theatres were

232

covered with an awning, and the sunlight would therefore be diffused; nevertheless, the level of illumination of the open stage must have been significantly higher than that of the discovery-space, set back under the balcony, and thus shielded from the direct light of the sun. The visual effect is similar to that experienced by an observer standing in a sunlit road and looking into the window of a house. From inside the house, the room looks well-lit, but from outside it gives the impression of being dark, owing to the difference in levels of illumination. A large number of plays can be cited in support of this theory, which explains why the discovery-space is so often used to represent a prison, cave or grotto.

The discovery-space is used for four main purposes, of which the most common is the representation of a prison or cave. It is also used to disclose the results of violence, as in the final cuadro of Calderón's El alcalde de Zalamea, when the dead body of the Captain is revealed sitting in a chair, and the King is urged by Pedro Crespo to look behind him:

> Si no créeis
> que es esto, señor, verdad,
> volved los ojos, y vedlo.
> Aquéste es el Capitán.[10] (907-10)

In Calderón's El médico de su honra, doña Mencía is thus discovered on three occasions. In Act II she is revealed sleeping: Descubre una cortina donde está durmiendo (SD 881); and in Act III she is discovered writing a letter: Alza una cortina, y descubre a doña Mencía escribiendo (SD 410). On both occasions the husband, don Gutierre, is led by circumstantial evidence to fear the worst, and these two discoveries therefore lead up to the final discovery, the chilling revelation of the dead body of the murdered wife:

> D. Gut.   Vuelve a esta parte la cara
>   y verás sangriento el Sol,
>   verás la Luna eclipsada . . .

> Descubre a doña Mencía en una cama, desangrada.

> Rey.   ;Notable suceso! (Ap. Aquí
>   la prudencia es de importancia.
>   Mucho en reportarme haré.
>   Tomó notable venganza.)
>   Cubrid ese horror que asombra,
>   ese prodigio que espanta,

espectáculo que admira,
símbolo de la desgracia.[11]   (815-31)

As can be seen from the dialogue, the dead body is
displayed to the audience for a short space of time
only. The discovery-space could also be used for the
revelation of symbolic or emblematic scenes, as in
Tirso de Molina's La prudencia en la mujer (Acts I
and II), or La venganza de Tamar (Act III). It could
also be utilized, more prosaically, as an extension of
the main playing area and for the introduction on to
the open stage of bulky furniture and properties, as
in the garden scene of Act II of the Alcalde de
Zalamea.[12]

    The use of the discovery-space to represent a
prison is well illustrated in the first cuadro of Act I
of La vida es sueño. The play begins with Rosaura
making her entrance on the balcony which ran across
the rear of the stage: Sale en lo alto de un monte
Rosaura, vestida de hombre en traje de camino, y en
diciendo los primerosa versos, baja (SD 1).[13] Her
first speech consists of 22 lines, and allows sufficient time for her to appear on the balcony and
descend to stage level in the sight of the audience:
"ciega y desesperada, / bajaré la cabeza enmarañada /
deste monte eminente / que abrasa al sol el ceño de
la frente" (13-16). She is followed by Clarín, who
similarly descends. On the open stage, she descries
the prison, represented by the discovery-space. The
stage direction reads: Descúbrese Segismundo con una
cadena y la luz, vestido de pieles (SD 102), and
Rosaura's simultaneous speech stresses the darkness
of the prison and the feeble light of the candle which
can be seen within:

              ¿No es breve luz aquella
              caduca exhalación, pálida estrella,
              que en trémulos desmayos,
              pulsando ardores y latiendo rayos,
              hace más tenebrosa
              la oscura habitación con luz dudosa?
              Sí, pues a sus reflejos
              puedo determinar (aunque de lejos)
              una prisión oscura
              que es me un vivo cadáver sepultura;
              y porque más de asombre,
              en el traje de fiera yace un hombre
              de prisiones cargado,
              y sólo de la luz acompañado. (85-98)

Segismundo is dressed in skins, and his symbolic costume links him as prisoner with the monsters who inhabit caves or are incarcerated in other Calderonian works.

One such monster is Semíramis in La hija del aire. The Primera parte of this play opens with antithetical speeches off stage and a contrast between sweet and harsh music. A grotto or cave is seen at stage left, and within Semíramis, hammering at the door and demanding to be let out: Ha de haber una puerta de una gruta al lado izquierdo, y dentro den golpes, y dice Semíramis dentro (SD 13).14 I do not wish here to discuss whether La hija del aire was written for corral or for Court performance, nor to consider the question of the authorship of the Segunda parte. The text of the Primera parte in Calderón's Tercera parte (Madrid, 1664), suggests a performance in the commercial theatres, but it could well be that the play is printed from a text of what was originally a Court play adapted for the corrales. At all events, as we shall see later, caves and grottoes are to be found in both Court plays and corral plays; what is unusual here is that the cave is not centre stage, but to one side. Enter Tiresias, dressed in skins, and torn between the demands which come from both sides of the stage, and those of Semíramis in her prison. He unlocks the door of the prison, and enter Semíramis, vestida de pieles (SD 43). She has been imprisoned from birth and now hears the strains of music for the first time; significantly, she is more attracted to the harsh music of trumpet and drum, "de Marte bélico horror" (18), than to the sweet music of love. Prophecies at her birth had foretold that she would be "horror / del mundo" (134-5), that her love would turn a great King into a tyrant, and that finally she would be the cause of his death; it was for this reason that she was imprisoned, but it is also clear that imprisonment has wrought her temper to the point where she may well, if permitted, bring about the evils prophesied at her birth. Semíramis, then, is, like Segismundo, a "fiera racional" (179), and so she will prove herself to be in the course of the play. She is now returned to her prison. In the second cuadro, Lisías describes her prison, beside a lake amid harsh mountains. The approach is through a tangled wood--"confuso laberinto / de bien marañadas ramas / y de mal compuestos riscos" (702-4)--the image of the labyrinth or maze which is also associated with the prison of Segismundo.15 Taking pity on the sighs and groans of the prisoner,

Menón breaks down the door of the prison (773-7) and
liberates, not the horrible monster which had been
feared, but a beautiful woman, a "divino / monstruo"
(778-9). Semíramis now tells her tale: the product
of a rape, born under an evil star, her mother died
in giving birth to her. Despite all warnings, Menón
takes her with him, overcome by her beauty. The motif
of the prison reappears at the beginning of Act II;
kept in isolation in a beautiful garden by Menón, Semíramis is as much a prisoner of his love as she was
before in her cave. One prison has been exchanged for
another, although Menón claims rather to be himself the
prisoner of her beauty. She decides to flee: "¿jamás /
más que un bruto no he de ser?" (1255-6). In Act III
Semíramis has gained the love of King Nino; Menón in
desperation seeks at night to enter the palace garden
in order to see her. Discovered, Nino at the request
of Semíramis grants Menón his life, but has his eyes
put out. Menón thus at the end of the play finds himself in another prison, that of blindness, echoing the
imprisonment of Semíramis at the beginning of the play
and underlining the manner in which Nino is himself a
self-inflicted prisoner of his sensuality and Semíramis
of her fate. The _Primera parte_ ends with Menón's
prophecies of destruction and death, and with dire
portents in the heavens. The action of the _Segunda
parte_ takes place after an interval of years. Menón
has committed suicide, Nino has died, and Semiramis
rules in place of their son Ninias. She is victorious
over Lidoro, and commands him to be imprisoned and
treated like a dog. In the second _cuadro_ Ninias is
acclaimed by the common people, and Semíramis vows to
retire to a voluntary imprisonment:

> el más oculto retiro
> deste palacio será
> desde hoy sepulcro mío,
> adonde la luz del sol
> no entrará por un resquicio.   (848-52)

The figure of the chained Lidoro, who appears at the
end of the Act, is a reminder of the unstable nature
of human affairs (1050). In Act II, blinded with rage
Semíramis has shut herself away in a gloomy self-imposed
prison (1263-4). By the third _cuadro_ she has repented
of this rash action, and decides to take her own son,
the young king Ninias, prisoner. She will blindfold
him and conduct him to a dark cell: "podré ciego
traerle / donde el sol otra vez no llegue a verle"
(2142-3). The blindfolding of Ninias thus echoes the

physical blinding of Menón and the moral blindness of other characters, and is equated with and reinforced by night imagery. In Act III Lidoro, freed from prison, is again threatened with imprisonment and, at the end of the play, Ninias is freed and Semíramis's treachery discovered. This bald summary has concentrated on the use of one image in the play: that of imprisonment.[16] Extended during the two parts of the play to include the physical darkness of the night and that of blindness, and to encompass the self-imposed blindness of those who trust only to their own judgment and are swayed by their passions, the image is built on the appearance in Act I of the Primera parte of Semíramis in her grotto-prison, dressed in skins, the fiera racional whose freeing will bring about the disasters foretold at her birth.

The cave is used for a different purpose in El mágico prodigioso. In the third cuadro of Act II, the Devil, successful in his temptation of Cipriano, has drawn up a cédula. The text suggests that they are on the balcony of the corral stage--"¿Qué ves desta galería?" (1912)[17]--and the scene has parallels with the Temptation on the Mount. In order to impress Cipriano, the Devil literally moves mountains: Múdase un monte de una parte a otra del tablado (SD 1926). The Devil then displays to Cipriano the sleeping form of Justina, contrasting the dark setting with the beauty of the girl:

> Pues rasgando
> las duras entrañas, tú,
> monstruo de elementos cuatro,
> manifiesta la hermosura
> que en tu oscuro centro guardo.

Abrese un peñasco y está Justina durmiendo.

(1939-44)

Probably the effect is staged elsewhere than in the discovery-space, which would not have been visible to actors located on the balcony. Impressed by the Devil's power, Cipriano signs the bond with his blood. The Devil warns him that he can teach him his magic arts in one year, provided that "en una cueva encerrados, / sin estudiar otra cosa, / hemos de vivir entrambos . . ." (1993-5). At the beginning of Act III, the cave is clearly located in the discovery-space, and Cipriano enters on to the platform stage from it: de una como cueva (SD 2026). He contrasts

237

"este monte elevado / en sí mismo al alcázar estrellado"
with "aquesta cueva oscura, / de dos vivos funesta
sepultura"; nevertheless, both have been the "escuela
ruda" in which he has learnt the magic arts of the
Devil (2032-9). The mountain, then, aspires to Heaven,
and the cave, in the bowels of the earth, is cut off
from the natural harmony, the equivalent of the grave;
the images of movement upward and movement downward
symbolize the falsity of this knowledge, which vies
with Heaven and at the same time debases the human
being. The magic is infernal, and will cause discord
in nature (2044-63). But in coming out of the cave
into the sunlight, Cipriano has made use of his free-
will, as the Devil realizes:

> ¿A qué, usando otra vez de tu albedrío,
> más que de mi preceto,
> con qué fin, por qué causa, y a qué efeto,
> (Enojado.)
> osado o ignorante,
> sales a ver del sol la faz brillante?
>
> (2065-9)

Although Cipriano is still capable of making use of
his free-will, his reply to the Devil reveals his infernal pride: ". . . aún tú mismo no puedes / decir,
si es que me igualas, que me excedes" (2074-5). It
is a dark knowledge that he has been taught:

> pues la nigromancia he penetrado,
> cuyas líneas oscuras
> me abrirán las funestas sepulturas,
> haciendo que su centro
> aborte los cadáveres, que dentro
> tiranamente encierra
> la avarienta codicia de la tierra,
> respondiendo por puntos
> a mis voces los pálidos difuntos. (2079-87)

The cave in this play is, therefore, the image of an
attack on God's order, the centre of an underground
cult of power aimed at the destruction of the harmonious world which God has created. But the Devil's
schooling can only be self-imposed; man has always the
power to make use of his free-will, and to step forth
from the dark cave into the sunlight.

When we turn to examine plays which were undoubtedly written for performance at Court, we run into
problems. The published texts very often do not give

detailed stage directions, and their paucity can
clearly be seen by comparing the text of Andrómeda y
Perseo published in Parte veinte i una de comedias
nuevas, escogidas de los mejores ingenios de España
(Madrid, 1663) with that of the manuscript recently
discovered by Phyllis Dearborn Massar.[18] The drawings
of Baccio del Bianco, preserved in that manuscript,
indicate clearly that it was possible for a cave or
grotto to be placed at the rear of the sets of perspective flats which made up the visible-change stage
machinery of the theatres of the Coliseo of the Buen
Retiro and the Salón dorado of the Alcázar. I shall
return to this play shortly. In Act I of Calderón's
Eco y Narciso, written for performance in 1661, the
shepherds of Arcady speak with horror of the "horrible
monstruo fiero" that inhabits "lo oculto / . . . deste
monte inculto" (148-57).[19] In the second cuadro we
are introduced to Narciso and to his mother Liríope,
both dressed in animals' skins. Narciso is anxious
for freedom and, like Segismundo, asks why he should
have less liberty than bird or beast (238-92).
Liríope promises to enlighten him, and Narciso leaves
the stage. Liríope, bearing bow and arrows, is then
confronted by Anteo, armed with a javelin. Each is
about to attack the other. As Anteo tries to capture
Liríope, she overstresses her bow and the bowstring
breaks (a foretaste of the end of the play). She
calls Narciso to her from his cave, and it is therefore at her bidding that for the first time in his
life he confronts another human being. As Narciso
asks her "Quién soy, y cómo me niegas / la libertad"
(440-1), the wind whips away half the reply. "¿Nada,
sino a hablar, me enseñas?" (450), he asks his mother
accusingly. Narciso calls on the gods and on all
natural things for help, thus revealing a desire to
live in harmony with the universe; his natural tendency is towards good, but he needs, and lacks, gui-
dance. In the third cuadro the mystery of his birth
is revealed. A shepherdess of Arcady, Liríope had
been loved by Céfiro; she had not returned his love
and, in desperation, he had carried her off, borne by
the wind, the instrument of discord, to a lofty mountain in which was a dark cave, and there had raped
her. Abandoned by Céfiro, she had been left in the
care of Tiresias, an aged magician. Liríope tells
how Tiresias had wished to make himself the equal of
Jupiter and, for his pride, had been imprisoned in
darkness. Liríope too was imprisoned--"presa allí,
y ciega también" (817)--although innocent of all
wrong. But in her imprisonment she gains knowledge

from Tiresias, although the learning she acquires is not necessarily for good; Tiresias's knowledge produces discord in the heavens. In due time she bore a son, Narciso. Before his death Tiresias had foretold the birth of Narciso and warned Liríope that "una voz y una hermosura / solicitarán su fin, / amando y aborreciendo" (834-5), and had advised the mother to keep her child from knowledge. Narciso, thus, is another being who has grown up in an enclosed world, symbolized by the cave, and who is now to be exposed, against his mother's wishes, to the society of other human beings. The horoscope is both true and false and, as Basilio in endeavoring to frustrate the auguries at the birth of Segismundo brought about the very dangers he was trying to prevent, so Liríope has misunderstood the prophecy and brings disaster on her son. She had understood the augury to refer to the voice and beauty of another. She tells her son: "tú sólo no más / podrás guardarte a ti mismo" (1423-4), but, in her attempts to avoid destiny, she has destroyed this possibility. When Eco falls in love with Narciso, Liríope reacts selfishly. In imprisoning her son, she had violated a natural law and broken the great chain of being. And now she kills love, reducing it from a dialogue to a mere echo, a reflection of self-love, rounding out the circle and preventing the possibility of any escape for Narciso. "Cumplió el hado su amenaza, / valiéndose de los medios / que para estorbarlo puse" (3221-3).

The cave as a philosopher's retreat appears at the very beginning of La estatua de Prometeo, when the protagonist emerges from the "triste pavorosa gruta" (10).[20] He symbolizes man's "anhelo de saber" (88). Without knowing it, he already possessed "la lógica natural" (106), and with good teaching new paths were opened up and darkness became light. He hoped, with his newly-acquired knowledge, to govern his native land wisely, but had been overthrown by a "ciego popular furia" (159). He therefore retired to the cave and studied the lessons of the heavens and of nature. Mankind had rejected knowledge (199-200), but the gods praised it. Prometeo pays homage to Minerva, goddess of learning, and decides to make a statue of her, thus creating a neo-Platonic reflection of absolute knowledge. The statue is to remain in his cave until a suitable temple is built. Minerva makes her appearance in the guise of a wild beast pursued by Prometeo--an emblematic picture of the difficulty of grasping knowledge--but takes off her animal skins and reveals

beneath the costume in which Prometeo had portrayed
her in his statue: she is the true version of what
he had copied in "sombras" and "fantásticas ideas"
(473-4). At the behest of Minerva, Prometeo flies
up to the golden castle in the sky. Enter Prometeo's
brother, Epimeteo, searching for the "funesta boca" of
the cave (597). Martial music issues from within the
gloomy cavern, and Palas, goddess of war, commands
Epimeteo to find and smash the statue of Minerva. In
Act II Prometeo descends from heaven with the gift of
fire, stolen from the sun, enters the grotto and dedi-
cates the torch to Minerva, leaving it in the hand of
the statue. When Epimeteo endeavors to steal the
statue, it comes to life: the torch of the sun has
breathed life into it. It is not Minerva, however,
who steps down from the pedestal, but Pandora, and
Prometeo confuses the living statue with the goddess
(the two being differentiated for the audience by contrasting Minerva's recitative and song with Pandora's
spoken lines). Prometeo is now confusing human knowledge with the divine. The cave in this play, therefore, represents the acquisition of knowledge through
intellectual effort undertaken in solitude; as Minerva
says to Prometeo in Act I: "que te aparte / de todos
donde a solas pueda hablarte" (504-5). The play
teaches us not to confuse human science with the
divine knowledge of which it can only be a pale reflection.

The creation in a court spectacle or play of a
scene set in a cave or grotto had become a commonplace
device, and is echoed by Baccio del Bianco's design
for Hell in Act II of Calderón's Andrómeda y Perseo.[21]
The previous scene had been of snow-covered rustic
cottages, and the fires of Hell provide an abrupt
contrast. The complicated setting, with its remini-
scences of Callot and Hieronymous Bosch, was disclosed
to the audience for a relatively short space of time,
and was followed by a woodland scene. Such a scene
had its counterparts in many Italian productions of
the seventeenth century. Of more interest for the
present paper is the use of the cave at the beginning
of Act II. The grotto of Morfeo is disclosed,[22] with
the figure of Morfeo, viejo venerable, sobre unas
hierbas de su significación, como son beleños y
cipreses.[23] Perseo demands:

> ¿Qué lóbrega estancia es ésta,
> en cuyos cóncavos hondos
> delirios son cuantos veo,

fantasías cuantas toco?

He falls asleep and, as he sleeps, Morfeo discloses
to him the secret of his origin:

> Representadle, ilusiones,
> su nacimiento, de modo
> que le vea, y que no sea
> creído después de los otros.

According to the stage direction, descúbrese el
retrete de Danae, vestida de Dama, y cuatro Damas
en ella cantando y una dueña.[24] Danae is revealed
in her chamber within the grotto of Morfeo, which
opens to disclose a scene-within-a-scene, with its
own proscenium and the illusion of perspective created
by means of a backcloth on which are painted doors
and galleries. Jupiter descends from aloft on a
golden eagle, and the episode shows how he took possession of Danae in the shape of a shower of gold.
The mystery of Perseo's birth thus revealed, cúbrese
toda la gruta de Morfeo y el retrete, y vuelve a
quedarse como antes estaba, con las caserías nevadas.
The action of the play-within-the-play is thus taking
place in the mind of the sleeping Perseo, and the
characters are enacting in plastic form the thoughts,
visions, dreams of the protagonist, a device familiar
enough in comedia and auto sacramental.

The auto version of La vida es sueño uses the
cave to represent the "lóbrego seno / de la tierra,
el duro silo / de sus entrañas, el ciego / vientre
de su oscuro limbo" where Man, before his creation,
is imprisoned "sin ser, alma y vida, / discurso,
elección ni aviso" (342-7).[25] Man is revealed in
the cave, dressed in skins, and with Gracia at his
side bearing a torch, symbolizing the ability to
choose between good and evil (652-7). Tempted by
the Devil, man eats the apple and is consigned again
to his prison, where he is revealed once more clad
in skins (SD 1372) and chained (SD 1377). He escapes
from his prison once he has recalled to him Entendimiento and, with his help, summoned Albedrío. Once
Man realizes that, by making use of his reason and
free-will, he may call on God's grace, his chains
fall away from him. His place in prison is assumed
by Christ, who thus takes upon himself Man's suffer-
ings, symbolized by the chains and the dark imprisonment (SD 1682). Christ is finally revealed on the
cross in the same location (1742-5).[26]

The cave as a symbol of womb/tomb is explained by
Pecado in El pleito matrimonial del cuerpo y del alma:

> los ojos vuelve, a mirar
> Abrese una gruta como de una peña y estará
>   EL CUERPO como echado y dormido
>   el corazón de esa gruta,
>   cuya boca se espereza
>   para que su centro escupa
>   el Cuerpo, que en ella ahora
>   como en el seno se oculta
>   materno, que poco o nada
>   la significación muda
>   la explicación del concepto
>   porque sean peñas duras
>   las entrañas que le aborten,
>   puesto que su primer cuna
>   el centro fue de la tierra
>   que ha de ser su sepultura,
>   donde el nacer y el morir
>   son dos acciones tan una
>   que no son más que pasar
>   desde una tumba a otra tumba.[27]   (169-86)

The implications of the cave setting are therefore multiple. Segismundo's prison/cave is at once
tomb and womb, the symbol of the enslavement of the
free-will and of man's imperfection, and Plato's
cave.[28] The discovered play-within-a-play in Andrómeda y Perseo is the shadowy illusion of what is
passing through the mind of the protagonist. The
cave as the beginning of a process of education merges
with the topos of the anchorite/philosopher removed
from the world to produce the philosophic figure of
Prometeo in La estatua de Prometeo, and a parodic
counterpart in the satanic magician of El mágico
prodigioso. Whilst Prometeo seeks true revelation
by retreat into a secluded world of study, the acquisition of knowledge is symbolized by the torch; in
El mágico prodigioso, the dark knowledge imparted by
the Devil is contrasted with the light of God's sun.
Physical darkness is equated with physical blindness
in La hija del aire, and in the same play and in El
médico de su honra, with moral blindness. The repeated
use of the discovery-space as a gloomy setting--the
theatre of violence, the home of dark mysteries, the
cave or prison of non-being--is suggested by the different levels of illumination which would make a discovery-space in the corrales or in the lower storey of
an auto cart appear dark by contrast with the open

stage. In Court plays, with an artificially illumi-
nated stage, the contrast would be simpler to achieve
and even more effective. The connection of many of
these symbolic interpretations with the grave--the
dark prison, the gloomy grotto, the cave in the bowels
of a mountain, the tomb of non-existence--when read
together with the symbols of upward and downward movement, recall the use of three levels in religious performances of medieval origin in the churches of Eastern
Spain, where Heaven was represented aloft in the
vaulting of the church, the earth by the actors who
appeared on a scaffold or on the level of the spectators, and the location of Hell at a lower level was
suggested by a trapdoor or Hell mouth. Many plays
written for the corral stage certainly use the upper
level to suggest moral superiority, and, as has been
demonstrated in the present paper, the use of the
discovery-space or "inner stage," whilst on the same
level as the platform stage, time and again gives the
impression that the action therein is connected with
the grave, or with the infernal regions.[29] This is
of course not always so, and many plays use the
discovery-space for other purposes: nevertheless,
I hope to have demonstrated that the staging of many
corral plays embodies a reminiscence, perhaps uncon-
scious, of the three levels of Heaven, Earth and Hell,
and that the symbolic significance is made easier to
grasp by the ingenious use of the staging potentiali-
ties of the apron stage, the balcony and the discovery-
space of the corrales de comedias, and of similar
effects in the Court theatre and on the carts of the
autos sacramentales.

Westfield College, University of London

Notes

[1]Ignacio de Luzán, La poétics, ed. Russell P.
Sebold (Barcelona: Labor, 1977), 467.

[2]J. E. Varey and N. D. Shergold, "Tres dibujos
inéditos de los antiguos corrales de comedias de
Madrid," Revista de la Biblioteca, Archivo y Museo
del Ayuntamiento de Madrid, 20 (1951), 319-20.

[3]N. D. Shergold, A History of the Spanish Stage
from Medieval Times until the End of the Seventeenth
Century (Oxford: Clarendon, 1967), 202-3.

[4]Alvaro Cubillo de Aragón, La perfecta casada,
Act III; in Dramáticos posteriores a Lope de Vega,
ed. Ramón de Mesonero Romanos, BAE 47 (Madrid: Suc.
de Hernando, 1913), 122.

[5]Antonio Enríquez Gómez, La prudente Abigail, in
Academias de las Musas (Bordeaux, 1642).

[6]Tirso de Molina, La celosa de sí misma, in
Comedias escogidas, ed. Juan Eugenio Hartzenbusch,
BAE 5 (Madrid: Atlas, 1944), 137.

[7]Anon., An Account of Spain (London: Joseph
Wilde, 1700). See Gerald E. Wade, "A Note on a
Seventeenth-Century comedia Performance," BCom, 10,
1 (1958), 10-12 (p. 11).

[8]Quotations are from Pedro Calderón de la Barca,
Los cabellos de Absalón, ed. Gwynne Edwards (Oxford:
Pergamon, 1973).

[9]The Reglamentos de teatros of 1608 stipulate that
performances should begin at 2 p.m. from October to
March, and at 4 p.m. from April to September, "de
suerte que se acaben vna hora antes que anochezca";
J. E. Varey and N. D. Shergold, Fuentes para la historia del teatro en España, III. Teatros y comedias
en Madrid: 1600-1650. Estudio y documentos (London:
Tamesis, 1971), doc. núm. 2, p. 48. In 1641 it was
laid down that the plays should begin in winter at
2 p.m., in spring at 3 p.m. and in summer at 4 p.m.,
"de modo que se salga siempre de dia claro"; Fuentes
III, doc. núm. 38, p. 93.

[10]The quotation is from Pedro Calderón de la Barca,
El alcalde de Zalamea, ed. Peter N. Dunn (Oxford:

245

Pergamon, 1966).

[11]Quotations are from Pedro Calderón de la Barca, Dramas de honor, II, ed. Angel Valbuena Briones, Clásicos Castellanos, 142 (Madrid: Espasa-Calpe, 1965).

[12]See my analysis in "Espacio escénico," in II Jornadas de Teatro Clásico Español. Almagro, 1979, ed. Francisco Ruiz Ramón (Madrid: Ministerio de Cultura, 1980), 19-34 (p. 27).

[13]Quotations are from Pedro Calderón de la Barca, La vida es sueño, ed. Albert E. Sloman (Manchester: UP, 1961).

[14]Quotations are from Pedro Calderón de la Barca, La hija del aire, ed. Gwynne Edwards (London: Tamesis, 1970).

[15]M. S. Maurin, "The Monster, the Sepulchre and the Dark: Related patterns of imagery in La vida es sueño," HR, 35 (1967), 161-78.

[16]On the symbolism of the prison in the plays of Calderón, see Alexander A. Parker, "Metáfora y símbolo en la interpretación de Calderón," in Actas del Primer Congreso Internacional de Hispanistas, ed. Frank Pierce and Cyril A. Jones (Oxford: Dolphin, 1964), 141-60; Gwynne Edwards, The Prison and the Labyrinth: Studies in Calderonian tragedy (Cardiff: Univ. of Wales Press, 1978); and P. R. K. Halkhoree and J. E. Varey, "Sobre el tema de la cárcel en El príncipe constante," in Hacia Calderón. Cuarto Coloquio Anglogermano. Wolfenbüttel 1975, ed. Hans Flasche, Karl-Hermann Körner and Hans Mattauch (Berlin-New York: de Gruyter, 1979), 30-40.

[17]Quotations are from Pedro Calderón de la Barca, Comedias religiosas, I, ed. Angel Valbuena Prat, Clásicos Castellanos, 106 (Madrid: Espasa-Calpe, 1930).

[18]Phyllis Dearborn Massar, "Scenes for a Calderón Play by Baccio del Bianco," Master Drawings, 15, 4 (1977), 365-75, and Plates 21-31.

[19]Quotations are from Pedro Calderón de la Barca, Eco y Narciso, ed. Charles V. Aubrun (Paris: Institut d'Etudes Hispaniques, 1963).

[20]Quotations are from Pedro Calderón de la Barca, *La estatua de Prometeo,* ed. Charles V. Aubrun (Paris: Institut d'Etudes Hispaniques, 1965).

[21]Massar, Plate 27.

[22]Massar, Plate 25.

[23]Quotations are from Pedro Calderón de la Barca, *Obras completas,* I. *Dramas,* ed. Angel Valbuena Briones (Madrid: Aguilar, 1966), 1641-80.

[24]Massar, Plate 26.

[25]Quotations are from Pedro Calderón de la Barca, *Autos sacramentales,* I, ed. Angel Valbuena Prat, Clásicos Castellanos 69 (Madrid: Espasa-Calpe, 1942).

[26]For a further consideration of this play, see my forthcoming article "Calderón's *auto sacramental, La vida es sueño,* in Performance," to appear in *Iberoromania.*

[27]The quotation is from Pedro Calderón de la Barca, *Autos sacramentales,* II, ed. Angel Valbuena Prat, Clásicos Castellanos 74 (Madrid: Espasa-Calpe, 1942).

[28]On the connection between Plato and *La vida es sueño,* see Jackson I. Cope, "The Platonic Metamorphoses of Calderón's *La vida es sueño,*" *MLN,* 86 (1971), 225-41; Michele F. Sciacca, "Verdad y sueño de *La vida es sueño,* de Calderón de la Barca," *Clavileño,* I, 5 (1950), 1-9; and Harlan G. Sturm, "From Plato's Cave to Segismundo's Prison: The four levels of reality and experience," *MLN,* 80 (1974), 280-9.

[29]For a more detailed exposition of this idea, see my paper read at the Albany conference on Hispanism as Humanism, March 1980: "The Multi-Level Stage: Classical or Renaissance?" (in press).

Calderón: Imitator and Initiator

Vern G. Williamsen

As I spent the past several years working with the
minor dramatists of seventeenth-century Spain, I came
to realize that those dramatists who wrote during the
last half of the century, in competition with Pedro
Calderón and some of the others among the finest Golden
Age dramatists such as Agustín de Moreto and Francisco
de Rojas Zorrilla, were following the trends of the
times in which they wrote. Actually, it is possible
to see those changing qualities most clearly in the
works of the minor dramatists. This may be true since
they, as writers in competition with more illustrious
playwrights, placed greater emphasis on those elements
of dramatic structure and style that had the most appeal
for the audiences they were addressing.[1] Through more
careful plot construction they simplified the structures underlying their dramas. They made use of the
formal stylized poetic language of the high Baroque.
They sought a more systematic development of thematic
as well as of poetic unity. In part by being more
attentive to the principles of dramatic decorum, they
developed the characterization of the persons in their
plays to a higher level than that employed in earlier
works. Under the influence of the court theaters they
wrote plays that called for an increasingly complicated
staging. They spent a great deal of their creative
effort in reworking plays by earlier writers in order
to bring them into conformity with contemporary dramatic
practices. And, in general, they approached their
works from a more serious point of view, seeking to
achieve a greater intellectual and less emotional
dramatic effect. Edward M. Wilson and Duncan Moir
have reported that these are the very qualities that
identify them as belonging to the Calderonian School.[2]
Also to be noted is the fact that although these
writers continued to write comedias in the same vein
and dealing with the same themes as had been popular
earlier in the century, the growth in number and in
kind of two special classes of plays, the comic comedia
de figurón and the showy mythological drama, was
especially remarkable.

Antonio Hurtado de Mendoza consistently used
plots of socially significant themes: the social
climber's use of wealth as a means for gaining acceptance; the roguish veterans who, on returning from

foreign wars, depended on opportunity and wits as a means of gaining a living; and the problems of an unhappy marriage that could only be resolved through divorce. In each of his plays, the characterization is so carefully and well handled, so interesting in itself, that the thesis, though properly subliminal, is unmistakable in its presentation.

Alvaro Cubillo de Aragón is most interesting for the steps he took to simplify the structure of the comedia. He practically eliminated the subplot as a technique for providing complications or dramatic tension. He did this both in his original works and in those he rewrote from earlier models.

Antonio Enríquez Gómez stands out not only for his depiction of opportunistic characters forced to thread their way carefully around dangers thrown in their paths by the opposing forces they had to deal with, but also for the avoidance of accepted theatrical conventions in his works: his heroes may never marry or they may, indeed, marry early in the play. The more serious comedias of Enríquez Gómez do not necessarily revolve around problems susceptible of resolution through marriage.

Agustín de Salazar y Torres openly employed his audience's probable knowledge of literature and history to supply some of the expository material needed in his works, adding thus to the economy of words in his presentation. He also made heavy use of dramatic convention as the stuff from which to create humor. This is most clearly seen in the constant references made by characters in his plays to the fact that they were, after all, only figments of the theatrical world.

Sor Juana Inés de la Cruz is noteworthy for the perfectly symmetrical mode in which she cast her plays as well as for the novel, inventive way in which she applied conventional symbolism: bringing lights onto the stage to create chaos and putting them out as a means of bringing about a resolution, a clarification that results from the darkness; an escape from the labyrinth muddles matters, a return to the maze clears them up.[3]

Francisco de Bances Candamo deserves recognition for the perfection and three-dimensional quality of the characters in his works. They, like all real humans, have weaknesses and strengths, attractive as well as repulsive qualities that act in concert to create verisimile personalities.

In summary, there was, in the last half of the seventeenth century, a gradual movement towards the acceptance of the theatrical norms that were to govern the drama of the following century. We find in the plays written in this period the very qualities that became the hallmarks of Neoclassic theater. Ignacio de Luzán whose Poética of 1737 is still too frequently cited as having given birth to Neoclassicism in Spanish letters,[4] recognized as much when he praised the dramas of Bances Candamo for their perfection of style, good taste, verisimilitude, decorum and propriety of both action and character: qualities that, along with an observance of the basic dramatic unities define that which is Neoclassic.[5]

Naturally, a corollary problem came to mind as I examined these conclusions: the extent to which the definition of their works as Calderonian was a dependable one. What is Calderón's responsibility for those elements cited as the basis for grouping these poets under his aegis? Are the devices, structures, and procedures really Calderón's own? If not, if they are instead the result of a natural evolutionary process in the history of Spanish drama rather than a result of Calderón's direct influence, why have we so long recognized the existence of a Calderonian epoch (as following an earlier Lopean cycle) in the development of the comedia? Is such periodization a valid, meaningful process or does it only represent a convenient tag under which to bundle an otherwise amorphous mass of plays?

In determining the "Calderonian" nature of the final two-thirds of the seventeenth century, it must first be stated that no other dramatist of that period wrote as many of the extant texts as did Calderón. Of the comedias we have from his hand, fifteen were probably written before 1631 (for an average of one and one-half plays per year in the third decade of the poet's life). The twenty year period from 1631 to 1650 saw the preparation of between sixty and sixty-five of the extant plays, an average of more than three per year. In the last thirty years of his life (1651-1681), Calderón seems to have produced no more than thirty-five to forty comedias, only slightly more than one play per year, a high percentage of them in the nature of mythological works, court spectacles, or libretti for musical productions rather than true comedias. That the reduction in his production of dramatic works is not due to mere lack of creative energy is shown by the fact that this same period witnessed the writing of fifty-one of the seventy-one autos sacramentales that he wrote.6

I have previously shown how one poetic idea evolved in the theater of Antonio Mira de Amescua, in plays written between 1602 and 1630. That metaphorical system gradually took on the format of a décima with a repeated questioning refrain that re-appeared as Segismundo's soliloquy on liberty in the first act of Calderón's La vida es sueño (1634).7 The mutual admiration of the older Mira de Amescua and the much younger Calderón is demonstrated by far more than one such poetic interchange, but this one is most interesting because Calderón did not let it lie there untouched. He himself dragged it out for refurbishment. He made use of the same idea in Los tres afectos de amor (1658) in which Rosarda laments (Act I):

¿Qué ansia como que no encuentre
fiera que apenas cobrada
la primera piel se vea,
que a buscar al sol no salga?
¿Qué horror como que no mire
pez que la primera escama
arme apenas, cuando surque
vivo bajel de las aguas?
¿Y qué rigor como que
no halle flor que el primer nácar
apenas rompa al capillo,
cuando ya goce del aura;
y que yo con más instinto,
con más razón, con más alma
y con menos libertad
envidie, sin dar más causa
que el delito del nacer,
ave, fiera, pez y planta?8

Here we have an example of the process by which Calderón adopted an existing poetic structure and its metaphor, and adapted it twice to his own purposes. He later re-adapted it to fit still another context in his auto of 1673 La vida es sueño where it again wears its décima format.9

But Mira de Amescua was not the only poet whose work or ideas were appropriated by Calderón. As is well known, the third act of Tirso de Molina's La venganza de Tamar reappeared, practically verbatim, as the second act of Calderón's Los cabellos de Absalón. Various hypotheses have been advanced to explain this strange use by Calderón of another's text. Among them, Otto Rank who suggested that one of the reasons Calderón may have made use of the earlier materials was to avoid the need for treating the indelicate subject of incest himself.[10] Helmy Giacoman, however, found that the difference in themes of the plays may have been of greater importance. He felt that the main concern of Tirso's work was Amón's passion while that of Calderón's comedia was Absalón's lust for power.[11] Albert E. Sloman, whose monograph is the most valuable and thorough study we have of Calderón's use of earlier plays, found that in each of the cases he studied Calderón had so reworked the materials as to present an entirely new work, but that all have in common an unswerving search for dramatic unity not present in the original.[12] Tirso's third act, which became the second act of Calderón's play, deals with the vengeance exacted upon Amón at the hands of his half-brother, Tamar's brother, Absalón. Calderón uses this action not as the climax of a Biblical story of incest but rather as the turning point in the trajectory of Absalón's search for power, that point at which he is forced into open conflict with his father. This shift in focus results in real tragedy rather than in mere vengeance for and punishment of a horrendous sin as in Tirso's work. Thus, in spite of Sloman's reservations about the quality of Calderón's Los cabellos de Absalón, [13] the lifted portion of La venganza de Tamar becomes a jewel set into a new context, a centerpiece for the inherent tragedy of the Biblical tale as perceived by Calderón.

Calderón also made use of earlier works as a source for interesting episodes that he reset into new contexts with a more or less complete rewriting. In Claramonte's Púsome el sol, salióme la luna (written before 1625), the penitent Teodora, after having lost her virginity, dresses as a man and seeks admission to a Carmelite monastery where she hopes to live the life of a religious. The lascivious Alcina who had earlier opened Teodora's house to her seducer, herself attempts to seduce the new "monk" who is living temporarily in a hermit's cave outside the walls of the monastery. When Alcina is refused, she takes the "hermit's" cloak to use as proof of her story about having been raped by him. Later Alcina brings her baby to the monastery claiming that the new monk is the father. Teodora reveals herself as a woman in order to disprove the claim and is dismissed from the monastery. Calderón uses the same idea to bring his play based on the legend of St. Eugenia, El José de las mujeres (1640-1644), to an exciting climax when Eugenia reveals herself as a woman and, therefore, incapable of having seduced Melancia as was claimed. In both cases, the original motif rests in the Biblical story of Potifar's wife but with a change in the sex of the people involved.[14] As we have seen, that change of sex in the Biblical source was not original with Calderón; his use of it to underscore the emotional climax of his play with a pungent, dramatically ironic scene was.

Besides using episodes, poetic elements, and even entire acts from previous works, Calderón at times chose to rework an entire play. As Sloman has shown in dealing with Calderón's recastings (La niña de Gómez Arias originally by Vélez de Guevara, and El alcalde de Zalamea and El médico de su honra, both of which have been attributed to Lope de Vega, as well as in three rewritings of plays he had originally developed jointly with other poets), he consistently brought an original disorderly dramatic structure under careful control. The source plays are nowhere near the beautifully arranged and unified works that Calderón later prepared. Sloman's list is, however, incomplete since some of the refundiciones have not been noted, probably because the base work was a piece written by one of the lesser lights among the Golden Age dramatists, and, therefore, less commonly studied. The coincidences of theme, structure, and language between Calderón's Guárdate del agua mansa (1649) and Antonio Hurtado de Mendoza's Cada loco con su tema (1623-1630) are a case in point.[15] Valbuena Briones has cited Don Toribio of Calderón's play as prototypical of the figurón, a character type that came to have great importance in Spanish and in French theater of the last half of the seventeenth and all of the eighteenth centuries.[15] In pointing to the distinctive qualities of Don Toribio, Valbuena noted the peculiarity of the character in that he is an "hidalgote asturiano" to whom the wealthy but unlanded "indiano" uncle wishes to marry one of his two daughters. As a country cousin, the figurón shows himself to be completely lacking in courtly manners, a facet of his personality that gives rise to both problems and humor. This is precisely the theme of Hurtado de Mendoza's earlier play. In both works, the girls are of opposite personalities, one quiet and submissive, the other not. There are in both plays three other young suitors for the girls' hands. In both, this multiplicity of suitors gives rise to the comic action. However, again the play by Calderón is a more tightly woven, less disperse work in which scenes and speeches of questionable taste have been eliminated and a more regular structure derived for the whole. But even the process of so changing an earlier work was one learned from others. Mira de Amescua, for example, when he recast Salucio del Poyo's Privanza y caída de don Alvaro de Luna (written before 1605) as La segunda de don Alvaro (1623-1624) eliminated extraneous matter, sharpened contrasts, and added psychological depth to the characters as he shaped the story into one of the few fine tragedies of the so-called Lopean cycle.[17]

As an imitator Calderón used the techniques of reworking earlier plays that he learned from Mira and from others to make use of poetic ideas, dramatic episodes (in one case a large verbatim section), themes, and even entire plots to prepare new, improved plays. As an initiator Calderón so recast the plays and materials as to achieve greater unity of theme, poetic imagery, and characterization as well as the classic unities of action, place, and occasionally time. As he reached for these unities Calderón managed, in most cases, to present a work with clear and present didactic purpose. As Duncan Moir suggested in his study, "Las comedias regulares de Calderón: ¿unos amoríos con el neoclasicimo?", the qualities so achieved by Calderon were classic in their intent.[18] In order to appreciate the full meaning of this statement we must, of course, separate those of Calderón's works that moved away from the line of true drama towards the zarzuela, opera, and court spectacle. Moir was correct in his insistence upon using the word "Classicist" to refer to Calderón, but just as correct was the suggestion made in his title that this tendency on Calderón's part was a forward step on the path towards Neoclassicism.

The proof lies in the ways in which the minor writers who, in the period after 1650, replaced Calderón as the major providers of comedia texts followed his lead: Hurtado de Mendoza learned to handle characterization and so directed his works as to serve a social purpose; Cubillo de Aragón eliminated the distracting secondary plot as a means for achieving dramatic tension; Enríquez Gómez and Salazar de Torres worked with the artificiality of theatrical stylization; Sor Juana developed a perfectly symmetrical dramatic structure; and, finally, Bances Candamo, besides developing methods of presenting characters and actions in verisimile and decorous fashion, set forth a description of dramatic construction that led directly to Luzán's Neoclassic manifesto of 1737.[19] Calderón and the others who followed him, along with their contemporaries in France (Corneille, Molière and others) mined the rich field of earlier Spanish drama for materials they might recast into a more regular, less hectic mold. While the comedia format--a three act, polymetric play--remained constant in Spain, the drama was developing towards true Neoclassicism there just as it was in the land to the north.

Sufficient evidence exists to indicate the need for a more complete study of the relationship of Calderonian drama not only to that of the commonly studied poets of the Lopean period, but to the plays written by the less frequently studied, not necessarily weaker, dramatists of both preceding and following epochs. The focus of such a study should not be the facts or the process of transmission of structures, poetic expression, or themes but rather a description of the varying dramatic effects achieved and esthetic purposes served as the materials passed from one playwright to another. I believe that further study will show Calderón to have been a key transitional figure as the prevailing esthetic tone in Spain passed from the exuberance of the Baroque to the more staid and sober qualities of the Neoclassic.

University of Missouri, Columbia

Notes

[1]My study, The Minor Dramatists of Seventeenth
Century Spain, is now in press (G. K. Hall, Boston).

[2]The Golden Age: Drama 1492-1700 (New York:
Barnes and Noble Inc., 1971): 120-44.

[3]See my study, "Forma simétrica en las comedias
barrocas de Sor Juana Inés," Cuadernos Americanos,
224 (1979): 183-93.

[4]Nigel Glendinning, The Eighteenth Century (New
York: Barnes and Noble, Inc., 1972): 90ff.

[5]Ignacio de Luzán, La poética o reglas de la
poesía, ed. Luigi de Filippo (Barcelona, 1956): II,
125.

[6]These facts are garnered from Harry Hilborn, A
Chronology of the Plays of D. Pedro Calderón de la
Barca (Toronto: University of Toronto Press, 1938).
In general, I have accepted Hilborn's findings since
any variance between them and subsequent findings of
others is insignificant in terms of the present study.

[7]"The Development of a Décima in Mira de
Amescua's Theater," Bulletin of the Comediantes, 22
(1970): 32-36.

[8]Pedro Calderón de la Barca, Obras completas, ed.
A. Valbuena Briones (Madrid: Aguilar, 1966): I, 1186.

[9]These décimas are found in scene 5 of the auto
in the second speech of Hombre. The metaphor referred
to begins with the line "Apenas nacer se ve."

[10]Otto Rank, "Die Blutschande des Amnon mit der
Thamar," in his Inzest-motif in Dichtung und Sage
(Leipzig: Franz Deuticke, 1926): 66-73.

[11]Helmy F. Giacoman, "En torno a Los cabellos de
Absalón de Pedro Calderón de la Barca," Romanische
Forschungen, 80 (1968): 340-53.

[12]The Dramatic Craftsmanship of Calderón: His
Use of Earlier Plays (Oxford: Dolphin Book Co., 1969).

[13]He says among other things (p. 127), "Only a

lack of interest, probably after work on it had begun, can account, in my opinion, for the unsatisfactoriness of the play as a whole and for the wholesale appropriation of Tirso's act."

[14]Valbuena Briones, in Obras completas, I, 905.

[15]For the text of Hurtado's play, see BAE, 45: 407-76.

[16]Obras completas, II: 1289-90.

[17]For a more complete description of the recasting by Mira, see my forthcoming Minor Dramatists, Chapter Two. For a discussion of the work by Mira as tragedy, see Raymond R. MacCurdy, "Tragic Hamartia in La próspera y adversa fortuna de don Alvaro de Luna," Hispania, 47 (1964): 82-90.

[18]Hacia Calderón: Segundo Coloquio anglogermano, Hamburgo 1970 (New York: Walter de Gruyter, 1973): 61-70.

[19]Wilson and Moir cite and describe Bances Candamo's Teatro de los teatros de los pasados y presentes siglos (1689-1690) in their The Golden Age: Drama, pp. 139-40.

De Calderón a Lorca: el tema del honor en La casa de Bernarda Alba

Eduardo Urbina

Es justo y necesario el señalar al comienzo de una obra lo que se debe en concepto de inspiración y ayuda a otros. En mi caso la obra es pequeña pero la deuda grande, y, así, no puedo por menos de reconocerla abiertamente. Tratándose de un proceso de atar cabos sueltos, es decir, de rematar los puntos en coordenadas ajenas, empezaré mencionando los padrinos que han hecho posible esta ponencia, sin que por ello les toque parte ni culpa: Edwin Honig, Calderón and the Seizures of Honor (Cambridge, Mass., 1972) y Gwynne Edwards, The Prison and the Labyrinth. Studies in Calderonian Tragedy (Cardiff, 1978). Omito por impertinente aquí mi opinión sobre sus libros y dejo para más adelante el mostrar lo oportuno de sus contribuciones para el desarrollo de mi tema.

Y pasemos al caso. Viene siendo costumario el traer a colación el nombre de Lope de Vega al analizar el origen y carácter de la obra dramática de García Lorca, sin duda, por aquello de su capacidad de absorber los gustos y maneras del pueblo y hacer de ellos un arte tan tradicional como nuevo. Ya en 1936 Pedro Salinas señalaba la conexión entre ambos en torno al tratamiento y sublimación de lo popular, en relación con lo que denominara la española "fatalidad dramática del vivir terrenal."[1] Angel del Río, en su seminal estudio sobre la vida y obra de Lorca, habla de cómo éste bebió en los clásicos, y en particular en la obra de Lope--a pesar de lo que afirmara Montesinos sobre sus escasas lecturas--"hasta hacer de la tradición en sus formas más diversas algo consustancial con su propio mundo poético." Y en otro lugar añade: "La influencia al parecer más evidente (en García Lorca) es la de los clásicos españoles como Lope y Góngora, la poesía de los cancioneros anónimos, sin olvidar algunos autores románticos."[2] Muy al caso son las observaciones del primer historiador del teatro de Lorca, Roberto Sánchez, quien, tras señalar su "sentido popularista" paralelo al de Lope, afirma que en su teatro "el conflicto moral y espiritual se resuelve con la norma de un texto calderoniano," y que en él tuvo innegable influencia el auto.[3] Aunque

Sánchez no ofrece referencia textual alguna, valga su
intuición como primicia del tema aquí abordado. Y
para no extenderme en las citas mencionaré tan sólo
el eco continuado de la conexión Lope-Lorca en críticos
como Alfredo de la Guardia,[4] María Teresa Babín[5] y,
más recientemente, Francisco Ruiz Ramón.[6]

La mención específica de Calderón como posible
fuente e inspiración de Lorca es menos frecuente pero
no por ella menos significativa. Así, François
Nourissier, a pesar de considerar a Lorca como verdadero continuador de Lope, añade que "comme Calderón,
il discernera, posé sur les visages divers de la vie,
la même masque de la mort."[7] J. L. Flecniakoska[8]
señala de manera imprecisa la deuda de Lorca con los
autores de tragedias del siglo de oro, mientras que
H. Ernest Lewald, tras reconocer el papel central del
tema del honor en sus tragedias, no vacila en afirmar
(a propósito del alcalde y su hijo en El alcalde de
Zalamea) que son "forerunners of the guardians of
middle-class morality personified centuries later by
Bernarda Alba."[9] Cedric Busette,[10] en un estudio de
poco interés y desigual sobre su dramaturgia, menciona
la importancia del triángulo amoroso en El alcalde de
Zalamea como uno de los motivos temáticos de Lorca.
Sin embargo, utiliza La vida es sueño a fin de establecer la diferencia entre la tragedia clásica de Calderón,
en la que triunfa la justicia poética y el orden social
queda afirmado, y la tragedia lorquiana. Considera a
ésta moderna, es decir, carente de claridad y de
resolución, ya que el individuo es incapaz de sobre-
ponerse a su destino. Pero quien más lejos ha llevado
la oposición entre Calderón y Lorca es Francisco
Carenas.[11] En un artículo titulado "García Lorca y
el teatro del siglo de oro" aparecido en la revista
Espiral de Bogotá, niega toda deuda, atribuyendo cualquier correspondencia a una pura analogía formal.
Carenas considera el teatro del siglo de oro y el
de Lorca diametralmente opuestos. Por un lado ve un
teatro escapista, tradicional y burgués, que niega la
realidad histórica de su tiempo para afirmar en cambio
el poder absoluto del rey y de la religión, y por otro
un teatro al que considera instrumento de crítica
social y auténtico testimonio de una época. Para
demostrar su tesis compara Mariana Pineda y La vida
es sueño. Los resultados para Carenas son obvios
y la conclusión contundente: "oposición ideológica
que enfrenta a Calderón y a Lorca."

El silencio, confusión o disparidad ilustrados

en torno a la dramaturgia lorquiana y su relación con
el teatro del siglo de oro tienen su base en la
difícil y compleja naturaleza de tres términos:
tragedia, honor y realismo. No creo que sea necesario hacer referencia aquí a la polémica Bentley-
Reichenberger, ni a las teorías de A. A. Parker,[12]
cuando se trata, precisamente, de trazar un terri-
torio a compartir entre Calderón y Lorca y de dejar
al margen una visión excesivamente estrecha y dog-
mática de sus dramaturgias. Baste simplemente indicar
que la serie de posturas señaladas sobre el valor y
significado de los dramas de Lorca, vis-à-vis Calderón,
se debe a una polaridad crítica idéntica, es decir,
según se elija ver en ambos un mayor o menor grado de
conformismo o distanciamiento. Pero vayamos por partes.

En cuanto al binomio tragedia-Calderón y al tema
del honor, el haber antepuesto como padrinos a Honig
y Edwards me evita, espero, el tener que repetir o
resumir sus puntos de vista. He aquí, sin embargo,
un par de citas que creo ponen de manifiesto la correspondencia sugerida entre Calderón y Lorca. Honig, que
no se limita a las tragedias, sino que incluye en su
brillante estudio La vida es sueño y La dama duende,
afirma que en sus variantes o "seizures" del tema del
honor Calderón ilustra, más allá de convenciones y
tradiciones, su anhelo humanista de búsqueda de la
libertad, de afirmación del individuo en contra de un
orden social injusto y de un destino adverso. En sus
asaltos las demandas del código del honor "defeat the
hero's humanity instead of ennobling it, while the
pursuit of individualism, in testing the limits of
freedom and erotic curiosity, including murder, rape,
and brigandage, may be the road to salvation."[13] El
libro de Edwards, si cabe aún más sutil y magistral,
pone de manifiesto la constante preocupación de Calderón con la condición humana, el difícil ejercicio
de la voluntad y la búsqueda de libertad y salvación;
factores que caracterizan, asimismo, en mi opinión,
el teatro experimental y poéticamente apasionado de
Lorca. En lugar de estudiar variantes, Edwards
divide a las que denomina "secular plays" en dos
grupos. Unas, como La vida es sueño, presentan el
triunfo del hombre, de su libre albedrío sobre sus
circunstancias y situación, es decir, conquistando
el laberinto, escapando de su prisión. Otras, sin
embargo, a las que concede el título de tragedias,
y a las que dedica su estudio, presentan la visión
de un hombre derrotado, víctima de su destino y aún
de su propia naturaleza: "It is a situation of

helplessness made more helpless, of his vulnerability
cruelly and tragically exposed, and made more pitiful
partly by his efforts to redress the balance and swim
against the tide, partly by the fact that the very
expression of his positive qualities makes the tide
run faster."14

No es menor la polémica suscitada por el binomio
tragedia-Lorca. Se discute desde su número o clasificación hasta su intención y significado.15 Pérez
Marchand, comparándolas con las de los comediógrafos
griegos, las encuentra carentes de intensidad dramática, faltas de envergadura y dominadas por un fatal-
ismo pesimista. Señala, sin embargo, con temprano
acierto, su carácter como obras de arte no comprome-
tidas, de valor esencialmente poético-simbólico.16
No difiere mucho de lo apuntado por Sumner M. Greenfield, quien considera el teatro de Lorca como el
producto de la fusión de dos tradiciones, una culta
y otra popular, la tragedia y la farsa. Las tragedias
dan expresión al tema de la libertad, pero no en conexión con el honor, sino con lo que denomina integridad
personal.17 Tanto estos dos trabajos como el más
extenso de Luis González del Valle, La tragedia en
el teatro de Unamuno, Valle-Inclán y García Lorca
(New York, 1975), remiten las tragedias a un contexto
clásico distante y cometen el error de realizar el
análisis de las mismas omitiendo su base y fuente más
inmediata, la tragedia del siglo de oro y, en particular, la tragedia calderoniana.18

A la relación elaborada hasta aquí entre Calderón
y Lorca en cuanto a preocupaciones e intereses, acti-
tudes artísticas, paralelismos temáticos y analogías
formales, hay que añadir, como suceso clave y orienta-
dor, la creación y establecimiento--junto con Eduardo
Ugarte--del teatro universitario experimental La
Barraca, en el que Lorca toma parte en calidad de
director, adaptador, actor e inspiración constante.19
Resulta imposible desestimar el obvio y profundo
efecto que hubo de ocasionar en la sensibilidad de
Lorca, poeta dramático, la lectura, adaptación y
escenificación de los entremeses, comedias y autos
que produjo la Barraca entre julio de 1932 y abril
de 1936. Lorca absorbe una técnica y un método, una
temática y una poesía, directamente aprendidos de Gil
Vicente, de Cervantes, de Lope de Vega, de Tirso de
Molina y de Calderón. Y es en las fórmulas dramáticas,
en los conflictos humanos que en torno al tema del
honor se dan cita en las obras representadas donde

262

Lorca, en contacto íntimo con la tradición y con el pueblo, con el pasado y el presente, reconociendo su mágico poder, concibe la necesidad de crear un nuevo tipo de teatro, una nueva tragedia y una nueva comedia, capaz "de recoger el drama total de la vida actual . . . que apasione, como el clásico--receptor del latido de toda una época" (II, 1045). Es así como ya en 1934 declara: "Hay que volver a la tragedia. Nos obliga a ello la tradición de nuestro teatro dramático" (II, 1207). Planea, pues, una trilogía trágica sobre el pueblo, al parecer inacabada, y, siempre en la vena experimental que le caracteriza, decide aún ir más lejos, crear un teatro más fiel a la realidad, simplificando y esquematizando aún más conflictos y personajes. He aquí el momento donde, en mi opinión, juega un papel fundamental la influencia de Calderón y, particularmente, del auto. Lorca se mueve hacia un simbolismo intensificado que llama "realismo,"[20] hacia la expresión esquemática, casi abstracta, de la condición humana que le atormenta de manera constante: la falta de libertad de la mujer en lucha con un destino injusto--o en las palabras de Ruiz Ramón, el conflicto entre el principio de autoridad y el principio de libertad.

Llevado de la lección de misterio y símbolo, pasión y alegría que vive en contacto con el público como representante de comedias, Lorca se propone revitalizar la escena dando nueva vida como autor a un teatro que, como el representado por La Barraca, sea todo "emoción y poesía en la palabra, en la acción y en el gesto" (II, 1011), un teatro, en fin, "para sentirlo" (II, 1037). Lo que intenta llevar a cabo en La casa de Bernarda Alba es la novedad de un drama que integra experiencia y poesía, sentimiento y símbolo, un drama que capta y expresa fielmente la esencia y espíritu de un pueblo, a la vez que lo universal del conflicto humano entre individuo y sociedad, instinto y orden, predestinación y libre albedrío.

Sucede, pues, que el auto de Calderón La vida es sueño fue la obra más representada por La Barraca, en la que Lorca mismo hacía el papel de la Sombra. Luis Sáenz de la Calzada, actor que fue también en el auto y miembro del grupo, se pregunta extrañado en su libro de memorias sobre sus años con Lorca, el por qué de la elección y continua representación de La vida es sueño. Como respuesta logra tan sólo aducir cierta afinidad personal por parte de Lorca, cierto gusto teatral, "la posibilidad de que el sueño se hiciera vida."[21]   Encuentro lo de la afinidad significativo pero creo que las razones de tal elección van más hondo.   Habiendo hallado en los pasos de Rueda, en los entremeses de Cervantes y en las comedias de Tirso y Lope un teatro capaz de dar cabida a una temática que es la suya propia, un teatro que el pueblo siente y ama, creo que en la elección del auto de Calderón puede verse la culminación de un proceso de identificación y absorción de ese teatro clásico que es ya lo que Lorca quiere que su teatro sea: "poesía que se levanta del libro y se hace humana. Y al hacerse, habla y grita, llora y se desespera" (II, 1078).[22]

El auto es alegoría a través de la cual se enseña dramáticamente al público una verdad.   Si bien es cierto que Lorca no enseña verdades, sino vidas en pena, no lo es menos que intenta crear un teatro popular y estilizado sin asomo de propaganda, que le permita "un contacto más directo con las masas" (II, 1041).   Su teatro ". . . depurado, con una visión y una técnica que contradicen la simple espontaneidad de lo popular" (II, 993), es una obsesiva especulación sobre el tema de la libertad,[23] sobre la condición humana, tal y como lo es el de Calderón, según han puesto de manifiesto Honig y Edwards.   El auto escenifica poéticamente por medio de símbolos y abstracciones un problema y una solución.   El teatro de Lorca, de trayectoria truncada, no ofrece soluciones, sólo conflictos irresolubles, pasiones ciegas. Sin embargo, en el auto, por extraño que parezca, se da con éxito la posibilidad de una fusión entre idea y símbolo, entre experiencia y poesía a la que Lorca se refiere al hablar del realismo de La casa de Bernarda Alba.   La intuición y sensibilidad artística de Lorca le llevan a reconocer en el auto de Calderón un aspecto esencial de su credo: un drama en el que todo es magia, misterio, capaz de conmover, de maravillar y de apasionar aún al más inculto con sus palabras, gestos y atmósfera.

Brenda Frazier en La mujer en el teatro de Federico García Lorca (Madrid, 1973), además de encontrar una relación temática entre Yerma y el auto de Calderón El pleito matrimonial del Cuerpo y del Alma--la oposición Cuerpo-Alma causa la muerte del hijo--dice de las cuatro hijas menores de Bernarda: "parecen cuatro Segismundas colocadas ante un mundo con la posibilidad de conocer otra manera de vivir y

264

sentir sin estar preparadas para ello."[24] Ciertamente,
a pesar de que se intente aquí relacionar la novedad
de La casa de Bernarda Alba, su realismo poético, con
Calderón, y en especial con el auto La vida es sueño,
no quisiera dar a entender que haya sido modelada
según el auto o que no tenga otras fuentes e influ-
encias. Se trata, por el contrario, más que de un
neo-auto, de una tragedia del tipo de las estudiadas
por Edwards, es decir, en donde "the nature of the
individual, the intervention of other people, and the
decisive role of chance and accident conspire to bring
about the tragedy."[25] El tema del honor, planteado a
raíz de la obligación de guardar luto, domina las
acciones de Bernarda en torno a la casa--su limpieza
y preservación--y sus habitantes, que se ven privados
en contra de su naturaleza de su libertad, en favor de
una norma externa de conducta y de un sentido de clase
falso. Valga notar, por otra parte, que el honor
supone un imperativo ético-moral equiparable a la
gracia, ya que su presencia significa vida y su ausencia muerte; mientras que como inversión del amor significa pecado y muerte en lugar de vida y esperanza.

En cuanto al auto propiamente dicho, quisiera
establecer las siguientes ecuaciones, todas ellas en
función de la deuda general que guarda Lorca con el
teatro del siglo de oro y del simbolismo, motivos y
temas que caracterizan las obras de Calderón (tragedias y auto), según lo hasta aquí discutido. Sin
duda, la casa de Bernarda, que es prisión trágica, no
dista mucho de ser también cueva, y como tal, cuna y
sepultura. El luto, como ocasión de encierro, supone
una imposición, un oráculo o un original pecado que
predetermina el destino de las hijas. La casa
materializa irónicamente en su blancura esta premisa.
De la trinidad que forman en el auto Poder, Sabiduría
y Amor, falta en la tragedia de Lorca el correspondiente personaje para el Amor; de ahí que no haya
salvación posible. El Poder, en términos negativos,
lo encarna Bernarda, mientras que la Poncia parece
actuar como la Sabiduría, ya que es ella quien aconseja y dispone; aunque por sus deseos de venganza, de
perder a Bernarda a través de sus hijas, parezca
actuar como la Sombra. Adela resulta ser, dada la
mencionada inversión, el Hombre. A pesar de su condición de heroína en la tragedia, Adela es un personaje ambivalente. Admirable por su determinación
y voluntad de vida, es decir, por el ejercicio de su
libre albedrío, pero cegada por la soberbia, por su
falta de Entendimiento. Pepe el Romano no es Luz

ni Angel, sino Lucero, Príncipe de las Tinieblas, y
como tal tienta al Hombre con la complicidad de la
Sombra--recuérdese que actúa siempre de noche y con
engaño--hasta perderle cuando, tras despeñar al
Entendimiento, come la fruta, que no es amor, sino
pecado.

Las circunstancias impiden en la tragedia la
intervención de la Sabiduría (la Poncia) en favor
del Hombre. Ahora la vida es realidad y no sueño.
En la imaginación poética de Lorca no cabe la medi-
ación de la Gracia vivificadora. Adela actúa afirmando su derecho a ser libre y se decide a obrar de
acuerdo con su instinto, siguiendo su libre albedrío,
en contra de un orden y un poder injustos. Sin
embargo, en el universo cerrado de la casa sus
acciones son signo de deshonor y la muerte, imagen
de la culpa, termina al fin por imponerse. En La
casa de Bernarda Alba la vida es un sueño irrealizado.
Y así, termino poniendo en boca de la desafortunada
Adela las palabras que pronuncia el Hombre al caer
víctima de su pecado y ser por todos abandonado:

> ¿Qué mucho, pues (ay de mí),
> si todos me desahucian,
> que en brazos de letal Sueño,
> negra Sombra de la Culpa,
> pues dejo a la Muerte viva,
> deje a la Vida difunta? (OC, 1400)[26]

Saginaw Valley State College
University Center, Michigan

Notas

[1] "Dramatismo y teatro en Federico García Lorca" (1936) en Literatura española del siglo XX (Madrid: Alianza, 1970), pág. 193.

[2] Federico García Lorca (1899-1936). Vida y Obra (New York: Hispanic Institute, 1941), págs. 15 y 67-68. José F. Montesinos, Die Moderne Spanische Dichtung (Leipzig, 1927), pág. 117. Citado por del Río, pág. 11.

[3] García Lorca. Estudio sobre su teatro (Madrid: Jura, 1950), pág. 122.

[4] García Lorca. Persona y creación (Buenos Aires: Sur, 1941), págs. 203-330, esp. 230-31.

[5] García Lorca. Vida y obra (New York: Las Américas, 1955), págs. 48-51.

[6] "García Lorca y su universo dramático," en Historia del teatro español. Siglo XX (Madrid: Alianza, 1971), págs. 187-227, esp. 191-92. Importantes, aunque de menor interés para nuestro tema, son los estudios de Edwin Honig, García Lorca (Norfolk, Connecticut: New Directions, 1944); Gonzalo Torrente Ballester, "Bernarda Alba y sus hijas, o un mundo sin perdón," en Teatro español contemporáneo (Madrid: Guadarrama, 2ª ed., 1968), págs. 111-126; y Francisco Mena Benito, El tradicionalismo de Federico García Lorca (Barcelona: Rondas, 1974).

[7] Federico García Lorca dramaturgue (Paris: L'Arche, 1955), pág. 34.

[8] L'Universe poétique de Federico García Lorca (Paris-Bordeaux: 1952), págs. 105-120.

[9] "Life and Death Archetypes in Fry's A Phoenix Too Frequent and García Lorca's House of Bernarda Alba," REH, 9 (1975), pág. 211. Véase también Andrés Sorel, Yo, García Lorca (Madrid: Zero, 1977), pág. 115 y siguientes.

[10] Obra dramática de García Lorca: estudio de configuración (New York: Las Américas, 1971), págs. 11-21.

[11] "García Lorca y el teatro del siglo de oro," Espiral (Bogotá), no. 118 (1971), 5-18.

[12]El ya legendario artículo de Arnold G. Reichenberger, "The Uniqueness of the Comedia," HR, 27 (1959), 303-16, se vio continuado polémicamente por Eric Bentley en "The Universality of the Comedia," HR, 38 (1970), 147-62, con respuesta de Reichenberger, en el mismo número, págs. 163-73. Reichenberger contrasta precisamente la tragedia del teatro del siglo de oro con la de Lorca, afirmando su disparidad ya que en éste, en sus dramas de honor, se da la catharsis y por lo tanto son universales. Véase también el posterior artículo de Reichenberger, "Thoughts About Tragedy in the Spanish Theater of the Golden Age," Hispano, special number 1 (1974), 37-45. Las teorías de A. A. Parker sobre el honor y la tragedia calderoniana pueden leerse en The Approach to the Spanish Drama of the Golden Age (London: Diamante Series VI, 1957) y en "Towards a Definition of Calderonian Tragedy," BHS, 39 (1962), 222-37.

[13]Honig, pág. 5.

[14]Edwards, pág. xxv.

[15]Véase en particular Jolianne Burton, "Society and the Tragic Vision in Federico García Lorca," tesis doctoral inédita, Yale University, 1972. No he visto Margaret Dewhirst, The Tragic Element in the Drama of Federico García Lorca (Eugene: Univ. of Oregon Press, 1947).

[16]Monelisa L. Pérez Marchand, "Apuntes sobre el concepto de la tragedia en la obra dramática de García Lorca," Asomante, 4 (enero-marzo 1948), 86-96. Véase asimismo F. Olmos García, "García Lorca y el teatro clásico," Les Langues Neo-latinos, 54 (1960), 36-67.

[17]"Lorca's Theatre: A Synthetic Reexamination," Journal of Spanish Studies, XXth Century, 5 (1977), 31-46. Véase también F. Lázaro Carreter, "Apuntes sobre el teatro de García Lorca," PSA, 18 no. 52 (1960), 9-33; María Teresa Babín, "Deslindes de la crítica en torno a García Lorca," SinN, 9 (1978), 13-30; y Edwin Honig, "Lorca to Date," Tulane Drama Review, 7 (1962), 120-26.

[18]Véanse págs. 101-168 y en esp. 148-68 y 31-34.

[19]Luis Sáenz de la Calzada pasa revista a las

obras estrenadas por La Barraca e incluye un reper-
torio completo de las representaciones dadas en "La
Barraca" Teatro universitario (Madrid, 1976), págs.
49-107. No he podido ver F. Masini, Federico García
Lorca e La Barraca. Documenti di teatro, 32 (Bologna:
Capelli, 1966).

[20] J. Rubia Barcia, "El realismo mágico de La casa
de Bernarda Alba," en Homenaje a Angel del Río, RHM,
31 (1965), 385-398; Miguel A. Martínez, "Realidad y
símbolo en La casa de Bernarda Alba," REH, 4 (1970),
55-66; James Dauphiné, "Le réalisme symbolique dans
La maison de Bernarda Alba," Les Langues Néolatines,
73, no. 231 (1979), 85-95. Los siguientes estudios
de Vicente Cabrera ponen al descubierto el intenso
simbolismo, casi alegoría, del drama de Lorca:
"Poetic Structure in Lorca's La casa de Bernarda
Alba," Hispania, 61 (1978), 466-71; y "Cristo y el
infierno en La casa de Bernarda Alba," REH, 10 (1979),
135-142. Véanse asimismo Sumner M. Greenfield,
"Poetry and Stagecraft in La casa de Bernarda Alba,"
Hispania, 38 (1955), 456-461; Sam Bluefarb, "Life
and Death in García Lorca's House of Bernarda Alba,"
Drama Survey, 4 (Summer 1965), 109-120; R. A. Young,
"García Lorca's La casa de Bernarda Alba: A Micro-
cosm of Spanish Culture," ML, 50 (1969), 66-72;
Wilma Newberry, "Patterns of Negation in La casa de
Bernarda Alba," Hispania, 59 (1976), 802-809; y
Robert C. Spires, "Linguistic Codes and Dramatic
Action in La casa de Bernarda Alba," TAH, 3, no. 23
(1978), 7-11.

[21] Sáenz de la Calzada, págs. 56-57.

[22] Allen Josephs y Juan Caballero, editores de
La casa de Bernarda Alba (Madrid: Cátedra, 6ª ed.,
1980), a la que en un amplio estudio introductorio
clasifican por razones poco convincentes de drama en
lugar de tragedia, consideran la obra "un nuevo
experimento de forma," escueta, poética y en la que
se plantea un problema moral y humano. Cf. María
Teresa Babín, "García Lorca, poeta del teatro,"
Asomante, 4 no. 2 (1948), 48-57; y Marie Laffranque,
"Federico García Lorca. Le théâtre et la vie," en
Réalisme et poésie au théâtre (Paris: CNRS, 1960),
págs. 147-171.

[23] Además de los estudios mencionados en la nota 7
arriba, véase Robert Lima, The Theater of García Lorca
(New York: Las Américas, 1963); y Michael C. Wells,

"The Natural Norm in the Plays of Federico García Lorca," HR, 38 (1970), 299-313.

[24] Véase pág. 138, y sobre el mismo tema Joseph W. Zdenek, "La mujer y la frustación en las comedias de García Lorca," Hispania, 38 (1955), 67-72.

[25] Edwards, pág. 177.

[26] Para La casa de Bernarda Alba, así como para las declaraciones de García Lorca sobre su teatro y La Barraca, he utilizado la edición de Arturo del Hoyo en Obras Completas (Madrid: Aguilar, 20ª ed.), II, 835-930 y 931-1030, y para el auto La vida es sueño la edición de A. Valbuena Prat en Obras completas, vol. III, Autos sacramentales (Madrid: Aguilar, 1952), págs. 1381-1407.

Notes on the Contributors

Born in Buenos Aires in 1940, MARÍA AMADEI DE
PULICE is presently a doctoral candidate at UCLA.
While at UCLA, she has been a teaching assistant and
received the department's Outstanding Teacher of the
Year Award in 1971. From 1968 to 1972 she held a
UCLA Regents Fellowship. Her dissertation, written
under the direction of Carroll Johnson, is on Cal-
derón's theater.

CESÁREO BANDERA is Professor of Spanish and Comparative Literature at the State University of New
York, Buffalo, Born in Málaga in 1934, he studied at
the universities of Seville and Salamanca and received
the Ph.D. from Cornell University in 1965. He taught
at Cornell before moving to Buffalo in 1969. In addition to several articles on Calderón's work he has
published the book Mímesis conflictiva: Ficción
literaria y violencia en Cervantes y Calderón (Madrid,
1975).

HANNAH E. BERGMAN is Professor of Spanish at
Lehman College and Graduate Center, City University
of New York. Born in 1925, she studied at the Carnegie Institute of Technology (now Carnegie Mellon
University) and at Smith College and received the
Ph.D. from the University of California, Berkeley,
in 1953. She has taught at Smith College, Brandeis
University and Hunter College and has been at Lehman
College since 1961. She serves on the editorial board
of Bulletin of the Comediantes and was elected Corresponding Member of the Hispanic Society of America in
1974. Specializing in the entremés, she has published
two books on Luis Quiñones de Benavente and two editions of his entremeses.

DONALD T. DIETZ is Professor of Spanish at Texas
Tech University. Born in 1939, he studied at the Uni-
versity of Notre Dame and received the Ph.D. from the
University of Arizona in 1968. He has taught at the
University of Dayton, Ball State University and the
University of Louisville and has been at Texas Tech
University since 1976. He served as a judge at the
Fourth Golden Age Drama Festival at the Chamizal
National Monument in 1979. His book The Auto Sacra-
mental and the Parable in Spanish Golden Age Literature
appeared in 1973.

MANUEL DURÁN is Professor of Spanish and Chairman of the Department of Spanish and Portuguese at Yale University. Born in Barcelona in 1925, he studied in Spain, France, Mexico and the United States, obtaining the degrees of Licenciado en Derecho and Maestro en Letras at the Universidad Nacional Autónoma de México and the Ph.D. in Romance Languages and Literatures at Princeton University, where he studied with Américo Castro. He has published several volumes of poetry, a number of language textbooks and many books and articles of literary criticism dealing with authors of all periods of Spanish literature. In 1976, in collaboration with Roberto González Echeverría, he published the important two-volume Calderón de la Barca: Crítica y antología.

HANS FLASCHE is Professor Emeritus of the University of Hamburg, where he taught from 1963 until his retirement. Born in 1911, he received the Ph.D. from the University of Bonn in 1935. He was elected Corresponding Member of the Hispanic Society of America in 1971 and Corresponding Member of the Real Academia Española in 1977. He was awarded an honorary doctorate from the Catholic University of Portugal in 1979. In addition to numerous critical studies and the book Über Calderón (Wiesbaden, 1980), Professor Flasche is now publishing a monumental Konkordanz zu Calderón in collaboration with Gerd Hoffmann.

EDWARD FRIEDMAN is Associate Professor of Spanish at Arizona State University. Born in 1948, he studied at the University of Virginia and received the Ph.D. from Johns Hopkins University in 1974. He taught at Kalamazoo College before going to Arizona State in 1977. He has published many articles on Spanish Golden Age literature, and his book The Unifying Concept: Approaches to the Structure of Cervantes' Comedias is scheduled for publication in 1981.

SUSANA HERNÁNDEZ-ARAICO is Associate Professor of Spanish at California State Polytechnic University, Pomona. Born in Mexico in 1947, she studied at Mount St. Mary's College and received the Ph.D. from UCLA in 1976. Her dissertation, written under the direction of Enrique Rodríguez-Cepeda, was on "El concepto de ironía en la tragicomedia calderoniana (del humor al determinismo)." She participated in a panel on "Women in Spanish Golden Age Literature" at the National Hispanic Feminist Conference in San Jose, California in March 1980. Her article "La Semíramis calderoniana como compendio de estereotipos femeninos" is to be published in the National Hispanic Feminist Conference Anthology in 1981.

EVERETT W. HESSE received his Ph.D. from New York University. He has taught at the Universities of Wisconsin, Southern California, Arizona, Maryland and San Diego State. He has published numerous articles on the comedia, Lope de Vega, Tirso and Calderón. His books include Calderón (Boston, 1968), Análisis e interpretación de la comedia (Madrid, 1968), La comedia y sus intérpretes (Madrid, 1973), Interpretando la comedia (Madrid, 1977) and New Perspectives on Comedia Criticism (Madrid, 1980). He was elected National President of the American Association of Teachers of Spanish and Portuguese in 1955 and a Corresponding Member of the Hispanic Society of America in the same year. He was decorated by the Spanish government in 1972 with the "Orden de Isabel la Católica" for his work on the theater.

J. RICHARDS LeVAN is currently a doctoral candidate at the University of Texas, Austin, where he is completing a dissertation entitled "From Tradition to Masterpiece: Circe and Calderón" under the direction of Stanislav Zimic. He studied at Davidson College and received his M.A. from the University of Texas in 1976. In 1978 he received a Fulbright-Hays Grant for study in Spain.

ALBERTO PORQUERAS-MAYO is Professor of Spanish at the University of Illinois. Born in Lérida, Spain in 1930, he studied at the University of Barcelona, received the Ph.D. from the University of Madrid in 1954 and did post-doctoral work at the University of Bonn in 1954-55. He taught at the University of Madrid, the University of Bonn, the University of Hamburg, Emory University and the University of Missouri before assuming his present position at the University of Illinois in 1968. He has served on the editorial boards of Segismundo and Comparative Literature Studies. In addition to numerous articles and reviews, he has published four books on the prologue as a literary genre, editions of Alfonso de Carvallo's El Cisne de Apolo (Madrid, 1958) and of Calderón's El príncipe constante (Madrid, 1975), Preceptiva dramática española del Renacimiento y Barroco (Madrid, 1965; in collaboration with F. Sánchez-Escribano) and Temas y formas de la literatura española (Madrid, 1972).

FRANCISCO RUIZ-RAMÓN is Professor of Spanish at Purdue University. Born in Spain in 1930, he received the Ph.D. from the University of Madrid in 1962. He taught at the University of Oslo and the University of Puerto Rico before going to Purdue in 1968. He was awarded a Research Grant from the Juan March Foundation in 1979. He is editor of the bibliographical section of Revista de Literatura, co-editor of Estreno and serves on the editorial board of Crítica Hispanica. Author of numerous articles on Spanish literature, he has also published several editions of plays by Lope de Vega and Calderón and an influential two-volume Historia del teatro español (3rd edition, Madrid, 1979).

ROBERT TER HORST is Professor of Spanish at the University of Arizona. Born in 1929, he studied at Princeton University and received the Ph.D. from The Johns Hopkins University in 1963. He has taught at the University of Wisconsin, Duke University and the University of Rochester and was Fulbright Visiting Professor of Spanish at the Université de Lille III in 1976-77. He has published a number of important articles on Calderón's work, and his book Myth, Honor and History in the Secular Drama of Don Pedro Calderón is scheduled for publication in 1981.

EDUARDO URBINA is Assistant Professor of Spanish at Saginaw Valley State College. Born in Spain, he studied at California State University at Hayward and received the Ph.D. from the University of California, Berkeley in 1979. While at Berkeley, he was awarded the Charles E. Kany Graduate Scholarship in 1978-79. He has read a number of papers on Spanish Golden Age literature at professional meetings and recently participated in the VII Congreso Internacional de Hispanistas in Venice.

ANGEL VALBUENA-BRIONES is Elias Ahuja Professor of Spanish at the University of Delaware. Born in Spain, he received his Ph.D. from the University of Madrid in 1952. He has taught at the University of Madrid, Oxford University, the University of Wisconsin, Yale University, the Universidad Autónoma de México and the Instituto Caro y Cuervo in Bogotá, Colombia, where he was Director of the Andrés Bello Seminar. He serves on the editorial boards of Arbor, Bulletin of the Comediantes and Hispanic Journal. He has edited more plays by Calderón than any other living scholar and has also published numerous articles and several books, including Perspectiva crítica de los dramas de Calderón (Madrid, 1965).

JOHN E. VAREY is Professor of Spanish at Westfield College, University of London. Born in 1922, he served in the Royal Air Force from 1942 to 1945 and received the Ph.D. from the University of Cambridge in 1951. He began teaching at Westfield College the following year. He is general editor of the Tamesis Collection, joint editor of Critical Guides to Spanish Texts and Research Bibliographies and Check-Lists, and has served on the editorial boards of Segismundo and Themes in Drama. In 1979 he was elected President of the Association of Hispanists of Great Britain and Ireland. In addition to numerous articles on Calderón he has published a 19-volume facsimile edition of The Comedies of Calderón (London, 1973) in collaboration with D. W. Cruickshank.

BRUCE W. WARDROPPER is William Hanes Wannamaker Professor of Romance Lanugages at Duke University. Born in Scotland in 1919, he studied at King Edward's School and at Cambridge University and received the Ph.D. from the University of Pennsylvania in 1949. He has taught at the University of Pennsylvania, The Johns Hopkins University, The Ohio State University, Harvard, the University of Pittsburgh and the University of North Carolina. He served on the executive board of the Asociación Internacional de Hispanistas from 1971 to 1977 and has been a member of the editorial committees of Modern Language Notes, PMLA and Revista Hispánica Moderna. He is a member of the Educational Advisory Board of the John Simon Guggenheim Memorial Foundation. His numerous books and articles reflect wide-ranging interests and an encyclopedic knowledge of Spanish literature of the Golden Age.

WILLIAM M. WHITBY is Professor of Spanish at Purdue University, where he has been teaching since 1968. Born in Philadelphia in 1920, he studied at Haverford College and received the Ph.D. from Yale University in 1954. He has taught at Yale, at the University of Southern California and at the University of Arizona. During the summer of 1964, he was a Visiting Associate Professor at the University of California, Berkeley. He was editor of the Bulletin of the Comediantes in 1964-66 and associate editor of Hispania in 1972-74. He is now general editor of Purdue University Monographs in Romance Languages. He has published an edition of Lope de Vega's La fianza satisfecha (Cambridge, 1971) in collaboration with Robert R. Anderson. Several of his important articles on Calderón's work have been reprinted in Critical Essays on the Theatre of Calderón (New York, 1965), Critical Studies of Calderón's "Comedias" (London, 1973) and Calderón y la crítica: historia y antología (Madrid, 1976).

VERN G. WILLIAMSEN is Professor of Spanish at the University of Missouri, Columbia. Born in 1926, he studied at San Jose State College and the University of Arizona and received the Ph.D. from the University of Missouri in 1968. He taught for seventeen years in elementary and secondary schools in California and Arizona and was Assistant Professor of Spanish at Westminster College from 1965 to 1968. In addition to many articles he has published editions of plays by Mira de Amescua and Ruiz de Alarcón, a book on The Minor Dramatists of Seventeenth Century Spain (Boston, 1981) and An Annotated, Analytical Bibliography of Tirso de Molina Studies (Missouri, 1979).

Cubillo de Aragón, A.,
    231, 250, 256; cited,
    245n

Dauphiné, J.: cited, 269n

Derrida, J., 20

Descartes, R., 4, 29

Dewhirst, M.: cited, 268n

Dietz, D., x, 271; cited,
    185n, 186n

Díez Borque, J. M.: cited
    225n

Dillon, E.: cited, 91n

Diodorus Siculus: cited,
    92n

Domínguez Ortiz, A., 8

Dostoievski, F., 17

Dunn, P. N., 151; cited,
    153n, 245n; quoted,
    145, 155n

Durán, M., vi, 1, 2, 272;
    cited, 15

Eco, U.: cited, 225n

Edwards, G., 51n, 107,
    261, 264; cited, 115n,
    116, 245n, 246n, 259,
    268n, 270n; quoted,
    261-2, 265

Einstein, A.: quoted, 28

Eliade, M.: cited, 88n

Empson, W.: cited, 155n,
    quoted, 148

Enríquez Gómez, A., 231,
    250, 256; cited, 245n

Entwistle, W. J., 144,
    145, 153n, 167; cited,
    140n, 152n, 155n, 173n;
    quoted, 143, 148

Enzina, J. del, 36

Erasmus, D., 27

Erikson, E., 20

Faber, J. N. von, 9

Fernández Montesinos, J.:
    cited, 267n; quoted, 259

Ficino, M., 77, 83; cited,
    87n, 92n

Filippo, L. de: cited, 257n

Flasche, H., xi, 192, 193,
    272; cited, 16n, 197n,
    246n

Flecniakoska, J. L., 260;
    cited, 267n

Fontana, G., 219

Forner, J. P., 9; cited,
    16n

Fothergill-Payne, L.:
    cited, 184n; quoted, 175

Frazier, B.: cited, 264,
    270n

Freud, S., 48, 228n;
    quoted, 17

Friedman, E., ix, 272

Frutos Cortés, E., 20, 21

282

Mariana de Austria, 36, 85, 92n

Maritain, J., 16

Martínez, M. A.: cited, 269n

Martorell, J., 170n

Marx, M., 182; cited, 184n; quoted, 175

Masini, F.: cited, 269n

Massar, P. D., 239; cited, 246n, 247n

Mattauch, H.: cited, 246n

Maurin, N. S.: cited, 246n

McGarry, M. F. de S.: cited, 185n

Mela, Pomponius, 85

Mena Benito, F.: cited, 267n

Mendeleiev, D. I., 29

Menéndez y Pelayo, M., vi, 6, 6-11, 16n, 53, 157; cited, 15n; cited and quoted, 139n; quoted, 7

Menéndez Pidal, R., 1

Mesonero Romanos, R. de: cited, 245n

Michelangelo, 41, 46

Migne, J.-P.: cited, 195n

Mira de Amescua, A., 34, 195n, 252, 253, 255, 258n, 276

Moir, D., 249, 255; cited, 257n, 258n

Molière, 256

Monte, G. del, 228n

Montemayor, J. de, 54

Mora, J. J. de, 9

Moratín, L. F., 9

Morel-Fatio, A.: cited, 226-27n

Moreto, A. de, 75n, 249

Newberry, W.: cited, 269n

Newton, I., 29

Norval, M., 151; cited, 153-54n, quoted, 148

Nourissier, F.: cited, 267n; quoted, 270

Olivares, Count-Duke of, 23, 36, 38

Olmos García, F.: cited, 268n

Orozco, E., 8

Ortega y Gasset, J., vi, 5, 8, 16n; cited, 15; quoted, 2, 3, 4, 6

Ovid: cited and quoted, 90n

Pabst, W.: cited, 172n

Palley, J., v

Pagés Larraya, 76n

283

Parker, A. A., 11, 26, 124n, 127, 261; cited, 16n, 115n, 128n, 153n, 184n, 189, 195n, 196n, 197n, 246n, 268n; quoted, 196n; cited and quoted, 139n, 185n

Parr, J. A., v

Patch, H. R.: cited and quoted, 116n

Pavis, P.: cited, 225n

Pellicer, C.: cited, 90n

Pérez, C., 65, 75n

Pérez de Ayala, R., 2

Pérez Marchand, M. L., 262; cited, 268n

Pérez de Montalbán, J., 195n

Pérez de Moya, J., 78, 79, 81, 85; cited, 88n, 91n, 92n; cited and quoted, 93n

Philip II, 36

Philip IV, 23, 36, 38, 39

Philip V, 36

Phillipson, H.: cited, 229n

Pico della Mirandola, G., 27

Pierce, F.: cited, 246n

Pietshmann, K. R.: cited, 171n

Plato, 17, 27, 77, 83, 243

Porqueras-Mayo, A., x, 273; cited, 152n, 154n, 170n, 171n; quoted, 144

Porta, G. della, 35

Poyo, S. del, 255

Pring-Mill, R. D. F., v, 11; cited, 16n

Prudentius, 176

Pythagoras, 29

Quevedo, F. de, 6, 196n

Quilligan, M.: cited, 139

Quiñones de Benavente, L., 271

Rachet, G.: cited, 128n

Racine, J., 200

Rada y Delgado, J. de la, 9; cited, 16n; quoted, 10

Ramírez, B., 65

Rank, O., 253; cited, 257n

Reichenberger, A. G., 261; cited, 268n

Reichenberger, K. and R.: cited, 87n, 170n

Rennert, H. A.: cited, 87n, 227n

Río, A. del: cited, 267n; quoted, 259

Ríos, B. de los, 7

Riber, L.: cited, 91n, 92n

Riquer, M. de: cited, 170n

Weightman, J. and D.: cited,
  88n

Wells, M. C.: cited, 269-70n

Whitby, W., ix, 275; cited,
  154n

Williamsen, V., xii; cited,
  257n, 258n

Wilson, E. M., 11, 29, 51,
  85, 144, 177, 249; cited,
  92n, 143, 152n, 155n,
  172n, 185n, 257n, 258n

Wise, D.: cited, 173n

Wölfflin, H., 158

Young, R. A.: cited, 269n

Zamora, A. de, 9

Zamora Vicente, A.: cited
  and quoted, 152n

Zdenek, J. W.: cited, 270n

Zimic, S., 273